# FICTION
## *first aid*

Instant Remedies
*for Novels, Stories and Scripts*

 Raymond Obstfeld

**WRITER'S DIGEST BOOKS**
Cincinnati, Ohio
www.writersdigest.com

Fiction First Aid. Copyright © 2002 by Raymond Obstfeld. Manufactured in the United States of America. All rights reserved. No part of this book may be reproduced in any form or by any electronic or mechanical means including information storage and retrieval systems without permission in writing from the publisher, except by a reviewer, who may quote brief passages in a review. Published by Writer's Digest Books, an imprint of F&W Publications, Inc., 1507 Dana Avenue, Cincinnati, Ohio 45207. (800) 289-0963. First edition.

Visit our Web site at www.writersdigest.com for information on more resources for writers.

To receive a free e-newsletter with tips and updates about writing and Writer's Digest products, subscribe online at http://newsletters.fwpublications.com.

06   05   04   03   02      5   4   3   2   1

Editors: Jack Heffron and Brad Crawford
Production coordinator: Sara Dumford
Cover designer: Lisa Buchanan
Interior designer: Mary Barnes Clark
Cover photography by Photonica

# Acknowledgments

To Sandy Watt, retired from agenting, but still my dear friend. And to Brad Crawford, whose heroic efforts in editing this book are deeply appreciated.

## About the Author

Raymond Obstfeld is the author of twenty-seven novels in a variety of genres, including mysteries, suspense thrillers and mainstream novels. He also has sold ten screenplays, thirteen books of nonfiction, including *The Novelist's Essential Guide to Crafting Scenes*, and numerous short stories, poems and articles. He lives in Tustin, California, and heads the writing program at Orange Coast College in Costa Mesa, California.

(1) bland wallpaper that just lies passively in the background, not actively contributing to the story; or (2) gaudy wallpaper that screams for attention and distracts the reader from the story.

**Symptom: Description overload**

*Common Ailment*

**Symptom: Low-impact settings, off-beat pacing**

*Common Ailment*

**Symptom: Bland phrasing; writing that echoes published writers but is less effective**

*Common Ailments*

**Symptoms: Monotonous phrasing; overwritten and confusing passages; muddled details**

*Common Ailment*

**Symptoms: Oversimplified, emotionally shallow characters; major cross-gender characters who seem minor; inaccurate gender-specific details**

*Common Ailment*

the voice of characters who are not the same gender as the author.

# CHAPTER ONE

# Plot

**Symptom: "Writer's block"**

*Common Ailments*

**The Flypaper Effect.** Overwhelmed by all the plot possibilities, the writer is stuck, unsure what should happen next.

**Symptom: Predictable plots**

*Common Ailments*

**Rushing.** Where do you come up with your ideas so quickly? From the thousands of story plots filed in your head from every other story you've seen or read.

**Underexposure.** We distinguish bad writing from good by comparing it to other works in the same genre. The more works you're exposed to, the better idea you have about the quality of your work.

**Overly Mechanical Plots (Joseph Campbell Syndrome).** Connect-the-dots plots that are as predictable and dull as if they'd been stolen from Plots 'R' Us.

**Symptom: Ho-hum suspense**

*Common Ailments*

**Uninvolving Characters.** Characters don't have to be likable to be involving, but they do need to generate empathy in the reader. To do that, readers need to know why characters are the way they are.

**Low Stakes.** Readers don't care sufficiently about the characters or see the events as important enough to read on.

**Symptom: Flat payoff scenes**

*Common Ailments*

**Promising Too Much.** When the plot promises more than can reasonably be delivered, the reader feels let down.

**Paying Off Too Little.** The key payoff scenes of the story do not meet readers' expectations, either in emotional intensity, plot clarity or thematic development.

## FAQs Frequently Asked Questions

? What is plot? page 6

? How do I come up with plots? page 7

? Should I make an outline? page 23. See also 241-245

? Should I skip ahead in my manuscript if I don't know what will come next? page 6

? How does plot relate to my characters? pages 11-15, 31-33, 40-44, 61-64

? What's the difference between a character-driven story and a plot-driven story? pages 13-15

? Should I follow a plot template? How much leeway do I have to be original? pages 28-31, 33

? What do I need to know about pacing? pages 23 and 24

? How can I come up with the right ending for my story? pages 15-22

---

## Symptom: "Writer's block"

### Ailment: The Flypaper Effect

The Flypaper Effect is not "writer's block," but merely an *inevitable part of the writing process*. Typically, it occurs at three particular points: once each in the first, second and third acts (see treatment on page 8 for a discussion of three-act structure).

**Flypaper trap #1.** The opening thirty to fifty pages of a three hundred-page novel are the honeymoon chapters for a writer. (In a short story, this is the first few pages; in a screenplay, the first twenty-five to thirty pages.) Yes, they're challenging because the opening pages drive the rest of the novel. But they are also the easiest part of the plotting because everything is fresh and doesn't require explanation. It's all character and plot hook. But once you've finished introducing the major characters and the plot hooks,

2

which usually takes thirty to fifty pages (more if the book has multiple points of view or many subplots or is longer than 350 pages), the writer must now start to explain things; the characters, which just seemed to tell you what they needed to do in the first few chapters, now sit on your shoulders impatiently waiting for instructions.

Flypaper trap #2. Having finally extracted himself from the first flypaper trap, the writer is confronted with a second, which occurs roughly halfway through the novel, short story or screenplay. This is the point at which the writer has the end in sight, may even know exactly how the story will end, but isn't yet sure how to get there. It's as if the end is a distant island paradise and the writer is sitting atop the first 150 pages salivating to get there. But how, damn it, how?

Flypaper trap #3. The last hundred pages of a novel can cause writers to lock up faster than the small intestine after a five-cheese pizza. You're finally on the island, but it's not quite the paradise it seemed like from a distance. All the plot and character conflicts must be resolved in a believable and satisfying way; the reader must be impacted by the ending on both an emotional and intellectual level; she must close the book with a sigh and the overwhelming impulse to rush out and buy another book by this author. All the pieces of the puzzle are in front of you on copious notes and detailed outlines pinned to your corkboard, but the maddening challenge is how to fit them all together. (See "How to Choose an Ending" on page 15 for treatments.)

### Diagnosis

The good news is that this problem is not only common, but often the sign of a dedicated and conscientious writer. Questioning oneself is a crucial part of the writing process. Having doubts is merely the residue of that questioning process. In fact, the Picky Critic who resides in the back of your mind is a writer's best friend and should be nurtured and honed, not ignored.

Beginning writers often write by the seat of their pants, meaning they may have a plot idea, but they don't really know what to do with it. So they write, write, write—sometimes faster than they can think. Then suddenly the book comes to a halt because the author doesn't know where to go. Now she faces two choices: aban-

3

don the novel for a while (translation: forever), or push ahead, screw the Picky Critic. This latter choice usually means the book will be unsalable at the end and the writer will be forced to do many more drafts.

Picky Critic is the distillation of instinct and experience. Listen to this voice!

It is telling you that certain choices are too familiar, predictable or not right for your story. Writers often try to ignore this voice, rationalize it as a part of themselves that's being too demanding. But the experienced writer comes to cherish it.

## Treatment

Because problems with plot choice are so universal among writers, there are many techniques, from quick fixes to more elaborate considerations. Often the writer will use a combination of techniques, because rarely are two flypaper traps the same. Following are three quick fixes. Even if one doesn't work in one situation, it may in the next, so don't abandon any of them.

**1. Change the names.** It sounds almost too easy to work, but it does. Sometimes you get stuck in the plot because you have trouble envisioning a key character. You're used to the way he walks and talks and acts to the point that he's become too predictable. In such a case you may be able to get fresh perspective on the character simply by changing his or her name.

**2. Add new character trait or detail.** Teenagers change their style more often and rapidly than most others because they are neck-deep in discovering exactly who they are while at the same time trying to define that person for themselves and others. This may result in new hairstyles, various body piercings or tattoos. Each time they do this, it allows them to see themselves differently, see if the person doing this is who they really are. Imagining it sometimes isn't enough; they have to experience the change. The same principle is true with characters. You may have trouble believing a character's action because she is not necessarily the character you've described so far. You now have three choices: eliminate the action, have a different character do it or fine-tune the character so that we believe she would do it. (See also "Contrived Pivotal Action" in chapter two, especially physical therapy on page 73.)

Sometimes that character can be nudged toward the one you had in mind simply by adding a new trait. For example, in my suspense novel *The Reincarnation of Reece Erikson*, I had an assassin villain who traveled around with toy soldiers and a fold-out map of Little Big Horn. He was an expert on the battle, and each night he would carefully recreate it, sometimes trying to figure out how Custer might have won. Why the obsession? Because he was descended from the one man tried for desertion in the battle, the one man who probably made the right choice. But the choice went against the mythology of Custer, and the deserter became a scapegoat. My intention was to use this trait to make the assassin more interesting. Give him a memorable personality. But I also wanted to show how he used this to justify in his own mind what he did for a living.

**3. Change the setting.** (See also the Wrong-Address Settings ailment on page 132.) There have been times when I've been stuck in a scene and can't seem to find my way out. It's like being in a dream in which you know something bad is about to happen and you can't decide whether you're in a dream or whether it's real. I usually just decide it's a dream and transport myself out of the scene. Same in writing. Sometimes you're stuck because whatever is happening is happening in the wrong place. The shoot-out in the warehouse isn't working because we've seen it a million times and you can't seem to break out of those too-familiar images. So, move the shoot-out to a museum hosting a Rembrandt exhibit. Right away you can see new ways of having the characters interact. In addition, relocating a scene may force you to do research, which in itself can trigger a rejuvenation in the story.

When adapting the novel for the film *Chocolat*, screenwriter Robert Nelson Jacobs changed the time period of the novel, which was contemporary, to the 1950s. In an interview in *Creative Scriptwriting*, he explained how this change liberated him: "It enabled me to see things more specifically. . . . [It's] invigorating to find some place, research it like crazy, and become part of that world. There's something very exciting about that."

## STAYING THE COURSE VS. SKIPPING AHEAD

Beginning writers often ask whether they should just skip the part that's got them stuck and move ahead to a section in which they already know what will happen. My advice is not to do that. Here's why: The Picky Critic is telling you that there's something wrong with the passage you're stuck on. The resolution to that problem may involve rethinking the plot altogether. If you skip ahead, continuing on with an earlier plot choice, you could find yourself locked in. You need to have all your options open when trying to break through a plot-stall. You may realize that your original intention of bringing the characters together at the Grand Canyon three chapters later won't work. But if you skip ahead and write the Grand Canyon chapter, you now have a commitment to it and the effort that went into writing it. Sometimes getting unstuck means re-envisioning who the characters are and what they might do. In fact, you may be stuck because you've imagined them too narrowly and now they are bristling at those confines. So, work through the plot-stalls as they come; they may take the novel in a new, much better direction.

I've had many students with completed novels in my workshops who, after our discussions on plotting, have blurted, "If I'd known this before, I could have saved myself writing a few drafts of the novel." No guarantees, but it's worth a look.

## WHAT PLOT IS

Plot is what happens in your story, the events that take place. There are two basic parts to plotting:

1. choosing what happens in the story
2. choosing the scenes that show what happens

**1. What happens.** The first part is the Big Picture: the plot of the entire story. It's like building a robot that will help out around the house. The second part is trickier because you're now choosing the best way to implement the Big Picture. Now you have to decide what it will look like, what source of power will be, how many arms and legs it will have, if any.

**2. Choosing scenes.** The scenes you choose will establish the kind of story you're telling. For example, the difference between *drama* ("serious" mainstream literature) and *melodrama* (soap opera) is the selection of scenes and the focus. Melodramatic scenes focus on titillating the emotions, kind of like poking a bear with a stick. The point of the melodramatic scene is to elicit some emotional reaction. Dramatic scenes also attempt to elicit emotion, but the scenes are constructed to then make us *think* about the emotion, to see it in a larger context. Drama wants us to explore why we have those emotional reactions, what they say about us as individuals, as a culture, as human beings.

### The Source of Plot

How do you know where your plot should go? There are three basic sources of plot (four, if you count stealing from other writers).

**1. Plot based on factual events.** Here the author is following some historical event, either that happened to herself or to someone else. The problem here is that there are so many more events than you can use in a story. Or that the real events may seem boring in the telling. A character may do an extraordinary thing but be a boring person. This is when you sacrifice "reality" and replace it with "realism." That means you're replacing facts with scenes that make a better story. The key to writing a good story based on actual events—even if they happened to you—is to remember this: The story is about truth, not facts. The truth is the impact the events had, not what the character had for breakfast.

**2. Plot based on theme.** Here the author chooses plot events based on the thematic approach. If the story is a classical tragedy (e.g., *One Flew Over the Cuckoo's Nest*, *Five Easy Pieces*, *King Lear*), then certain plot points must take place. However, as you can see from the vast differences in the three examples, despite the fact that they all have the same basic plot events, the scenes they use to present these events are quite different. See chapter five for more about theme-based plots.

7

**3. Plot based on a genre template.** Here the author accepts that there are certain conventions in each genre. These conventions dictate the larger structure of the plot. However, making each of those conventional scenes interesting and somehow surprising is the author's challenge. Many writers have successfully met that challenge. (See page 13 and treatments on page 28.)

## Three-Act Structure

The three-act structure of a story is easy to learn. It's pretty much like a bedroom dresser with three drawers. ("Hmm, socks and underwear in the top drawer, complication of conflicts in the second drawer. . . .")

Act 1. The beginning of the story should introduce the three main features:

1. major characters
2. conflict
3. setting

1. **Characters:** Make us care about the protagonists. This is achieved through a variety of techniques: tone, style and stakes (discussed in "Two Major Plot Elements" on page 11). (See the Uninvolving Protagonist ailment in chapter two.)

2. **Conflict:** There are two kinds of core conflicts: plot (external) and character (internal). Here you establish exactly what the character wants to change about his or her life and what the obstacles are. (See the chart and "Two Major Plot Elements.") Stories often begin with a misdirection conflict, a conflict designed to create suspense and reveal something about the character; it isn't the core conflict, merely a device. For example, a story may begin:

> James saw the Honda CRV's backup lights flash on from two aisles away. He floored the gas pedal and swerved around the Toyota truck that, like him, had been desperately trolling the campus parking lot for the last fifteen minutes. James didn't care that it wasn't fair, or neighborly, or Christian or any of the other moral buzzwords his mother would say if she was here beside

him. What he cared about was that he was already ten minutes late for English class and the professor had warned him to never be late again, "if you entertain any fantasies of graduating, Mr. Klein."

Being late is not a major conflict of the story. But it's presented in such a way that it could be. It has stakes (will James be kicked out of class?) that create suspense, so we are committed to the action and the character.

**3. Setting:** The setting must be believable and interesting. Just enough texture (details about the setting) must be supplied to make the world seem real. This amount of texture depends upon the type of story you're telling and how important the setting is in influencing the plot and the characters.

**Act 2.** The middle section is where the plot complications are more fully developed. For example, in a genre story, the one person who can reveal the identity of the villain and save the world is murdered. In a more literary mainstream novel, the estranged husband and wife may be about to reconcile when she discovers she is pregnant by the man she dated while she and her husband were separated. The idea here is to provide obstacles that challenge the characters to delve deeper into who they are, to have to confront their internal demons and past mistakes and make decisions that could redefine who they are. The best of genre fiction will also include this mainstream concern, but make it subordinate to the genre conventions.

**Act 3.** The last section must resolve all of the conflicts—though not necessarily happily. Resolve means to bring closure to the plot and character conflicts that motivated the action and emotion of the story. That doesn't mean that the characters' lives must be neatly resolved, but that everything is resolved in the *reader's mind*. The reader must feel as if she's standing on a mountaintop, viewing the whole story for the first time, and understanding why everything happened as it did. (For more on endings, see "When Endings Attack" on page 19.)

**ACT 1 (BEGINNING)**
*create suspense by presenting
plot and character conflict
to establish stakes*

**PLOT CONFLICT** Make clear what the characters want and some of the obstacles in their way.

**CHARACTER CONFLICT** Make clear why what they want is so important to them.

**STAKES** The intensity of the suspense is the result of how well plot and character conflict are presented.

**ACT 2 (MIDDLE)**
*increase suspense by
complicating plot through
increasing stakes and/or
decreasing ability of character
to achieve goal*

**INCREASE STAKES** For example, competing in the race is no longer just for glory, but for the prize money that will pay for the protagonist's education now that her family has lost all its money.

**DECREASE ABILITY** The characters have additional obstacles that inhibit their ability to get what they want (e.g., they lose a job, break a leg, loved one becomes ill, etc.).

**ACT 3 (END)**
*resolve suspense with payoff*

**PAYOFF** Payoff scenes must equal or surpass the promise that is made by the suspense. Say someone at work promises to tell you a "very personal secret," but every time you ask what it is, he says he'll tell you later. After work, that secret had better be worth the suspense of waiting all day.

who i am
what i have

who i want to be
what i want

PLOT CONFLICT

CHARACTER CONFLICT

## What This Chart Teaches You About Plotting

The chart above illustrates the basic structure of most, if not all, plots. Act 1 of a story presents a protagonist, defining *"Who I Am,"* for that character, meaning the strengths and weaknesses of her personality (e.g., funny, emotional, ambitious, etc.), and *"What I Have,"* meaning where her life is at this time (e.g., job, romantic relationships, money, etc.). Also introduced here is some notion of how the character wants to change her life: *"Who I Want to Be"* (e.g., more in control of my emotions, less manipulated by my need to please, etc.) and *"What I Want"* (e.g., better job, the Lost Ark of the Covenant, a million dollars). Plot is how she goes about trying to achieve these goals while overcoming the various obstacles (plot conflicts) that are thrown at her.

**The lesson:** It's much easier to plot when you understand what your characters want—and why. Knowing these elements provides a general but inevitable path that the novel will take. The obstacles then will depend upon the kind of novel you are writing. If it is a genre story, many of the obstacles will be conventions of that genre; if it's mainstream, the obstacles will often be based on the character's own flaws. Beginning writers may think this makes plotting somewhat mechanical. Well, it is. The impact of a good plot isn't based merely on the events that occur but in the way they are presented to the reader through style, tone and various other techniques. Two artists may paint the same subject, but the outcome can be universes apart.

### Two Major Plot Elements: Conflict and Stakes

More important than being a slave to the three-act structure (the three dresser drawers), is understanding the elements that go into those drawers (*"Become* your underwear!"). Basically, plotting shares the same ingredients as advertising and politics: hope and fear. The writer creates a hope in the reader that the protagonist will accomplish something she wants, but continually builds a fear that she will fail. This interaction of hope and fear produces suspense.

**How conflict works.** This is the hope element of the story. There are two basic kinds of conflict: plot and character. Character conflict is emphasized in mainstream fiction, while plot conflict is emphasized in genre fiction. That doesn't mean that either type of fiction can't do a great job with both, merely that the focus is more on one. (Just as with songwriting, the emphasis is on the music more than the lyrics, whereas in poetry, the emphasis is on the word choices more than the rhythm.)

**Character conflict.** This focuses on a character's internal struggle. Usually it is something that is preventing the protagonist from progressing as a person. Perhaps she hates her mother for some past harm the mother caused the family. This hate keeps the protagonist from being happy. The story starts with "Who I Am" and soon reveals "Who I Want to Be." The struggle to become that person, which the character is convinced will make her happier, is the character conflict. Happiness, though, is achieved in incremental steps, like scaling a mountain. Each increment is a defining moment: It demonstrates knowledge (that the character knows what will make her happy), and ability (that she is capable of achieving it). Also, achieving one increment is sometimes crucial to give the character the strength/knowledge/tools to move on to the next step, as in a video game where power bars or extended life energy is absorbed through a trial.

Building effective character conflict requires that you imply specifically what the character needs to achieve happiness. First, what does she need in the long run to achieve substantial happiness? Second, what does she need in the short run to achieve immediate relief from misery? Example: To be happy, Beth must reconcile with her estranged mother. This is the short run, because it is a trial to demonstrate Beth's desire and ability to overcome whatever has caused the estrangement. Once she is able to do this, she proves she has the knowledge she needs to deal with emotional conflicts and be happy, and she proves she has the ability to use this knowledge to change who she is and how she deals with emotional conflicts in the future. (Take a closer look at how Beth's emotional conflicts and bigger-picture knowledge relate to theme in chapter five on page 175.)

**Plot conflict.** The obstacles in her way of achieving her goal are the plot conflicts. Plot conflict is an external event that complicates the protagonist's life. As described above, the focus here is on introducing "What I Have" and showing "What I Want" (and how badly the protagonist wants it). At first, the external conflict may seem totally unrelated to the character's internal conflict, but it often becomes obvious (usually in the second act) that the external conflict is a manifestation of the internal conflict. For example, a mother comes to visit her adult daughter—we now have external conflict. But the reader soon realizes (even if the unreliable narrator-daughter doesn't) that the protagonist's emotional trauma is due to how she chooses to react to the mother, not the presence of the mother herself. The conflict is self-induced. Yet, sometimes the plot conflict is just an external force that is not a manifestation of the character's internal conflict, nor is it self-induced. A hurricane, a murderer, a sudden loss of a loved one—these are external conflicts thrust into the character's life to test him, to provide an opportunity to overcome them or be destroyed by them.

Let's take another look at the conflict introduced above: Beth needs to overcome her estrangement with her mother. That's a plot conflict, but the character conflict addresses why she needs to do this and what impact this conflict has had on her life. For example, Beth's estrangement was caused by her mother's drinking while Beth was a child; Mother did not protect her when it was needed. Now Beth is struggling to work things out in a rocky relationship with her husband when Mom arrives, adding stress to the already-troubled marriage. Beth must overcome her hatred of someone who doesn't exist anymore (the drunken mother, now sober); Beth's tie to the past and her resentment for not being protected may have manifested itself in her as either distance because she trusts no one to protect her, or excessive need of protection. She sees neither in herself. To triumph, she has to slay Beth, the Beth whose ego still makes her seek revenge/anger, etc. Then she will be able to love her mother *and* her husband.

Typically, a story will be character-driven or plot-driven, meaning that either character conflict or plot conflict will dominate the story by motivating the action. Usually, genre stories are more plot-driven, while literary mainstream stories are character-driven; however, this is not always true. For example, the sports genre has certain plot conventions: troubled outsider, a romance, the big game. The genre demands these elements be included. When the audience's focus is on the drama of these plot points—and suspense is built on the outcome of events—then the story is plot-driven. Examples include the films *Any Given Sunday, The Karate Kid, Varsity Blues, Rudy, The Longest Yard* and *The Replacements*. Being plot-driven is not a slight, nor does it mean that the characters don't go through changes or have insights, nor that we don't intensely enjoy the story. It means that most of our enjoyment is directed at the turn of plot events. Not all genre stories are plot-driven, however. The sports films *Bang the Drum Slowly* (novel by Mark Harris), *The Hustler* (novel by Walter Tevis), *Lucas, The Gambler, Hard Eight* and *Vision Quest* (novel by Terry Davis) are character-driven. Character-driven stories focus on character reactions to events, chronicling character changes as a result of the plot events.

**How stakes work.** This is the fear element of the story. The power, impact and suspense of the plot depend on the stakes. What exactly are we playing for? Most genres use the character's life or death as the stakes: Overcome plot obstacles or die. (A variation is the threat to the life or lives of his loved ones.) Some

## Case Study: Plot-Driven vs. Character-Driven Stories

*Vision Quest* almost blows being character-driven by conceding to an expected genre convention that seems contrived. The story is about a high school wrestler who decides to drop two weight classes to wrestle the state's undefeated champion. Why? Because he's just turned eighteen and feels he needs to "make his mark." My students often interpret this as his desire for recognition by others, but the fact that he endures the scorn of the rest of the team and school for his "selfish" goal shows that glory is not his motivation. He merely wants to define himself as a man and challenge his fears before he graduates because he wants to become the kind of man who will challenge his fears as an adult. He wants to set the pattern for who he will become rather than start rationalizing why he doesn't face fears.

The story focuses on this internal struggle and how he almost abandons it when he falls in love with a worldly, slightly older woman on a vision quest of her own. However, with her help, he realizes that the relationship was a way to avoid his quest, and he shows up at the end to wrestle the champion. Had the film ended there, with his bursting through the doors into the gym to face his opponent, it would have maintained the integrity of being character-driven. But the film then shows the actual wrestling match in real time, with the teen triumphing. By showing the actual wrestling match—with the predictable victory—the story shifts its focus from the teen willing to face his demons to our rooting for him to win the match. But initially the story wasn't about whether he would win, only whether he would go through with his quest. In fact, his quest wasn't to win, but merely to wrestle the champion. By presenting the actual match and freeze-framing on the teen as his teammates hoist him onto their shoulders, the story shifts from mainstream drama to generic melodrama.

throw in the fate of the world: overcome plot obstacles or the virus will be released and the world will die. Mainstream stories tend to focus on more intimate stakes. If the character doesn't overcome the obstacles, he will be miserable. This is one we can all relate to on a daily basis. Our lives are designed around goals (What I Want/ Who I Want to Be). Some are short-term goals, some are long-term goals. We believe achieving these goals will make us happy. That's what stories are about: the pursuit of goals. The genre story tends to limit the goal to a tangible overcoming of a villain; the mainstream novel tends to focus on the overcoming of some internal conflict that is smothering the character's pursuit of happiness. However, the mainstream story isn't just about the reader cheering the character on to be successful in achieving the goals, it is also about assessing the goals themselves. Are they worthy goals, or are the goals somehow misguided and therefore the true cause of the character's stalled happiness?

To give the plot stakes, the goal must be very important to the character. The failure to achieve that goal must carry with it an enormous penalty. On the surface, the goal might appear minor: for example, a character wishes to write a poem. But the significance of that goal must be presented in a way that the reader sees it for more than it appears to be. Using the poem example, let's say that the boy who wants to write the poem is generally inarticulate with girls. This has left him isolated but accepting of his lot in life. Then he meets a girl he truly likes. She's a writer and is applying to colleges to study writing. Desperate to stay with her, he applies to the college and is told that if he writes an exceptional poem, he will be accepted into the program. Now the writing of the poem takes on a life-impacting significance.

### How to Choose an Ending

The third most common place for writers to get stuck is the Act 3 resolution. *How should the story end?* Many a caffeine-fueled night has been spent by writers agonizing over this question despite the fact that there are only *five possible endings.*

**1. Get what you want—happy.** The protagonist has set out to accomplish something, succeeds and is happy with the results.

This would include romantic-comedies, romances and most Disney animated movies. Action-adventures, mysteries and suspense-thrillers also tend to have this chaos-to-order ending.

**2. Get what you want—unhappy.** The protagonist gets what he wants but discovers it doesn't bring him happiness. In the film *Heartbreak Kid*, written by Neil Simon, the protagonist goes through agonizing changes to win a woman. At the end, he's married her but is sitting in the reception party clearly shaken now that he realizes this is probably a mistake. It's the same feeling one gets at the end of *The Graduate*, when the young couple escapes the bride's wedding and rides away together on the bus, clearly with a look of trepidation. In *The Hustler*, Fast Eddy finally beats Minnesota Fats, but it's too late now; it brings him no joy.

**3. Don't get what you want—happy.** The protagonist sets out to accomplish something but fails. Nevertheless, he is happy because he gets something unexpected that is better, either in the form of something concrete, like money or a relationship, or in the form of a better understanding of his life. Many teen love stories follow this pattern: The popular boy chases the popular girl, only to eventually realize that the girl with glasses, braces and hair in a bun is his true love.

**4. Don't get what you want—unhappy.** The protagonist does not succeed in accomplishing his goal and is miserable. This ending is usually reserved for unlikable protagonists who get what they deserve. However, sometimes it's also a cautionary ending for characters we like, but who confront their own character flaws and refuse to acknowledge them or change their behavior (see "bad faith" in chapter five, on page 212). Woody Allen's *Manhattan* ends with the protagonist refusing until it's too late, to realize that he pushed away true love because he cared more about society's opinion.

**5. Change mind—you no longer want what you thought you wanted.** The protagonist realizes in Act 3 that the thing (or person) he's been obsessively chasing is not what he really wants. This ending has two possible ways to go: He gets something else that makes him happy (similar to ending number three above), or he doesn't get anything else but is content just having this new insight into himself. After pursuing a valuable artifact that will make him rich, he may instead, just as he has the object in his hands, sacrifice his life to save someone else.

The key to a good ending is that it must be appropriate for your story and not feel contrived. It's not just a matter of blindly selecting one of the above ending options; you must decide what kind of story you're telling and how the ending will reflect on the events and character struggles you've presented. (For more on how this works, see "Six World Visions in Search of an Author" in chapter five.)

**The danger is in trying to force an ending that doesn't fit with everything else that's happened. I once heard a famous writer at a conference say, "If you want to be taken seriously as a writer, your protagonist must die at the end."**

I could see all the beginning writers in the audience scribbling this down, their brows furrowed as they tried to rethink their endings to kill off the protagonist. Even if this famous writer is correct in her assumption, you can't suddenly force an inappropriate ending; the reader will recognize the contrivance and balk. Take a moment to read the *Chinatown* sidebar on page 18.

What have we learned from this? The three rules of endings:

1. An ending should be unforgettable.
2. A writer must be flexible.
3. An ending must seem inevitable without being predictable.

Read that last one again; it's important. "Inevitable without being predictable" means that when the readers arrive at the end of the story, they must read the last words and feel satisfied that this is the only way the story could have ended. Yet they shouldn't feel that they knew all along that this would happen. Obviously, some endings are predictable in that we know the girl will get the boy or that the bad guys will be defeated. In such cases, the ending isn't about *what* happens, it's about *how* it happens. How does she get him? How are the bad guys defeated? Especially when the ending is known, the reader is counting on you to make it somehow surprising.

## Case Study: *Chinatown's* Ending

When the classic film *Chinatown* was released to rave reviews, one of the aspects that everyone praised was the brutal but realistic ending. On the dark streets of Los Angeles' Chinatown, the love interest (Faye Dunaway) is shot dead through the eye trying to save her daughter from her powerful, incestuous father (John Houston). Dunaway's daughter, the product of her father raping his own daughter, witnesses the shooting. While she screams in horror, the evil but politically powerful father comes over to hug and comfort her and the audience knows that the sexual abuse that happened to the mother/daughter will happen to the daughter/granddaughter. The private detective hero (Jack Nicholson) is outraged and starts after the evil father. But Jack's partner holds him back and says, "Forget it, Jake. It's Chinatown." Meaning, of course, that in the real world—for which Chinatown is a metaphor—there's no way to fight the rich and powerful. Pretty grim ending, especially for Hollywood, where conventional wisdom states that an unhappy ending costs the film anywhere from $10 to $20 million at the box office. But *Chinatown*'s honesty and refusal to pander nevertheless made it a critical and financial success. (Though, who knows, if Jake had saved Faye Dunaway and killed the evil father, it might have made even more money.)

After the film came out, the screenwriter, Robert Towne, complained about the ending. He had in fact written a happier ending and was angry that director Roman Polanski had changed it. "That's not the ending I wrote," he said to interviewers. Polanski's response was, "No, but this ending is unforgettable." Last year, Towne was asked whether he still thought Polanski's ending was the wrong one. He said he now realized that Polanski's was the better ending.

For me, the ending is like arriving at the end of a dimly lit tunnel and flipping a light switch. Then when you look back, you can see what the tunnel looked like for the first time. So too in a story, the ending casts a light on all the pages that you've read and illuminates them for the first time.

## The Difference Between Short Story and Novel Endings

First, we need to make some technical distinctions. The final scene in a story is different from that in a novel. In a story, the final scene may be only a few paragraphs, an addendum or continuation of action from the climactic scene. In a novel, the final scene is often a separate chapter—which may include several scenes—after the climax. In a story, the final scene is generally punchier, insistent, more like the last lines of a poem. It wants to leave you with an emotional and/or intellectual jab. In a novel, the final scene tends to be a wrap-up scene, in which the larger scope of the events are brought into clearer focus. It's usually less intense (the intensity having come from the climax), but still has a great deal of impact. The ending of a novel tells us how to feel and what to think about the events that just happened. This scene is more like a debriefing: gathering people who've been through an intense emotional experience and talking them through it so they can get greater perspective on what just happened to them.

## When Endings Attack

There are a few categories of conventional endings that are so common they have names. They are distinguished by their predictable and disappointing nature. Do not befriend or feed them, or they will hang around and devour your story. Among those to avoid:

**No-ending ending.** This is when the story just abruptly ends and you keep turning the page wondering if there's a page missing from your copy. You suspect that there must be a deeper meaning that you just aren't getting because you can't imagine why the person would end the story here. Of course, it's possible that there's a deeper meaning, but it's just as possible that the writer couldn't figure out how to resolve the story and just hoped being vague would be enough.

Sometimes the ending doesn't seem to resolve the conflicts of the story, but that doesn't mean it's a no-ending ending. It might be that the author thinks leaving the ending hanging tells us there is no resolution for these characters. This is a legitimate way to end a story.

**Twilight-Zone ending.** As much as I enjoyed the old Rod Serling TV series, I sometimes curse its influence on budding writers. Rather than compose an ending that evolves out of the conflicts the characters face, they often slap on a twist ending that they obviously think will give their story some depth—or at least entertainment value. Wrong on both counts. The twist ending offers no depth because it is a contrivance that roughly elbows its way into the story. Everything that came before is reduced to mere setup for this "punch line" ending. The characters are no longer as important and all our caring about what happens to them is sacrificed on the alter of "Surprise!" True, there could be some entertainment in terms of the shock value, but that is generally short-lived and once again reduces the rest of the story to an elaborate artifice to support the twist. To count on the shock value, it would have to accomplish two things: (1) truly take us by surprise, and (2) not seem too contrived. Considering the number of plots the average reader is exposed to through the various media, it would be the rare twist that actually surprises us. As for contrivances, the twist ending is by nature artificial, pulling the reader out of the story to marvel at the ending as if it were a sideshow freak.

What's especially annoying about this kind of ending is the writer's smug sense of being clever. For example, there are stories in which someone wishes for something only to have a demonic presence give her what she asked for, but in some punishing, literal manner that only torments her for eternity. In the famous "Monkey's Paw" story, a mother wishes for her dead son to come back, only he comes back as a corpse. This offers no insight into the nature of our wishes or fantasies; instead it suggests that satanic demons are basically strict grammarians.

**This-really-happened ending.** Sometimes writers present a bland or unbelievable ending, which they then justify by saying, "But this really happened to me." Stories aren't about facts, they're about truth. Save the facts for your diary. Rather, you should be asking what truths are revealed by those facts (meaning plot). The writer needs to examine why certain events took place, ask how the characters got themselves into such a situation, then—before deciding on whether to end with what really happened or to devise an ending of his own—consider what that ending has to say about the characters and the situation.

**Poetic justice ending.** Let's say a villain decides to kill someone by injecting him with a lethal virus. He sneaks up on the guy, syringe poised, needle only inches from the victim's neck. Suddenly a door opens bumping the villain's arm, forcing the needle into the villain's own chest. Beginning writers love this kind of ending because it's so tidy. And ironic. "Look, it's ironic," they say. To which one responds, "So?" Irony is one of the lowest levels of payoff. It seems contrived and phony and is therefore disappointing to the reader.

**The Tiger-or-the-Lady ending (hanging ending).** There's a famous short story entitled "The Tiger or the Lady" in which the hero is placed in front of two doors. Behind one is a hungry tiger that will devour him; behind the other is a beautiful lady who will become his lover. Only he doesn't get to choose the door, his lover does. This is the punishment for their illicit love. The story ends without the reader knowing which door his lover chose. We are left wondering whether she chose the lady, knowing her lover would then live with this other woman, or the tiger, choosing to kill him rather than give him to another woman. This is the hanging ending because it leaves the reader wondering what happens next. This is another favorite of beginning writers because it saves them the agony and hard work of actually coming up with a good ending. Readers do not want to care about characters and be anxious about what happens to them only to have the writer cheese out by leaving the ending up to the reader. If readers wanted to choose endings, they'd write their own stories and not read yours.

**You-figure-it-out ending.** Also known as the "huh ending" because you just stare, scratch your head and say, "Huh?" This ending is so obscure and unintelligible that you're tempted to think it must be meaningful—as with the no-ending ending. For example, *The Blair Witch Project* is a spooky little film with a lot of good characterization and suspense. But the ending is so undecipherable that no one knows what exactly happened. The problem with such an ending is that the focus then is on the puzzle aspect of the film, and figuring it out becomes a game. Instead of the audience receiving pleasure and satisfaction from the work as a whole, this treats your characters and plot as if they were nothing more than an elaborate crossword puzzle, easily disposable.

Proper plotting is difficult to learn from stories that are well-written because they seem so effortless. That's because they appear inevitable without being predictable. It's easier to learn plotting from bad stories because you can see what the writer did wrong and try to avoid it yourself. For me, watching bad movies and reading bad novels is a form of aversion therapy. I see the terrible mistakes these writers have made and am so afraid that I will make the same mistake that I redouble my plotting efforts.

 ## Physical Therapy

There are four things you can do to improve your plotting.

1. **Note pads everywhere.** This is one of the simplest and most effective ways of improving plotting, yet it is often ignored. *You must carry a pen and notepad with you wherever you go.* Spread them throughout your home, office and car. Next to toilets. Beside the bed. On the kitchen counter. Writers constantly get ideas that they think they will remember—but don't. You are lying in bed at night and have a great idea, but, too lazy to turn the light on and jot it down, you convince yourself you'll remember it in the morning. You almost never do. In addition, when you're busy trying to remember a line or concept, your mind isn't free to keep going with that train of thought. You've cut yourself off at your most productive moment. The second advantage of all these notepads is that merely seeing them sometimes nudges you to start thinking about the story again, examining your plot choices, running through variations of them.

2. **The harsh review.** One method many writers use to unstick themselves from plot flypaper is the harsh review. Imagine writing a review of your book from the point of view of someone who doesn't like you. What will he find to criticize in your novel? Plot

too predictable? Dialogue flat? Characters directly from Central Casting? When I do this during my own writing, I am brutal. But as soon as I'm done, I reread my manuscript with a more critical eye—and nervous fear that maybe my review was accurate. This forces me to think harder about my plot choices and sometimes seek more interesting alternatives.

**3. The slap-dash outline.** Some writers get mired down obsessing over their outlines; others hit a wall because they have no outline at all. An effective compromise is the slap-dash outline (detailed further on page 241). In essence, it means that you should outline only a few chapters at a time for the first half of the novel. This outline should be brief—two or three sentences describing each chapter. Once you hit the halfway point, your outlines will need to be progressively more detailed as you wrap up all the plot points and character conflicts.

**4. Pacing yourself.** I think it was director John Ford who said that making a movie is like taking a stagecoach ride through the Old West: At first you hope for a pleasant journey filled with wonderful sights and exciting people, but halfway through you just want to get the hell to where you're going! Writing is like that. The mistake writers often make is to be so excited about finally nearing the finish that they rush the ending. I made this same mistake many times at the beginning of my career. I would slavishly craft every word for the first 95 percent of the story, then in a white-hot rush of adrenaline, I'd gobble down the last 5 percent. It would take me a year to write two hundred pages of a novel, but the last fifty I would finish in two days of nonstop writing. And it showed.

Beginning writers often think that it's OK to write quickly at the end—to "get it all out on paper"—because they can fix it later. What they mean is that they can fix the style later, polish the prose, add nice metaphors and descriptions, tweak the dialogue. That's sometimes true. But generally that's not what's really wrong with the endings. It's like starting with a spoiled piece of beef and saying I can fix the flavor with spices. Indeed you can, but those who eat it will still get sick. The problem often comes because the author has not spent enough time thinking about the ending.

Forget the writing for a moment; put down the pen and shut off the computer. What's required here is some time spent just thinking through the variations of what might happen and what effect each variation will have on the reader.

Most writers need to maintain a pretty strict writing schedule to produce quality pages. That means writing a certain number of hours every day, including revising for a specified number of hours. Try to stick to this same schedule at the end of a story or novel. If you write three hours a day, keep writing that same amount of time, maybe a little more. But then stop! Don't keep going just because you have the energy or time. Instead, make some notes about what you will write tomorrow. It's much better to come back already knowing what you want to write. Plus, the extra time gives you a chance to think about what you intend to write. Sometimes that extra thought will allow you to reconsider and come up with a better way. Or it will provide you with time to enhance the original idea. Either way, the story is better off.

## Symptom: Predictable plot

## Common Ailments: Rushing; Underexposure; Overly Mechanical Plots

## Ailment: Rushing

Writers are neurotic; we write *despite* ourselves. It's a lonely occupation, often undertaken with little support from others. ("Are you nuts?! You know how hard it is to make a living as a writer?") Yet, despite the internal conflict of wondering if this isn't indeed nuts, we push on. We write. But on some subconscious level we agree that this very well might be a waste of time; after all, no one's paying us. This self-doubt often results in rushing our writing. The sooner I'm finished, the sooner I may sell it and show everyone I'm a real writer. There are other reasons writers rush their work. Professionals often have deadlines and are juggling several projects at once. They rush to finish them, and all the projects are the worse because of it.

We read fiction because, on the most basic level, we want to know what will happen next. Sure, we want insight into the human condition and all that, but we could get insight by reading philosophy and religion. So, it's not just *what* we get out of fiction, it's *how* we get it. Besides, sometimes we don't want insight, we just want a thrilling ride through the lives of characters much more exciting and daring than we are. But thrills and excitement are created through the element of surprise. The outcome of an event must be in question. People don't tune in to a sporting event in which the outcome is a foregone conclusion; they go when two evenly matched teams face each other. Anything could happen. When a writer rushes through his story, he makes plotting decisions too quickly. Where do you come up with your ideas so quickly? From the thousands of story plots filed in your head from every other story you've seen or read. Your mind flips through for a similar situation and pops up with the one you're most familiar with. It fills in the blanks by analyzing the patterns stored in your memory. The good writer recognizes this process and uses it to his advantage. If your mind came up with this plot suggestion, so will the minds of your audience. You can use that anticipation to surprise them, thereby increasing the suspense.

In the excellent book *Hitchcock*, French filmmaker François Truffaut (*400 Blows, Jules and Jim*) interviews Alfred Hitchcock, asking in-depth questions about each of Hitchock's films. Several times, Hitchcock describes how he chose a plot twist based on audience anticipation of what they were familiar with. For example, he picked Janet Leigh to play the doomed shower victim in *Psycho* because she was a pretty big star at the time and audiences would not suspect she'd be killed so early in the movie; they were used to the main star surviving to the end. Many filmmakers have used this technique since, so now the pattern has been added to the audience consciousness. Yet, the film *The Sixth Sense* manages to catch most of the audience by surprise because it took that same idea as in *Psycho*—using audience anticipation of familiar plot patterns—and gave it a new twist.

## Diagnosis

One familiar result of rushing is the emphasis on plot to the detriment of character. This is often the case in melodrama, which focuses on scenes of emotional reactions without developing substantial characters to make us care about those emotional reactions. For example, in the recent movie of the week, *Judy Garland: Me and My Shadows*, the film alternated, for four hours, between two types of scenes: Judy singing and Judy on drugs (or Judy crying about being on drugs). Scenes were not developed to make us care about Judy Garland, but each of those scenes was so similar to the previous one that there was no suspense about what was to come. The audience probably knew she'd died of a drug overdose before they started watching the movie, so the ending isn't the major suspense point (as in *The Sixth Sense*). When basing a story on a real person's life, you still must choose which scenes will best illuminate our understanding of the plot events, not just present the same plot event over and over. The fact that the movie lost one third of its audience from the first night to the second night suggests that familiarity had bred contempt. (See page 28 for treatment.)

## Ailment: Underexposure

Sometimes it's difficult for a writer to know what's predictable and what isn't. My students will often be surprised by some plot event in a book or movie that I saw coming from the story's opening. That's because I've seen and read much more than they have. In my scriptwriting class, students are asked to see a current movie in the theater, which we then dissect in class. Sometimes they come in all excited because they've never seen anything like it before. Then I list a dozen other films that did the same thing, sometimes better, sometimes not as well. For example, the film *Last Man Standing*, starring Bruce Willis, is a remake of *A Fistful of Dollars*, starring Clint Eastwood, which is a remake of the Akira Kurosawa film *Yojimbo*. Each is set in a different place and period of time. *A Fistful of Dollars* is a respectable remake because, though it mirrors the plot of *Yojimbo*, it does it with a style that is compelling and a character who is different enough to be interesting in his own right. However, *Last Man Standing* follows the plot pattern with nothing new to offer, making it bland and predictable. *A Bug's Life* is a clever adaptation of the same basic plot as *The Magnificent Seven*, which was an adaptation of the plot of *The Seven Samurai*. The test of originality in these films isn't in the basic plot pattern (all three have the same structure) but in how each develops those plot points, through characterization, dialogue, setting and sub-plots, to surprise and delight us.

Now the writer has a point of reference to compare. And that's how we tell good writing from bad writing: We compare it to other works in the same genre. Therefore, the more works you're exposed to, the better idea you have about the quality of your own work. This is important because the target audience for your work is usually in the following order: agents, editors, paying public. All three of these groups are usually well read in the genre in which you are writing. Let's say you write a mystery. It gets sent to an agent who's read a lot of mysteries. She will judge your book based on how it stacks up against other mysteries she's read. If the plotting is predictable, she won't want to represent it. Editors are even more selective: They've read many more mysteries that they've rejected than have accepted. If your mystery plot is the same as all the others that have been rejected, why purchase yours?

### Diagnosis

The most common result of a predictable plot is the most fatal: The reader stops reading the story. You know how it works: The story starts with an alarm clock going off. The character reaches out and throws it across the room, breaking it. (Now an alarm goes off in your head: I've seen that scene many times before.) His phone rings; it's his boss, a cigar-chewing cop who plays by the book. "Get your ass down here, Finnegan! You're in trouble!" (Uh oh, seen that scene a billion times.) Finnegan gets up and we see his place is a mess. Empty beer cans and pizza boxes. (Good Lord, not more empty pizza boxes!) Already we know everything that will happen in the rest of the story. No surprises.

**Lesson:** Read, see movies, study the patterns that you observe. Then take your time figuring out how to make your plot surprising. (See page 28 for treatment.)

### Ailment: Overly Mechanical Plots (Joseph Campbell Syndrome)

More than fifty years ago, Joseph Campbell published *The Hero With a Thousand Faces*, a book that showed the similar patterns shared by stories throughout time and from all over the world. This book was known mostly in the academic community, where it probably would have stayed if not for the film *Star Wars*. Following the success of the movie, when everyone was interested in anything to do with *Star Wars*, writer-director George Lucas revealed that he had consulted with Joseph Campbell in mapping out the plot for all the Star Wars stories. Joseph Campbell became a celebrity, and his many works on mythology became best-sellers. Since then, his ideas about plot patterns have been incorporated into many writing courses and books about writing. Understanding these plot patterns can indeed help a writer plot better. But there is also danger, Will Robinson.

Writers are often desperate for any tool that will help them write better. That's admirable because it shows they want to be better writers. But the danger is in using tools improperly and thereby destroying the work. I have read way too many stories and seen way too many movies that were written by writers who had obviously taped a copy of Campbell's "Quest of the Hero" chart to their computers, consulting it for plot decisions the way some people consult the I Ching, runes and astrologers. This resulted in connect-the-dots plots that were just as predictable and dull as if they'd been stolen from Plots 'R' Us. Just following the patterns isn't going to help your plotting become less predictable, but understanding how to use those patterns will. (For my own version of how to use Campbell's ideas, see page 222 in chapter five.)

## Diagnosis

As with Rushing and Underexposure, Overly Mechanical Plots create an inferior clone of story lines the audience has seen before. Readers know what is going to happen before it happens, and there is no curiosity about how it will happen.

## Treatment: Rushing, Underexposure, Overly Mechanical Plots

1. **Plot: what you can't change—and what you can.** Think of plots as if they were human bodies. There are only a few different basic body types, just as there are only a few different basic plots. But within that confined structure of arms, legs, torso and head, there are many

variations of how to enhance, alter and decorate the body. We change hair, muscles, eye colors; we pierce, tattoo and dress up the body so it continues to surprise, amuse and entertain. Don't think of the limited number of plot types as confining, but rather freeing. Knowing that there are only so many options for the plot to go, you are free to concentrate on the elements that make the trip worthwhile.

For example, the mystery novel usually has the same structure:

1. someone discovers a dead body
2. detective interviews possible suspects
3. murderer is uncovered

Yet, within that structure are many variations: (1) **Discover body.** How was the victim murdered? In my forthcoming mystery novel, *Anatomy Lesson*, the victim is a wealthy industrialist. Nothing new there. Except he isn't the only victim. The body that is discovered has his head, but the head is sewn to the torso of a young woman; sewn to that torso are the arms and legs of four different people. Now the mystery isn't just about who killed the industrialist, but who the other victims are and why they were put together in this arrangement. (2) **Detective.** There are hundreds of variations regarding the building of a detective. There are professionals, such as cops (Ed McBain's 87th Precinct novels), private detectives (Sherlock Holmes, Philip Marlowe, Sam Spade), medical examiners/coroners (novels by Kathy Reichs and Patricia Cornwell), and lawyers (John Grisham's novels); there are amateurs (Miss Marple, Nancy Drew). There are reluctant detectives forced to uncover the murderer because (a) she loved the deceased and the professionals aren't doing a good job, (b) she's a prime suspect or (c) she's protecting someone. In addition, you've got the variations of motivation for why each is in his profession (Batman's parents were murdered in front of him when he was a child); their varying personalities (Nero Wolfe never leaves his home); their flaws (Philip Marlowe drinks, Sherlock Holmes takes drugs). Add to this the dozens of types of characters you can introduce as suspects, the hundreds of different motives each might have to murder and the thousands of possible settings for these interviews. (3) **Murderer uncovered.** Solving the case means figuring out who did it, why he did it and/or how he did it. That offers as many possible combinations as license plate numbers. And there are more. But you get the point: Don't worry that you're working in a familiar plot pattern. Concentrate on how to make that pattern interesting and surprising by manipulating all these other elements. A guitar has only six strings, but those strings make a lot of delightful notes.

**2. Write yourself into a corner.** Plotting scares writers. They know that they have to come up with something fresh and clever or the whole story will be dismissed as derivative (or more kindly, an "homage" to whomever you stole the plot from). Rather than face that fear, writers often skirt the edges of genre conventions, never straying too far from the expected, but trying to dress it up so readers won't notice. Believe me, they'll notice. The antidote is to be bold and charge ahead, even though you don't know where it will take you. In other words, write yourself into a corner.

This is the same idea as the cliffhanger hook of the old serials: At the end of each installment, the protagonist hangs from a cliff. Below, a pit filled with starving tigers; above, tribesmen with poison blowguns approach. Oops, one hand just let go of the cliff. The fingers on the other hand are slipping, slipping . . . tune in next week to find out what happens. What a wonderful opportunity for the writer to distinguish her story by coming up with some brilliant, unexpected, clever twist. Of course, that requires thinking a lot, rejecting a lot of ideas, wondering if you're really smart enough to come up with an original idea. But when you finally do, you will have elevated your story above the rest of the predictable pack piled in an editor's rejection basket. When asked about the danger of contrived plotting, writer/director Neil LaBute (*In the Company of Men, Your Friends and Neighbors, Nurse Betty* [director only]) replied: "Occasionally, you write yourself into a corner. I've done that many times. But I'd rather do that than have it feel like it's systematic and a foregone conclusion."

The danger of writing yourself into a corner is that you will solve the problem with an obvious contrivance that causes the reader to lose confidence in the story (see the Rushing ailment on page 24 and the Insufficient Character Motivation ailment on page 66). For example, in the movie *Traffic* the key witness to the government's case against the druglord is protected by government agents in a seedy hotel. The druglord's wife wants the witness killed. But how? That's the corner. Unfortunately, the writer solves the problem with a contrived cliché: A phony room-service guy delivers poisoned food. The audience immediately has to ask a series of questions: Why a seedy hotel? Isn't it easier to guard someone at a good hotel where there is better security (cameras, etc.)? Three or four cops sit with the witness in his room, but nobody checks the ID of room service? Plus, why take the chance of even using room service when you can bring in your own food? Haven't these guys seen the three hundred other movies that use phony room service to attack a witness (as in the much more believable scene in *La Femme Nikita*)? This is the trickle-down effect of solving problems by using what's been used before— even if it wasn't convincing before. I just finished reading a novel section by one of my students. In an otherwise clever and promising story, he gives the protagonist the obstacle of having to smuggle something into a guarded hospital room. This is a variation of the witness-in-seedy-hotel problem. The usual way this is solved is by having the stereotypical incompetent guard. Yup, that's always the guy they pick to guard something really important (in this case a thawed ancient Roman soldier).

> Vinny worried that the guard would also want to see what he had in his sack. Fortunately, he merely stepped aside and let Vinny pass.

What luck! Which is exactly what makes the reader wince: luck, coincidence, contrived circumstances. Writing yourself into a corner is an opportunity to shine as a writer and shouldn't be squandered away with the predictable.

**3. How to de-emphasize plot.** Not all stories wish to emphasize plot; some prefer to have the suspense generated by the characters. Rather than have the readers focused on what will happen next, the author wants them focused on why whatever happened took place. The suspense is just as great—perhaps even greater— because the reader (and writer) is relieved of the burden of worrying whether or not the plot will live up to preconceived expectations. It's like watching a movie for the second or third time. The first time you watched it, you didn't much care for it because the plot did not deliver enough on its promise. But when you watch it again, and you already know how it will turn out, you can appreciate other qualities that you might have missed while distracted by the plot suspense. You enjoy the subtle characterization, edgy dialogue, etc.

The way to de-emphasize plot is to tell the reader early in the story what will happen to the characters later in life. This technique has two effects:

(1) Whatever we're told about the character's future makes us look at him differently in the story; the information actually enhances the character. For example, if we're told that the cute little boy in the story who is saving the drowning dog will one day grow up to rob banks and murder an innocent teller, we look upon the boy with added sadness. Two emotional and intellectual reactions are developing in the reader: one for the current story and one for the later story.

(2) We also scrutinize the details of the story more carefully, looking for clues as to why this sweet boy changes so drastically. The author has focused the reader's attention more intensely on the events of the story and characters.

In her novel *The Prime of Miss Jean Brodie*, Muriel Spark employs this technique to great effect. She tells us very quickly in the novel that Sandy betrays Miss Brodie, which results in Miss Brodie being fired. She also tells us the fates of most of the girls from Miss Brodie's class. Several times we see the adult girls in their lives. Following are a couple descriptions of the girls from the first few pages of the novel: ". . . said Rose, who was famous for sex-appeal." And "Mary Macgregor, lumpy, with merely two eyes, a nose and a mouth like a snowman, who was later famous for being stupid and always to blame and who, at the age of twenty-three, lost her life in a hotel fire . . ." A few pages later, we meet another of the girls, who is now twenty-eight years older and discussing the events of her youth with her husband when she reveals when Miss Brodie died:

> "Just after the war. She was retired by then. Her retirement was rather a tragedy, she was forced to

retire before time. The head never liked her. There's
a long story attached to Miss Brodie's retirement.
She was betrayed by one of her own girls, we were
called the Brodie set. I never found out which one
betrayed her."

By telling us all this now, the melodrama of what happened is
removed and the reader is left to ponder how a woman of such
obvious influence and respect ("we were called the Brodie set")
could be betrayed. Our attention is on the theme of betrayal
rather than merely the drama of the event itself.

By contrast, the play based on the novel (as well as the movie
based on the play), tells a much more linear story. Here the betrayal takes place at the end, so the audience focus throughout is
on what will happen to Miss Brodie. The emphasis is more on
plot suspense than character suspense.

 ## Physical Therapy

**Locked-room mystery exercise.** Want to challenge your
ability to come up with clever, original plot choices?
Locked-room mysteries are a sub-genre of the mystery category.
There are many variations, but the basic setup is that a dead body
is discovered in a bare room in which the doors and windows have
been locked and bolted from the inside. Now, add to that an
unusual manner of death: The dead man was killed by being
hanged, but there is no rope in the room and there's nothing to
hang from. Can you come up with a scenario that explains this?
Remember, don't be too easy on yourself by going for the
obvious.

**Variations.** Although this exercise may seem useful for genre
writing that tends to be more plot driven, it's equally useful for
mainstream literary writing. It strengthens the plotting muscles.
Plus, you can change the situation from a locked room to something more realistic. For example, a husband and wife with two
small children are seeking a divorce. The plot calls for them to
reconcile. What event or series of events would bring them back
together? Make a list of every scenario you can think of. When
you can't think of one more possibility, put the list aside. Then

## Case Study: Fresh Plotting, Stale Plotting

You already know the stories in which the plotting is fresh and original because those are the stories that probably inspired you to write in the first place: J.D. Salinger's *The Catcher in the Rye*, Alice Walker's *The Color Purple*, Harper Lee's *To Kill a Mockingbird*, etc. Such a list could go on for pages, and there are plenty of other sources in which writers list the books that most influenced them. The problem with such books for the beginning writer is that it's difficult to see how well-plotted the story is because it's done so seamlessly. But when it's not seamless, bad plotting jumps up and spits in your face.

But we can examine one scene in one story to see how a writer working within conventions of a genre structure still manages to create fresh plotting. In the film *Marathon Man* (based on William Goldman's near-perfect suspense novel), Babe (Dustin Hoffman) is held captive by evil Nazis who are torturing him. He's just an average guy, a grad student, up against ruthless professionals, so the audience knows he has no chance to escape on his own. His only hope is the professional spy Janeway (William Devane). And, in fact, Janeway does rescue Babe, killing his captors and speeding off in the getaway car. While speeding away, Janeway explains to Babe why he's been kidnapped and questions him about any knowledge he has of the bad guys. When Babe cries out that he knows nothing, the car screeches to a halt, and Babe discovers he's right back where he started, with his tormentors, who only faked being dead. Janeway is in with them.

It's a neat scene because it plays on the audience's expectations of escape while simultaneously snatching them away. Babe is now on his own, and the audience doesn't know how he'll get out of it. A bonus of the scene is that the author explains the complex plot to the audience so they know what's been going on. In fact, the scene is so good that the more recent movie *Enemy of the State* copies the scene, this time with Gabriel Byrne as the phony rescuer and Will Smith as the trusting dupe. Unfortunately, this version is much more clumsy and obvious.

Now let's look at a film that was also working within a genre, but made some bad choices. *Family Man*, with Nicolas Cage and Téa Leoni, follows the structure and conventions of the traditional romantic comedy. (See chapter five for a discussion of romantic comedy structure.) Cage plays a wealthy bachelor businessman who is transported into an alternate reality in which he married his college sweetheart right out of school rather than splitting up with her. Instead of going on to become super successful, he's a family man with a crappy job, very little money and two small children. Naturally, he will come to recognize how precious the family is over the hollow wealth he had before. The fact that he will come to this realization is not bad. In fact, knowing it will happen is what keeps us watching—it's the payoff. The challenge for the writer now is to make the payoff believable and fulfilling. It isn't. Here's why:

**Act 1 Setup:** Part of the problem is with the setup: The film starts with Cage singing joyfully as he struts about his enormous penthouse apartment filled with expensive furnishings. His walk-in closet is bigger than most people's apartments and is packed with expensive clothing. He has a gorgeous, sexy girlfriend. No wonder he's singing so happily: To him, his life is perfect. The film must now show that his life isn't as perfect as he thinks. But it's very difficult to have a character arc proving that a character wasn't really happy when he so clearly was. Had he at least had some doubts about the direction his life was taking, some small sense that it wasn't fulfilling, we might believe his change of heart. As it is, there's

*continued*

something almost cruel about taking away his happiness just because it isn't the same happiness that others experience. When the angel-like character who causes this says to Cage, "Remember, you brought this on yourself," the audience can only wonder how. By being happy?

**Act 3 Resolution:** The ending dismisses the film's self-described theme. The final scene shows Cage and Leoni, both wealthy and successful in the original reality, as they sit down to talk. The implication, as the romantic music swells, is that they'll now get together and their lives will be on track with that family they were in the alternate reality. However, the difference—and it's a huge difference—is that, instead of being the plucky couple who struggles through life, sacrificing material comforts for the greater good of their family, which is what the film emphasized was so important to Leoni, they will now be an enormously wealthy couple raising children with hardly a struggle. This plot choice negates the whole point the film was making.

The otherwise fine film *Vision Quest* also compromises its theme by making a poor plot choice at the end. (See case study on page 14.)

come up with three more scenarios. Those are the three that will be the most difficult—but they will probably be the most original.

 **Symptom: Ho-hum suspense**

**Common Ailments: Uninvolving Characters; Low Stakes**

### Ailment: Uninvolving Characters

We don't necessarily have to like the characters, but we need to find them compelling. If we don't find them riveting, we don't really care what happens to them next. (See also Uninvolving Protagonist, page 89.) David Schickler (*Kissing in Manhattan*) emphasizes the importance of making your reader care: "A high school teacher of mine said, 'Assume that your readers would rather feed their children to piranhas than read your stuff.' It makes you keep asking the question 'Why should someone care?' "

**How it works:** In my scriptwriting class, five of my students are each writing scripts about a group of buddies who drink, do drugs and seek sex. The opening scenes involve them all indulging in these preoccupations. Obviously, a lot of films are produced that emphasize some or all of these pursuits (*Road Trip*, *Tomcats*, etc.). They are aimed at the teen audience. Consider, however, that there are five such scripts in my class (and multiply my class by however many other scriptwriting classes there are and . . . hell, you do the math). That's a lot of competition. Why write that story? Because the characters are compelling. A few of the scripts are comedies. For these scripts to distinguish themselves, they need to have wacky comic scenes. For the other scripts, which are dramas, we have to care about the characters. For that, we need to know why they do what they do, often to their own detriment. I asked one student why his twenty-year-old protagonist drinks two bottles of vodka a day. "I don't know," he responded. He needs to know, and so do we. Otherwise, he's just another poser who uses booze or drugs to create a romanticized persona of someone with depth. *Character depth is not created by the flaws in the character—they're created by the reasons those flaws exist. The motivation is where the suspense resides.* (See below for diagnosis.)

### Ailment: Low Stakes

The story doesn't generate enough suspense to maintain reader interest. A story must create an increasing level of suspense. It's as if a knuckle is pressed against the reader's solar plexus, and with each turn of the page, the pressure increases ever so slightly. As the pages mount, so does the pressure, with the only hope for release coming from turning the last page. And the higher the stakes, the more readers care.

### Diagnosis: Uninvolving Characters and Low Stakes

Healthy suspense means the reader is continually in a state of wanting to know what will happen next. This is true whether it is a mainstream literary story or a conventional genre story. If it is a literary story, the reader wants to know what will happen next because she cares about the characters so much that she needs to know what impact the plot will have on these characters' internal lives. If it is a genre story, the reader wants to know what will happen next because she needs to know what the characters will do to affect the outcome of the story. The best stories have readers wanting to know both.

Suspense is created when on Monday I tell my three-year-old son that I'm going to take him to Disneyland on Friday. This introduces the two main ingredients of suspense: (1) anticipation and (2) unpredictability. Anticipation is generated by having to wait four days. This waiting period also produces unpredictability because anything can happen that might prevent the payoff of going to Disneyland. The less time between the promise and the payoff, the less suspense. However, too much time can also lessen suspense.

Suspense is created by a series of these promise-payoff scenes. In the Big Picture, promise is established when character and plot conflicts are introduced in Act 1. Character conflict: The protagonist drinks because he's a lousy attorney who can't win a case. Plot conflict: He is asked to handle a big case that not only is worth a lot of money, but also pits him against a giant evil organization. That is the setup of *The Verdict* (both the novel and movie). With a little variation, it's also the setup of *Erin Brokovich*, *The Rainmaker*, *A Civil Action* and *The Insider*. The payoff: The plot payoff is that the giant evil organization will be defeated. The character payoff is that the protagonist overcomes the reasons he's a lousy attorney and recognizes his own moral obligations. This is really nothing more than a variation of the revenge genre. A villain does something bad in or before the first act; the rest of the story the protagonist chases after the villain seeking revenge (or justice, depending upon your take).

In the Little Picture, promise and payoff occur within individual scenes, with each scene continually cranking up the suspense. The promise and payoff interact like two sticks rubbed together to produce fire. For example, our alcoholic attorney is a promise to the reader that he will not always act nobly; the payoff is when he's given opportunities to act nobly and he doesn't. This creates a larger suspense because now the reader doesn't know how he will act as the pressure of the case increases.

Beginning writers often mistakenly believe a fancy style or slam-bang action will be enough to hold the reader's attention. This is wrong. Style alone can become intrusive, with the readers feeling the author's presence and thereby bursting the fragile suspension of disbelief. Slam-bang action can become monotonous because it's repetitious.

Sometimes writers confuse action with suspense. Director Alfred Hitchcock described the difference between action and suspense something like this (and I'm embellishing here):

• **Action.** We're in a schoolroom filled with high school children. The teacher is lecturing about fractions. "Tina, what are you doing?" the teacher asks as he sees her pass a note to the hunky boy beside her. The teacher walks back, grabs the note and announces to the class, "Would you all like to know what Tina thought was so important that she had to disrupt my class?" Everyone laughs and shouts, "Yeah!" He pockets the note without reading it. "It's none of our business." They groan in disappointment; Tina looks relieved. He smiles at her. "But what is our business is the mid-term on Thursday." And suddenly the room explodes. Fire engulfs everyone. No survivors.

• **How it works:** The action startles us. Tina's passing the note is a misdirection meant to create a false suspense. The reader thinks the scene is about the note, which makes the bomb explosion all the more surprising. If this scene comes at the beginning of a story, suspense is generated because we want to know why it took place.

• **Suspense.** Back to the schoolroom, only this time we show the audience the bomb under the desk and a clock with only two minutes until detonation. The teacher says, "I'm letting you all out a little early today because my daughter is in her first play and I don't want to miss it." The students all chorus, "Ahhhhh, how sweet," but we can see they like him. The students all start to leave. We see the clock: one minute to go. We sigh with relief. "Wait, Mr. Thomas," protests one nerdy student. "What about the midterm? You were going to give us prompts to study." A groan rises from the students. "Oh, right," Mr. Thomas acknowledges. "Everybody back in here while I look for those prompts." The students gather around the desk, only inches from the bomb. Tick, tick, tick. Mr. Thomas rifles through his briefcase. "Where the heck are they?" he wonders aloud. "Can't we just come by your office later and pick them up?" an impatient student asks. Show the clock: twenty seconds.

**How it works:** Here suspense is generated by giving the readers superior knowledge to that of the characters.

### Treatment

Uninvolving characters, predictable plots and low stakes all diminish the suspense a reader requires to continue reading the story. There are many opportunities to increase the suspense quotient. First, we need to examine the structure of a story as it relates to suspense. (Refer also to the chart on page 10.)

## ACT 1: THE SETUP

Suspense is first created in Act 1 when we establish three things: plot conflict, character conflict and stakes.

- **Plot conflict.** This focuses on what the characters are pursuing. It could be a romantic relationship, money, a new job, an education—anything they think will *make them happier.*
- **Character conflict.** This focuses on the internal/emotional problems that get in the way of the characters achieving what they think will make them happier. In fact, this conflict may involve the characters pursuing the wrong goal, one that the reader realizes *won't* make them happier.
- **Stakes.** This focuses on the intensity with which the plot conflict affects the characters.

### Act 1 Fixit: How to Manipulate Stakes to Increase Suspense

We interrupt the act-by-act analysis to concentrate on stakes because this is the most important ingredient in increasing suspense.

Each scene makes a promise to the reader. An action scene promises that by the end of the scene, the reader will be breathless with excitement and either relieved that the characters pulled through the adventure or sad that they didn't. A love scene promises that there will be an attempt to bring the couple together for physical contact and, though this attempt may succeed or fail, when it is over, the reader will feel satisfied with the outcome. And so on.

The promise is nothing more than a variation of one kid carrying a shoebox walking up to another kid and saying, "Wanna see something really cool?" Who can resist the thrilling anticipation as the kid with the box slowly, sooo slowly, lifts the edge of the lid, revealing nothing but a sliver of darkness? But wait, the overhead light in the boy's room begins to eat away the darkness in the box, and you can see something. A shape is forming. My God, it's a . . . whatever.

In the promise part of the scene, it doesn't matter what's in the box. The promise has only one function: to tease the reader into being compelled to see how the scene turns out. In other words, to get the reader as interested as possible in looking in that box. In the payoff part of the scene, we discover what's in the box and how it affects the two boys.

The main method of increasing the promise value is by increasing the stakes. I have a simple way of teaching my students about stakes. I walk into the room the first day of class, take out a quarter, and flip it into the air. I ask a student to call it, heads or tails. I then show them the results. Everyone looks curious ("What is he up to?"), but a bit bored ("So what?"). Then I offer a challenge: "I'll flip the coin again. This time, if you win, you get an automatic A in the class, you never have to show up or write any assignments. But . . ." (dramatic pause to increase suspense) ". . . if you lose, you get an automatic F, plus you must show up every day of class and do all the assignments, even though you will get an F. Any takers?" Now I have their full interest. A couple clowns always raise their hands to accept the challenge, but I give them the steely stare and say, "I'm serious. If you lose, you will get an F on your transcripts." They usually back down. One person always accepts the bet and I flip the coin high into the air. Every student watches the coin arcing up and dropping down. I slap it onto my wrist, peek, grin and say to the student, "Are you sure? Are you positive you want this bet?" He always hesitates. Others advise him ("Don't do it, man!" "Go for it!"). Of course, I back out of the bet: If they lose, I don't fail them, though I don't tell them that until the end of class, so the lesson of stakes sticks with them. If they win, I pocket the coin without showing them because I've already made my point. The higher the stakes, the greater the intensity of the promise—and, of course, the bigger the payoff must be. This is what I call the P3 Equation ("payoffs per promise"). The greater the promise section of a scene, the greater the payoff (see "Act 3: The Payoff" on page 46).

The two principal ways to increase the stakes are through character and plot. By enhancing either or both of these elements, the stakes go up—and so does the promise.

Let's take the same little-boy-with-shoebox scenario and crank up the stakes a bit more. As it stands so far, the kid with the box just wants to show it to the other kid. Simple transaction. But what if we add a little information?

> Bill leaned over the water fountain and let the cool water wash over his sore lip. Who'd have thought his baby sister would have such a grip? She was only ten months old, and face grabbing was her newest trick. The constellation of scabs on his cheeks proved that much. Still, it was almost worth it to see her laugh so much when she got a chubby fistful of his face.
>
> "Wanna see something cool?" the voice behind him asked.
>
> Bill straightened up, wiped his mouth. "I don't want to see your smelly old sneakers." He reached for the box.
>
> "Careful!" Carl said, pulling the box out of Bill's reach. "This ain't sneakers, my friend. Not by a long shot."

The difference here is that Bill is developed a little more as a character. The sentences describing his baby sister are there to create sympathy for Bill: He's the kind of kid who loves his ten-month-old sister. Because we like that about Bill, we don't want anything bad to happen to him. The stakes of opening that box have gone up.

Another way to go is to develop Carl's character, but not sympathetically:

> Bill watched Carl coming down the hall carrying a beat-up old shoe box in front of him as if it were filled with crystal and might break at the slightest bump. Not that there was any chance of a bump from any of the other students in the hall; they all kept their distance as usual. Nobody wanted to risk getting Carl mad. Not after what he'd done to Jimmy Pine last week. In fact, Bill was surprised to see Carl at school. Wasn't he still on suspension?
>
> Bill hurriedly grabbed his books out of his locker so he could escape before Carl got to him. For some unknown reason, Carl thought Bill was his friend. He yanked on his notebook, but it was wedged between his chemistry and history books. Come on! He yanked again, harder.
>
> "Hey, Bill, wanna see something cool?" Carl said behind him.
>
> Too late. And what was that *smell*?

In this version, the concentration is on making Carl's character as sinister as possible. The fact that Carl was suspended tells us he's done something bad—and may do something worse. The fact that he's in school when he's still on suspension suggests that whatever is in that box may be directed at the school. The stakes are greater now because the possibility of what is in the box may affect more than just these two boys.

Both of the above versions concentrate on character, but obviously there are also plot elements present. You can focus more on one element over the other, but you can't do one at the exclusion of the other. One of the techniques used when focusing on plot is foreshadowing, which is a kind of promise. There are different forms of foreshadowing. One form is a character trait: In the opening of *Marathon Man*, Babe's dogged competitiveness against

43

another, better runner demonstrates that Babe has an inner strength he can tap into. Another form is a physical item: In the beginning of *Moby Dick*, the inn has a dark painting of whalers being overwhelmed by a whale. Playwright Henrik Ibsen said that if there's a gun hanging on the wall in the first act, by the third act that gun must be fired. What he meant was that the gun is an implied promise for which there must be a payoff.

Let's look at the same shoebox scene written with a focus on plot:

> Carl felt the sweat drops etching down his forehead straight for his eyes. He let them. He couldn't risk taking even one hand from the shoebox. He shuffled down the hallway, afraid to lift his feet for fear he might trip. He was a star track and field athlete who hadn't tripped since he was five. But today was not the day to take that chance. Not with what he was carrying.
>
> "Hey, Carl, whatchya got there? Your smelly sneakers?" Bill appeared at his side, bouncing happily along. He reached for the box.
>
> "No!" Carl snapped, spinning away.
>
> "Jesus, man, take a pill. What the hell is that?"

Where the previous versions directed reader attention at the characters first and the box second, here almost every line is somehow about the box. The author is pointing at it saying to the reader, "Whatever you do, don't take your eyes off the box." Plot focus is on what will happen, whereas character focus is on whom it will happen to.

## ACT 2: THE COMPLICATION

The first act is relatively easy: pretty much anyone can generate some suspense by introducing a plot hook and characters with something to lose. Act 2 is more difficult because it involves complicating the story: making it more difficult for the characters to achieve what they want. There are two ways to complicate the story: increase stakes and decrease the character's ability to achieve a goal.

**Act 2 Fixit: How to Complicate the Story to Increase Suspense**
Increase stakes. Although we've established stakes in the first act, increasing them in the second act will result in more suspense. For example, in Act 1 we introduce Sedgewick, a struggling actor who's promised his father that if he hasn't gotten a major acting role in five years, he will quit acting and take over the family sock manufacturing business. The story opens with one month remaining of the five years—and still no major role in sight. His girlfriend, Lisa, is also a struggling actress, but she suddenly lands a great role in a major movie. She tells Sedgewick she will be able to get him a major role as well.

Act 2 complication: Sedgewick discovers Lisa is having an affair with the star of the movie, which is how she's able to get him a featured role. Lisa doesn't know Sedgewick knows. Should he tell her he knows? Should he break up with her? If he does, he won't get the role and he's off to making socks. Should he pretend he doesn't know, take the job, and then break up with her? Doesn't that make him dishonest, something of a prostitute? The stakes that have been increased here relate to his integrity, how far he's willing to go to get what he wants.

There are variations to increasing stakes. The character might be training for the Olympics. This has been his dream, which has been fully supported by his parents, especially his father, who worked two jobs to pay for his training. The Act 2 complication occurs when the athlete learns his father has a terminal illness and might not live to see him compete at the Olympics.

Decrease character ability. Suspense is also increased by introducing a complication that inhibits the character's ability to achieve the goal that he thinks will make him happy.

Act 2 complication: Let's use the Act 1 setup, but instead of complicating things with Lisa, we'll have Sedgewick get the role he's always wanted. Only the role requires someone who can ride a horse. He lies and says he's a great rider. He has two days to learn before they shoot the riding scene. That's one complication. While practicing, he's thrown from the horse and sprains his ankle, which could cost him the role. That's the second complication. Both are obstacles he must overcome. The suspense is in whether or not he will—and how he will.

## ACT 3: THE PAYOFF

This is where all your suspense "promises" must be kept. This is discussed more fully in the Paying Off Too Little ailment on page 55.

### Cutting: The Pen Is Mightier Than the Sword (Unless You're in a Sword Fight)

The most underused technique of writers is cutting. Suspense is often increased not by adding words, but by eliminating them. The key to cutting is to read the manuscript with only one goal: cut whatever word, phrase, line, paragraph, page or chapter that is unnecessary. Don't polish the dialogue, tinker with style or anything else this time through.

True, sometimes it's difficult to know what to cut. You will agonize over some words, while others will be so obviously expendable that you wonder why you wrote them in the first place. A simple rule of thumb is to ask yourself whether the passage contributes to furthering the plot or revealing character. I just read a student chapter about a woman enduring the aftermath of breast cancer surgery. Within the chapter is a ten-page flashback to when the protagonist was a child. The writing in the flashback is excellent and would make a very nice story on its own; however, it had no function in the chapter. It did not reveal anything about the character we didn't already know, either in terms of information or conflicts. So, it had to be cut.

A common hiding place for excess wordage is the end of paragraphs. I can pretty much guarantee that if you look closely at the last two sentences of each paragraph, especially descriptive ones, you'll discover that many of them can be trimmed. The reason for this is that writers start to panic in the middle of a paragraph. They worry that what they've just shown the reader through action or implied subtly through description or dialogue isn't clear enough. So they tack on a sentence or two that tells the reader what it all means. Each time this happens, the reader feels the author's breath on her shoulder, and the suspension of disbelief is thumped.

Dialogue is another area often begging for pruning. In an effort to write "realistic" dialogue, writers get all Tarantino on our asses and plug in lots of colorful but distracting exchanges. Sometimes the best, most character-revealing dialogue is indeed the colorful exchanges that seem to be about nothing. It's up to the author to know when that's the case. A scene is "talky" if the length isn't justified by what we get. Ask yourself, "What do I get, and what do I give up in exchange?" If you get only a little characterization or plot development in exchange for a lengthy, suspense-deadening scene, think about trimming.

### The Suspense Pocket

The suspense pocket is a little device that creates a misdirected suspense moment within a scene to reveal something else. Here's how it works: A woman is sitting at a restaurant. The table is set for two, but by the way she keeps glancing at her watch, we realize her companion is late. When he finally arrives, her face brightens: She's not mad, just relieved. His face, however, is grim and evasive. He sits down.

"Honey, I was starting to worry," she says.

"Sorry, had a last-minute phone call."

"Bad news? You look gray."

"Listen, Trish, there's no easy way to say this. It's best if I just get it off my chest right now."

"You're scaring me, Brad."

"I'm sorry, but you need to know that—"

The waiter arrives with menus. "Our specials tonight include a . . ."

Just when the reader is most curious, we suspend (the root of the word suspense) the payoff with a misdirection. The "pocket" is that brief time between the hook and the payoff when the reader is most attentive. This is an opportunity to introduce another element, usually setting or character. Because the reader is now so attentive, she will be more likely to take in and retain whatever happens in this pocket—provided the pocket is not extended too long.

**How it works:** One of my students is writing a story that begins with the protagonist, a high school girl, coming home, finding a letter on the table and going to her room to open it. This is a wasted opportunity for a suspense pocket. Instead of immediately open-

## My Own Private Editing

When my agent of twenty years retired, I contacted another agent, Laurie Liss of the Harvey Klinger Agency. She asked me to send her my recently completed novel. When she finished reading it, she suggested I cut fifty pages. She was completely right. On my first read-through, I cut twenty pages. I knew immediately the novel was better. The second time through I cut another ten pages and was convinced I'd cut as much as humanly possible. To cut any more would require removing vital organs from the body of the story. But this was my first book with a new agent, and I wanted to give her the benefit of the doubt. I read through again—and the scales fell from my eyes. Indeed, there was more to cut: dialogue exchanges, descriptive passages, etc. I sent the novel back to her, pleased that I'd cut forty pages. The day after she received it, she phoned me. "I just read the first hundred pages, and I think the opening two chapters are a little talky. We can cut some of that. Maybe the whole firing incident." Ironically, I had scribbled a note across those chapters: "Too long. Cut the firing scene." But I'd ignored my note because the dialogue was so clever, the characterization so nice. And it showed that the protagonist was fallible in her thinking—an important device to increase suspense. However, when I looked at it again, I saw I could show her fallibility later. I cut the scene, which meant eliminating a whole character and subplot, and that instantly jacked up the suspense.

**Caution:** Sometimes you have to write long in order to explore all the aspects of the story, for your own sake, so everything is fully developed. Don't edit yourself too much while you're writing. Throw in flashbacks if you want, introduce subplots, let your characters yammer as long as you're having fun writing their dialogue. That's what writing a draft is all about. But editing is where the amateur and the professional differ. The pro always looks to do what's best for the novel, not what shows off the author's writing ability.

ing the letter, there could be several stalls: As she's going up the stairs, her mother calls to her.

"I noticed you got a letter from Florida. I didn't recognize the handwriting. Who do you know in Florida?"

"No one. Maybe Grandpa is on another vacation."

"You've seen his handwriting. They'd need the CIA to decipher the address."

**Pocket:** This delay between discovery of the letter and opening it is an opportunity to meet the mother and learn a little about the family. Also, how the girl interacts with the mother is character development.

Now the girl goes to her room, tosses her books carelessly onto the bed. A couple fall onto the floor, but she ignores them. She starts tearing at the envelope, saying, "Finally." But just as she rips it open, her little sister comes in and says, "I think I lost my Barbie's head in here."

**Pocket:** The fact that the girl ripped at the letter and said "Finally," tells us she knows whom it's from. The fact that she lied to her mother about it makes the letter even more valuable and cranks up the suspense another couple notches. The reader is even more curious about the letter, so her attention is heightened. This is an opportunity to slip in information that the audience needs when they are most likely to pay attention to it. How she responds to her little sister will reveal character—will she tell her sister to get out or will she set aside the letter and help her search for the Barbie head? If she does the latter, we can see she's a nice person who we can care about. This immediately raises the stakes and increases the overall suspense. In addition, the contrivance to show her searching through her room is an opportunity to describe her room (books, CDs, posters, etc.) and thereby reveal her character.

All the stories you ever liked have strong suspense. If they didn't, you wouldn't have liked them. Sometimes it's easier to understand a writing technique when you examine an example that isn't completely successful. That way you know what to avoid. Let's take a look at Thomas Harris's novel *Hannibal* and see what went wrong.

### Five Things That Went Wrong With *Hannibal*

1. Because Hannibal is more of a protagonist than antagonist—unlike in *Silence of the Lambs*—he had to be made more likable. To make Hannibal more likable, his victims had to be more deserving of their fates. But once the victims are more deserving, we care less about them, and the suspense is substantially lowered. We don't care about the victims' fates as much, so the sight of him stalking them is substantially less involving. Both the film and novel tried to overcome this by raising the gross-out factor, that is, making the attacks more brutal (see "Graphic texture" on page 59). We cringe in anticipation of having our stomachs turned, but not out of sympathy for the victim.

2. The movie suffers even more than the book. Without a prominent villain to arouse fear or vulnerable potential victim to give us hope, there is little suspense. Making Hannibal likable and comic (he keeps saying cutesy phrases like "okey dokey") means we need a powerful and threatening villain to take his place, in this case Mason. The book demonstrates Mason's evilness by showing him with children he's molesting. The movie sanitizes him, but at the cost of not having him seem menacing enough. We are told he's bad, and we see others carrying out his violent plan, but we never *see him doing* anything evil. The movie needed a scene in which he does an evil act against someone who doesn't deserve it. Hannibal actually deserves the fate Mason has planned for him, so there's not much suspense there. The film relies on Mason's deformed face to make us loathe

him, which appeals to a part of ourselves that we don't want to nourish: the hatred of the ugly.

3. The co-protagonist, Clarice Starling, is not as dominant a presence in either the novel or the movie as she was in *Silence of the Lambs*. This is because she doesn't have much of a character arc. In *Silence*, she goes from a dedicated but naive agent to a more mature and seasoned person. Much of the suspense generated in *Silence* is based on how much we care about this vulnerable character. In *Hannibal*, she's hardened, depressed, disillusioned. In fact, she's very much like the protagonist of Harris's earlier novel *Red Dragon* who later becomes Clarice's boss. Her gloomy state stays pretty much intact throughout the story, which doesn't give the reader much chance to care about her.

4. The ending of the novel, in which Clarice and Hannibal are romantically linked, repels many readers, not just because it confuses their ideals of good and evil, but because it is such a hopeless gesture. It leaves the reader with the feeling that everything that just happened had no real meaning. The movie tries to redeem this by having her resist him, but it's too little too late.

5. The problem really isn't with the writing or the plot choices Harris made. He was obviously trying to deal with larger themes. Hannibal is portrayed more as Lucifer the fallen angel, not the crazed devil of other stories. In fact, he sees himself as Christ-like, killing the Italian cop because the cop acted as a Judas to him. He punishes the wicked ("the rude") and chooses for himself what is good and what is evil, which, to him, is the only rational thing to do in a world filled with so many evil people. The characters who persecute Clarice are ambitious and uncaring, creating a world that is unjust and cruel. Those are his victims. The fact that Clarice and Hannibal marry is the result of her rejecting a world that is ultimately unjust, ruled by a benevolent God, and embracing a more existential we-make-our-own-justice universe as embodied by Hannibal. This is all worthwhile and skillfully done. Except he chose to do this in the thriller/serial killer genre.

## Symptom: Flat payoff scenes

## Common Ailments: Promising Too Much; Paying Off Too Little

### Ailment: Promising Too Much

Readers can suffer from "hype syndrome." This is when the author promises more than can reasonably be delivered. It's like enduring a movie studio publicity campaign—for example, a new *Star Wars* movie. We see the characters everywhere: in every store, on our drinking cups, on cereal boxes, candy bars and the covers of news magazines. We see the ads on TV, in movies and on videotapes you rent. This can go on for many months before the movie even opens. Finally, you go, stand in the long lines, pay the money, sit excitedly in your seat. But there's usually no way the movie will meet your expectation.

### Diagnosis

Over-promising results in a loss of appetite for the story. It's as if you've been starving yourself all day in anticipation of a great meal at a fancy restaurant. Finally, the food arrives, you bite into the fancy chicken that has four foreign names you can't pronounce—and it's *raw*! You spit it out. The waiter apologizes profusely and orders a new meal for you. But it's too late. Your anticipation has not been rewarded. The job of the payoff scene is to reward the readers with a moment that equals or surpasses their expectation. If it doesn't, the reader experiences a feeling of being let down as well as a lack of faith that the rest of the story will get any better.

A healthy payoff scene will not only satisfy the reader, but it will increase his appetite for the next payoff scene—which results in heightened suspense.

### Treatment

1. **Keep plots and subplots to a realistic minimum.** Don't overload the first two acts with too many plots and subplots.

Each story has a certain number of plot complications it can handle; any more than that seems intrusive and requires so many additional explanatory scenes that it's impossible to meet your payoff obligations. It's like charging too much on your credit card and not having the means to meet the minimum payments.

**2. Don't overuse cliffhangers.** Avoid too many cliffhanging chapter endings, especially in multiple-POV stories. I see this a lot in my workshops. Every chapter will end abruptly just as something major is about to happen. Then we switch to another character's POV and follow her storyline until that too ends abruptly in a cliffhanger. That makes every chapter a promise, with very little opportunity for payoff. In fact, when the reader is returned to that cliffhanging ending, the payoff is often flat because you've removed some of the anticipation energy. The reader has to remember what the circumstances were, which lowers the suspense. The more cliffhangers, the more the reader has to remember, until the story feels more like a midterm exam.

**3. Don't overuse jump cut.** Many writers who use cliffhangers often cheat the reader by using jump cuts. Instead of presenting an active payoff scene, they jump cut ahead. For example, we are left at the end of a scene with the character returning home to find his beloved girlfriend in bed with his boss. The next chapter or two go into other characters' POVs. When we start the chapter back with our poor cuckolded character, he's driving somewhere and we're told about the confrontation in a flashback, usually as a summary rather than an active scene. This can happen because the writer is afraid to write the scene (see "Push past the 'comfort zone' " on page 57). Overuse of the jump cut will frustrate the reader, and she will lose faith that you will ever give her an active, fully realized payoff scene.

**How the jump cut works.** The first line of the scene or chapter is some action or line of dialogue, which has nothing to do with the previous scene, even though we're with the same characters. This creates a sense of suspense—the reader must now find out what happened between the time the last scene ended and this one began. Here's an example from *Earth Angel*. The last sentence of chapter seven is, "I cried all the way over the Rockies until a flight attendant knocked and asked if I needed help." Chapter eight begins

"This can't possibly work," he argued, twisting his napkin's neck for emphasis. "You'll just end up embarrassing me."

"You have to trust me," I said.

"I do?" He frowned.

There is no apparent relationship between the ending of chapter seven and the opening of chapter eight. The suspense here is what happened after her flight landed. Who is this man she's talking to? What "can't possibly work"? Will she get him to trust her? Is trusting her a mistake? In movies, this is called a jump cut, though fiction writers employed it long before there were movies. However, the influence of movies on fiction writing can't be ignored, and this technique has become more popular lately.

Here's another example from Jen Banbury's novel *Like a Hole in the Head*. The last lines of one chapter focus on a fight in which a man attacks the female narrator:

. . . I kicked out again, this time connecting with his lame wrist. He screamed and rolled over into a fetal position. I pushed myself up so I was squatting on the chair, facing him. I flipped the catch on the gun and yelled, "The safety's off! The safety is off! Do you hear me? You jerk you fucking jerk? It's fucking off!" I let out a single sob, then held it all in.

The chapter ends there. The reader is wondering what happens next: Does she pull the trigger, can she force him to reveal the whereabouts of the object she's after? The intensity is especially high at the end of this chapter because she's yelling and sobbing, showing that she's at an emotional edge. Also, we know her life is at stake and she's not good with guns—a volatile combination. But the next chapter doesn't answer our questions. Instead, it starts with "I was making good time until I ran out of gas a couple of miles outside Baker." Now we have a separate conflict—running out of gas—to add to wondering about what happened with the guy she was pointing a gun at. She's used the jump cut to double the suspense—but she follows through with satisfying payoffs later. Overuse weakens the setup for an effective payoff.

## Ailment: Paying Off Too Little

The key payoff scenes of the story do not meet the readers' expectations either in emotional intensity, plot clarity or thematic development. There are many payoff scenes in a story; if the early ones do not meet or surpass the readers' expectations, the readers probably will not continue to the next payoff scene.

Many beginning writers are more comfortable with promise than payoff, which is why the payoff part of the scene is where writers most often fail. Part of the reason is that there are many familiar techniques and blueprints for creating promise. But for a payoff scene to truly be satisfying to the reader, it must be more creative and original. The challenge is that, given any particular promise, there are usually only a few options for payoff. If it's a revenge story, the payoff when the protagonist confronts the antagonist is limited: Either he extracts his revenge or he doesn't. But within those two choices are many subtle, yet powerful, variations that can be extremely satisfying to the reader.

No one can tell you how to write a satisfying payoff; however, you can be taught what elements to look for and what pitfalls to avoid.

## Diagnosis

As with the promise, the payoff will concentrate either on plot or character. Plot payoffs will focus on startling the reader with a shift in plot: Something will happen to the characters, or they will do something that will alter their *external* circumstances. Character payoffs will startle the reader with a shift in character: The characters will be *internally* affected or changed by what has happened.

The key to a good payoff is not that you give the reader what you think they want. The hero does not have to succeed in each action scene; the lovers do not have to embrace in each love scene.

When you try to do that, you often end up writing a predictable scene that disappoints.

The same problem can occur in character-driven payoffs. A student in my novel workshop submitted a chapter in which the two main characters, who are on the verge of falling in love, coincidentally find themselves on the same flight home. They wish to sit together so the man, Cameron, asks the ticket holder beside the woman, Susan, to swap seats. He says sure and leaves. There's nothing wrong with that. It's realistic in that most people would accommodate it. However, because this is the first extended scene of the couple together, the tension (promise) would have been heightened if the stranger were not so accommodating. If Cameron or Susan had been forced to somehow convince him to move, either by bribery, cajoling, lying or some other interesting means, the plot would have been more interesting and their characters would have been richer. Instead of just talking and thinking about their relationship, this would have been an overt act that demonstrated not only how much they wanted to be together (the stakes), but the kind of people they are by how they go about achieving it. Are they clever, bullying, blunt, clumsy? Plus, there is an opportunity to see either their contrasting styles in approaching this problem, or that they work well together, picking up on each other's cues.

The payoff in this case is the conversation itself. For the payoff conversation to satisfy, it must do several things: (1) It must reveal more of the characters than we've seen before, both informationally and emotionally. Informationally (do not look this word up) in that the reader or character learns something about another character that she didn't know. This could be background from their past, or it could be something concerning the current plotline. Emotionally in that the characters' reactions to each other are different than they have been before, somehow intensified by the information they received or the situation they are in. The reader must feel as though she knows these characters' feelings more deeply because of this scene. (2) The dialogue itself must be fresh. This will be achieved by making sure each speaker's voice is distinct and reflects her personality. Every person has a unique rhythm to the way she speaks, just as she has a unique walk. Beginning writers often have their characters all speak in the same voice and cadence, making their dialogue interchangeable. (3) The final payoff is watching the impact of what has just happened on the characters. It's like the Academy Awards—when the winner is announced, the camera immediately cuts to reaction shots of the losers. In this case, the payoff conversation's impact can be visible or not, external or internal. It doesn't matter. What matters is that the reader feels that whatever impact the scene had on the characters is enough of a payoff to justify the existence of that scene.

 **Treatment**

There are several ways a writer can increase the intensity of the payoff:
1. heightened style
2. graphic texture
3. unusual setting
4. unpredictable plot
5. character revelation

However, before we address these specific techniques, it is important that the writer first recognize that these techniques serve the following two larger goals:

**1. Push past the "comfort zone."** The comfort zone is the point where the writer feels comfortable because he is writing in a familiar pattern. For example, a husband and wife are having an argument. Most of us know what it's like to argue with a loved one, so the familiar pattern of what is usually said comes easily to us. However, there's a point in every argument in which either words and complaints the participants rehearsed run out or they start to get responses from the other person that they weren't expecting. The argument degenerates into an uncomfortable emotional chaos. The novice writer wishes to avoid this gray area because it would require a lot of thought. Which is why the advanced writer embraces this part of the scene. Though frightened by the unknown as much as the novice writer, she loves the challenge, because it is in this part of the scene that the unique personality of the story will emerge.

2. Generate a "sense of consequence." You must generate a "sense of consequence" that whatever happens in the plot impacts the characters. The greater the impending impact, the greater the suspense and the greater reader involvement and loyalty.

## TECHNIQUES TO IMPROVE PAYOFFS

Think of the following areas as colors, the addition of which will add vividness to a payoff passage. Manipulating these colors will make your payoffs superior to the bland, tepid payoffs so common in beginning writing.

1. Heightened style. An obligatory scene can become an extraordinary scene in the hands of an accomplished stylist. Using metaphors and similes, poetic word choices, a particular rhythm—these stylistic techniques can elevate an otherwise conventional scene to a higher level. For example, in Leonard Michaels's short story "City Boy," a boy and girl make out in the living room of her parents' apartment. The parents are just down the hall, asleep in their bedroom.

> "Phillip," she said, "this is crazy."
> I didn't agree or disagree. She wanted some answer. I bit her neck. She kissed my ear. It was nearly three in the morning. We had just returned. The apartment was dark and quiet. We were on the living room floor and she repeated, "Phillip, this is crazy." Her crinoline broke under us like cinders. Furniture loomed all around in the darkness—settee, chairs, a table with a lamp. Pictures were cloudy blotches drifting above. But no lights, no things to look at, no eyes in her head.

Though the scene is typical, the style is anything but. The choppy sentences create a montage effect, like a series of photographs. The rich imagery reveals a narrator with a poetic eye: "Furniture loomed," and "Pictures were cloudy blotches drifting above." This makes us more interested in him and therefore the scene itself.

**2. Graphic texture.** The amount of detail provided can also intensify a payoff scene. For example, in the film *Gladiator* the opening battle with the German tribe shows decapitations, amputations, burning men, etc. The opening twenty minutes of *Saving Private Ryan* also show detailed graphic violence. Yet, there have been many other battle scenes in movies that were less graphic. How graphic the writer is depends upon the effect she wishes to achieve. The makers of both of these films knew their audiences had probably seen dozens, if not hundreds, of battle scenes before. The challenge then was to take a familiar payoff scene and evoke the appropriate reaction from a battle-numbed viewer. The reaction sought in both scenes was a sense of how brutal war is, how brutal the men fighting it had to become to survive. These scenes had to depict a world that is filled with danger and chaos to such an extent that a character would seem justified in turning his back on that world. Yet, the fact that they not only don't turn their backs but also forge a moral code out of this chaos reveals them to be exceptional people. For us to *feel* that, first we must experience their terror.

The above example is about violence, but the same technique applies to all payoff scenes: sex, romance, arguments, etc. However, more graphic may not always be the best choice. Sometimes a reserved scene—one with fewer graphic details—can be more effective. That is usually the case when one is focusing on character revelation (see page 61).

**3. Unusual setting.** How many filmed chase scenes have you witnessed? A thousand? More? The more you've seen, the more likely you are to tense with annoyance when you see another one about to occur. I used to go to the movies once a week with a friend who, as soon as a familiar payoff scene would start to roll, would pretend to flip a switch on his head and say, "Time to turn off the brain." Then throughout the scene he would check off an imaginary list of predictable moments: car drives up on sidewalk, pedestrians scatter (check); huge truck backs out, blocking off the escape route (check), etc.

The way to add a little more interest to the payoff scene is to change the setting to one that may not be as familiar. In *Lady From Shanghai*, director Orson Welles created the classic chase among the funhouse mirrors, which has since been copied in several other films, including Bruce Lee's *Enter the Dragon* (see also Wrong-Address Settings on page 132). A typical chase scene might be more interesting through a sausage factory because the average reader isn't familiar with the workings of the factory. This way they are distracted from the conventions of the chase by the freshness of the setting. The same principle would hold true for any payoff scene, whether literary or within a genre.

**4. Unpredictable plot.** In William Goldman's novel and movie *The Princess Bride*, the grandfather who reads the fairy tale constantly challenges the little boy's conventional notions of how a story should proceed. When the handsome hero dies, the boy can't believe it and starts complaining that the story isn't fitting into the pattern he's used to. When the grandfather threatens to stop reading because the story is upsetting the boy, he pleads to hear more. Of course, in the end, the story will have the conventional ending the boy so wants, but the trip there will be filled with unpredictable wonder because the payoff scenes will not follow the usual pattern—or at least seem not to.

James Goldman, William Goldman's brother and author of the classic plays *They Might Be Giants* and *A Lion in Winter*, wrote the script for the film *Robin and Marion*, the story of Robin Hood and Lady Marion twenty years after we last left them. Robin (Sean Connery) returns from the Crusades an older, wearier, less idealistic man. After a failed suicide attempt caused by missing Robin so much, Marion (Audrey Hepburn) has become a nun. The story climaxes with Robin battling his old nemesis, the Sheriff of Nottingham (Robert Shaw), who is not evil in this story, and is in fact as noble in his way as Robin. The one-on-one battle is long and tiring for both aging men, though Robin finally wins. What do you think happens next? What do you think should happen? (Go ahead, take a moment to think about it.)

Here's what happens: Robin rushes to Marion's room, excitedly retelling the details of the battle, giddy with his victory for Right. A serene Marion offers him a drink to celebrate. A few minutes later, Robin's legs go numb, he starts to fall. Marion is already weak, lying on the bed. She tells him that she's poisoned them both. He roars with anger, calls for Little John. But she explains: This was his most glorious day and he will never have another like it. The rest of his life will be spent longing for such days as this. Robin realizes she's right and lays down and embraces her. Little John rushes in. Robin asks for his bow and shoots an arrow out the window. Where it lands, he tells Little John, is where he and Marion shall be buried.

Now that's an unpredictable payoff scene. There are many unpredictable tweaks you can do, big and small, throughout payoff scenes to make them less familiar. To do this, you need to be aware of what the audience is expecting and then divert from that. The benefit isn't just that the scene is better, but that whatever twist you give might lead the whole story in a fresh direction.

5. **Character revelation.** A familiar payoff scene can be made more compelling by focusing less on the action of the scene— what the character will do—and more on the impact of what's happening on the character. For example, in Stanley Elkin's short story "A Poetics for Bullies," a payoff scene involves a fight between the high school-age narrator, Push, and another boy, John, whom Push resents because he seems so perfect. John hits Push, knocking him to the ground, then offers his hand to Push.

He offers his hand when I try to rise. It is so difficult to know what to do. Oh God, it is so difficult to know which gesture is the right one. I don't even know this. He knows everything, and I don't even know this. I am a fool on the ground, one hand behind me pushing up, the other not yet extended but itching in the palm where the need is. It is better to give than receive, surely. It is best not to need at all.

The payoff here isn't the fight but this moment, when the hand is offered. This moment reveals all of Push's self-doubts, his personal conflict, making what he does next all the more intensely anticipated.

Sometimes a writer has the right instincts about how to offer character revelation, but fumbles the actual scene. In the following excerpt by student Christian Lozada, a likable aspect of the father is about to be revealed:

> Turning off the TV, he told his sons that he was going to teach them how to fish after he had dug up his father's fishing pole out of the hall closet. He brought it back to the TV room where there was more space. Gripping the stick with one sweat-filmed hand placed over the other, Thomas whipped it forward to cast out an imaginary line from his pole. Then, pumping the reel with his left hand, while rocking forward and stopping to yank back on it, he pulled in a rainbow trout for his kids and himself to imagine. He did all this without telling them what he was doing beforehand, so his jerky movements only confused and frightened them. But when he started describing the characteristics of a rainbow trout, they seemed genuinely interested. The boys had only seen fish on TV, but didn't know about different kinds until their father started talking about them. Thomas repeated his fishing movements, this time telling his kids what he was doing and why.

The first ten lines are fine; they are active and descriptive, all contributing to the readers' caring more about Thomas. But then things go wrong: Instead of continuing this moment in an active way, the author backed off and synopsized the action. Rather, he should have made this scene as active as possible. The last half of the paragraph should be expanded, complete with dialogue about the fish and what Thomas is doing. This is a payoff scene and needs to have more impact.

## Effective Payoffs: A Star Called Henry

The opening of Roddy Doyle's novel *A Star Called Henry* flashes back to describe the wedding of the protagonist's teenaged mother, Melody. After enduring endless and stupid marriage advice from the women guests, Melody feels "as if she was going to die, just a few more whispered words would kill her. . . ." This wedding reception scene is a payoff scene because it is meant to establish the influences on Melody that result in the dreadful life that the narrator endures. The challenge for the writer is how to end the scene in a memorable way that startles the reader in such a way that she cannot only understand these influences, but experience them on a visceral level. What plot choice should the writer make to accomplish all that? Doyle chooses to introduce a couple "moochers," who have attended the wedding reception to steal what little food there is. Only Melody's mother, Granny Nash, spots them.

> Granny Nash jumped onto one of them and bit him on the cheek. His screams saved Melody. She got away from the women. But the sight of her mother hanging on the poor man's face filled her with fresh terror. Was this part of the wedding? Would she have to do it? The man was trying to save his face but his arms were stiffened by all the bottles and sandwiches stuffed up his sleeves. His friend was being pounded by Melody's father, using her new husband's leg. And her Henry sat on the table guarding the rest of the bottles. The neighbours queued up to have a go at the moochers but Granny Nash wasn't ready to give up and hand over. She was growling and chomping like a scorched bitch from hell; her dirty old thumbs were crawling across the man's face, looking for eyes to gouge.

*continued*

This paragraph is the emotional payoff to the scene; it not only fascinates and entertains because of the dynamic plot activity and comic tone, but it also reveals a lot about why Melody is fated for the life she ends up with: (1) Melody's mother is presented as an animal ("scorched bitch from hell") who chews the intruder's face; (2) the neighbors are mindlessly violent, lining up to beat the men; (3) the new husband guards the booze, suggesting where his priorities lie; and (4) the moochers are presented as a common occurrence, revealing that given abject poverty, nothing is sacred.

 **Physical Therapy**

**Changing focus.** Select a payoff scene in one of your stories and rewrite it five times, each time focusing on a different technique: (1) heightened style, (2) graphic texture, (3) unusual setting, (4) unpredictable plot and (5) character revelation. I know it seems like a lot of work—and being a writer, you'll want to avoid this much work—but doing this exercise will better enable you to not only use these techniques, but also be better able to select the appropriate one for each payoff scene.

# CHAPTER TWO

# *Characterization*

**Symptom: Contrived pivotal action**
*Common Ailment*
**Insufficient Character Motivation.** Character's motivations are not defined enough to make actions believable.

**Symptom: Flat scenes, predictable traits**
*Common Ailment*
**Cardboard Minor Characters.** Minor characters are too thinly developed.

**Symptoms: Low stakes, bland personality**
*Common Ailment*
**Uninvolving Protagonist.** Protagonist isn't likable or compelling enough.

**Symptoms: One-dimensional antagonist, overly evil antagonist**
*Common Ailment*
**Stereotypical Antagonist/Villain.** Everything the character does or says is predictable.

## FAQs Frequently Asked Questions
? What's the one quality my protagonist must have? page 90
? How can I make sure the reader is invested in my protagonist? pages 91–96
? What's the secret to creating a convincing minor character? page 83–84
? How can I flesh out minor characters? pages 75–79
? What makes a minor character archetypal? page 85

65

? How might I resolve the conflict between protagonist and antagonist? page 108
? How can I heighten suspense through my antagonist's characterization? page 104

## Symptom: Contrived pivotal action

### Ailment: Insufficient Character Motivation

A character's key actions that drive the plot are not believable to the reader. When this occurs, the reader is jolted out of the story, and the rest of the events will now seem contrived.

### Diagnosis

For any plot to progress believably, characters must perform certain pivotal actions: They must fall in love, quit a job, break up with a loved one and so forth. These pivotal actions trigger the conflicts that make up the story's core plot and theme. In a healthy story, the reader is fully involved in these crucial moments and never doubts the characters' actions.

However, when characters appear to be just going through the movements to create conflict, we have melodrama instead of drama. Now their actions seem forced, the result of the author intruding into the story, and the readers can feel the writer's sweaty desperation. When the readers question why a character would perform an action, the story has lost credibility, which is nearly impossible to reestablish. You've cheated the readers and they don't trust you anymore.

There are two varieties of this malady: (1) There is no clear motivation for the character to perform the action, or (2) the motivation provided is not sufficiently developed. Both causes are common among beginning genre writers who concentrate too much on following the template of their selected genre. Yes, a mystery will usually have a dead body and some sort of detective, amateur or professional, trying to solve the crime. The writer will dutifully provide these elements. But they often leave out why the characters do what they do. For example, Eddie Murphy used to do a comedy routine about horror films. He wondered why, when a haunted house says, "Get out now or I will kill you!" white people in movies stay. Why indeed?

In the play (based on the novel) *Woman in Black*, which has been running many years on the London stage, the title ghost curses anyone who sees her by having that person's spouse and child die in horrible accidents. I took a class of thirty-five students to see the play, and we were all frightened by the sudden screams and theatrics common to the genre. But at the end, when we were supposed to feel an eerie pity for the protagonist, instead we all wondered why the ghost bothered. There's an explanatory line in the play, as there is in most of these works, about how she lost her own child in a horrible accident. But that isn't enough. We understand the agony of her loss but not why she needs to inflict it on others—and only those who see her face, which no one would see if she'd quit jumping out at them. Because this motivation is perfunctory, the story is reduced to a generic routine.

This same problem occurs in the film *What Lies Beneath*. The explanation for Harrison Ford's respected professor character being the killer is that the student he was having an affair with was going to reveal the affair and destroy his career. Now the ghost of the dead woman has been not only haunting the house, but on and off inhabiting the body of wife Michelle Pfeiffer. The ghost likes to open and close doors, turn lights and computers on and off, and sometimes write on steam-covered mirrors. But if the ghost has the power to do all that, why not just spit it out and tell Pfeiffer what the hell happened? More problematic is that Ford had been able to hide his homicidal mania for eighteen years from everyone. He not only kills, but in the climax when he chases Pfeiffer, he apparently enjoys it in a sadistic way, though that was not part of the character developed to that point. The filmmakers needed a villain we would hate in order to justify his horrific death. So he was suddenly a merciless homicidal maniac. The pivotal action is his attempting to kill Pfeiffer; no believable motivation is provided, just a cursory one that the filmmakers hope the audience won't notice because of the continual action at the end.

The filmmakers had two choices: make the film a psychological thriller in the tradition of Hitchcock, or make it a supernatural thriller in the tradition of *Sixth Sense*. Although they used the style of Hitchcock to tell the story (in the homage-not-ripoff tradition), the film detours away from the psychological to the supernatural. There really is a ghost, albeit a remarkably inefficient and inarticulate one. Instead of a climactic payoff scene that reveals character, it opts for one that reveals special effects (the movie version of author intrusion). However, if instead of hauling out the ghost, they'd stuck with the psychological, the story would have been more convincing. Here's how: Pfeiffer spends much of the film in the process of recovering the memory of something that she saw while Ford tries to convince her she's just imagining things. It's a bit disappointing to the audience when it turns out to be the standard I-saw-you-with-another-woman memory that implicates him in the coed's death. What if, instead, the memory Pfeiffer recovers is that *she* killed the coed? Then the reason Ford is trying to keep her from pursuing the investigation is that he doesn't want her to remember her crime; he both loves her and feels guilty for the affair that caused the death. This is better motivation, but doesn't provide us with the more cliched but cinematic chase ending. Obviously, it's possible to combine both the supernatural and psychological effectively, as is done in the very fine *Sixth Sense*. (Remember, films can often get away with making these kinds of errors because they have so much other stuff occupying your senses that you aren't always thinking about motivation. With written stories, readers move at their own pace and can stop to think about what's going on, which explains why so many novels are abandoned before the reader finishes.)

How does this happen? Again, two causes: (1) the author deliberately sacrifices motivation to push the plot in a certain direction, or (2) the author is unaware that the motivation is weak. The first cause is exemplified by the description of *What Lies Beneath*. The filmmakers believed the audience would be more satisfied by the chase and the special effects than by believable characters. The second cause is one of omission, usually caused by oversight or, more commonly, nearsight. *Nearsight* is the result of knowing the story so well that the author can't see that the motivation is not sufficient. Instead, the author is focused on getting the character to perform the pivotal act so the next phase of the story can take place. You know what has to happen in the plot. A character must do A for B to happen. Sometimes writers rush through the pivotal scenes that connect the plot because they are in a hurry to move on to the next scene.

Many times at the end of thrillers, the writer is left with trying to explain how the murderer could be a maniac because that person was so normal throughout. Too often the motivation is cursory, slapped onto the story like a ragged piece of duct tape: uh, he was abused as a child, yeah, that's it. Or his mother was overbearing. The curse of pop psychology is that everyone thinks he knows enough to use the buzzwords and that the reader will just nod in acceptance. Not so.

## Treatment

The most effective treatment is providing proper motivation for a character to perform the required pivotal action. You can do this by fashioning a character and motivation appropriate to the pivotal action or by creating a more believable action for your characters existing motivation.

To tailor motivation to the action, ask yourself the following questions:

**1. Why would the character do this?** This requires more thought than you might first realize. Your first reason might be too superficial or predictable. Beginning writers often make choices based on genre conventions rather than thinking about what their character might realistically do. For example, a recent student manuscript in one of my workshops had two men in a Western shootout. The good guy waits until the bad guy draws first before going for his gun. Lovely sentiment, but bad gunplay. Such courtesy in the face of bullets is less the result of characterization than it is of those old movie and TV codes that demanded a good guy could only fire his gun if someone was shooting at him first. We've seen it so many times that many of us think a guy who draws first and nails his adversary can't be heroic. That's what makes cliches and bad characterization.

In John Updike's short story "A&P," we have a showdown of a different sort. Teenage protagonist Sammy quits his job as a supermarket cashier when the store manager berates three teenage girls for wearing bathing suits while shopping. At first, you might say he quits because he wants to show off for the girls, be their hero. After all, he quits in front of them. But Updike wants you to know that, although being their hero would be a bonus, that's not Sammy's main motivation. He accomplishes this in two ways: (1) By having the girls immediately leave after Sammy announces he quits. This allows the manager, a friend of Sammy's parents, to ask Sammy to repeat what he's just said. Sammy could deny he said anything; that's what the manager wants him to do. This, however, is an opportunity for the author to prove Sammy's ultimate motivation is not about the girls, but about not wanting to be part of a group with arbitrary morals. (2) By showing us throughout the story leading up to the pivotal action that Sammy is unhappy in his job and with the people at his job, though he doesn't know why. He can't articulate his dissatisfaction, nor is he consciously aware of it. So, when he does quit, it seems inevitable.

**2. Does the character know why he or she is doing this action, or is there a deeper subconscious reason?** Sometimes there are two motivations for an action: the one the character believes to be the reason he or she is doing it, and the one that the readers recognize to be the unconscious reason. For example, a man runs into a burning building to save a trapped child, even though he doesn't know the child. He may do that because he values that child's life above his own. Or he may do it because there are a bunch of other children and elderly people nearby watching him. He fears their disapproval more than he fears the flames. If that's so, is his action—motivated by fear rather than in spite of it—still heroic? Many stories (*Catcher in the Rye, High Fidelity, The Rachel Papers*, "Naked" by Joyce Carol Oates, "In the Garden of North American Martyrs" by Tobias Wolff) have unreliable narrators who tell us why they are doing an action, but because the readers have witnessed the pattern of their behavior throughout the story, they recognize that what the character is saying isn't true, even though the character believes it to be true. That gap, by the way, is the heart of many stories.

To make the action fit your character's existing motivation, ask, **Is there an alternative action that might work better?** So far we've concentrated on fixing the scene by developing the motivation, but sometimes it's better to create a whole new action that might be more in line with the kind of character you've created. Keep in mind that although a skillful writer can make us believe that any person will do any act given the right circumstances, some acts are inherently more believable than others.

Following is a pivotal action scene from "Canyon," a story by Patricia Fitzgerald, a student in one of my fiction workshops. This section is a flashback in which the narrator reveals how she met her current boyfriend. She has placed an ad in the newspaper for a female nonsmoker with no pets and no boyfriend. One day Guy shows up without phoning first, as the ad requested.

I opened the door and he thrust the newspaper in my face, my ad circled in red marker.

"I'm here about the room for rent," he said. He took a drag from a cigarette, dropped it on the walkway and stamped it out with his foot.

I blinked at him. "Did you happen to read the ad?"

"Yeah," he said, squinting in the morning sun. He was sweating, even though it was only nine o'clock. I let him in. I fed him a ham and cheese sandwich and poured cup after cup of coffee.

The next day he pulled up my driveway in a rusted-out Volvo with a mattress strapped to the roof and a mangy cat named Mr. Reagan.

This is good writing. The style is smooth, clear, not intrusive, but with a definite voice and tone. The problem is that the reader can't fully believe that the narrator would rent the room to Guy. And because this first meeting establishes the basis of their relationship, it's crucial that we believe it. Yes, the reader could fill in the blanks: she takes him because he's so forceful, confident, everything she's not. Possibly. But that's a generic reason, one we'd find on soap operas, an easy explanation not worthy of a good story. Patricia recognized this problem and a few days later turned in this remarkable revision.

I opened the door and he thrust the newspaper in my face, my ad circled in red marker.

"I'm here about the room for rent," he said.

I blinked at him. "Did you happen to read the ad?"

"Yeah," he said and took a long drag from a cigarette. I waited for him to exhale, but he never did—at least not that I could see. I imagined what his lungs must look like. Two Brillo pads. Or infected clusters of coral. The other day, I had watched a documentary about the coral reefs off the Florida Keys. How the coral was dying, an oatmeal-ish kind of disease spreading like a rash across their colorful surfaces, caused by the daily assault of tourist scuba divers touching them, pawing them with grubby hands.

This is what happens when you live alone. You watch documentaries and you worry.

I stood my ground, striking what I hoped was a confident pose in front of my open door. "You're not exactly what I had in mind," I said.

"People change their minds. It happens quite often, or so I hear." He was sweating, even though it was only nine o'clock. He lifted his tee-shirt and used it to wipe the sweat from his forehead. His chest was narrow and pale, the skin stretched thinly over ribs that looked perfectly snappable.

Although this rewrite fleshes out Guy's character a little, its strength is in how it fleshes out the narrator. Her fascination with him, her mental digression about his lungs and about her own living alone is a trigger for why she accepts this guy into her admittedly drab life. We buy it now. A lesser writer would have focused on doing more with Guy, or having her explain to us why she's taking him in. The imagery she uses is poetic, making us like her even more.

Look at the dialogue she gives Guy. It suggests a brusque charm; tells us he doesn't change his mind—but instead of a stiff manly guy, he's witty, more appealing. Plus the physical description—ribs snappable—makes him seem boyish, needy, vulnerable—at least in her interpretation (which also reveals more about her).

 ### Physical Therapy

Go through your story and mark each place where a character has to make a crucial action. Examine those scenes closely asking, "Do I believe this character would do this? Why would he or she?" You have to realize that, as the author, you know why you need him to do that action. You may even have a reason interjected into the story, but making that motivation believable requires that the motivation is blended and woven throughout the story.

 ### Symptoms: Flat scenes, predictable traits

### Ailment: Cardboard Minor Characters

Minor characters are not developed sufficiently either to be believable or to make the readers care about them. Without strong minor characters, the entire story may seem anemic, shuffling along like a convalescent. When this happens, the impact of the plot on the main characters is severely reduced—thereby lessening reader involvement. When we don't believe the minor characters, we don't believe *in* the main characters.

When a reader sees a peripheral character's name continually and wonders, "Which one is he again?" the author has a problem with minor characters. Minor characters are as crucial to the texture and impact of a story as is a major plot event. Cardboard minor characters float through their scenes without leaving a trace in the readers' minds, haunting rather than inhabiting the story.

### Diagnosis

There are two types of cardboard minor characters: (1) underdeveloped and (2) stereotyped. The underdeveloped minor character simply lacks enough brush strokes to be visible; he's a literary vampire who has no reflection on the page. With the character stereotype, the writer has developed the character with a lot of traits, quirks, background and emotional baggage—it's just that all that "characterization" adds up to a char-

73

acter type that the reader has experienced many, many times before (e.g., the prostitute with a heart of gold; the chatty, thickly accented cabdriver; etc.). Such a character is so familiar that the reader can often predict what that character will do or say in any given scene. This immediately makes the scene less compelling and damages the entire story. For example, cop stories are overflowing with the gruff by-the-rules lieutenant who has to ride reign on the break-the-rules, live-by-the-hunch protagonist. This stereotype is so familiar it's been parodied in two films, *So I Married an Ax Murderer* and *Last Action Hero.*

 Once a character type is parodied, run as fast as you can from using that character.

Healthy characterization of minor characters is shown when each scene that such a character appears in is somehow improved and heightened by that character's presence. That means that the character, regardless of how much or how little she actually has to do, is an active participant in the scene.

She is a *presence.*

Think about the films and fiction in which the minor characters enhanced the work: Christopher Walken in *Pulp Fiction*; the hitchhiking women in *Five Easy Pieces*; Jack Nicholson in *Easy Rider*; the record store clerks in *High Fidelity* (novel and movie); Mr. Antolini in *Catcher in the Rye*; most of the minor characters in Stephen King's *The Stand.*

## MISTAKES WITH MINOR CHARACTERS

Writers sometimes put all their creative energies into the development of their main characters. As a result, they limit the development of their minor characters only to the specific function that the character serves in the story; that is, they define the minor characters by what they have to do to progress the story. This is a mistake. Scenes in which cardboard minor characters appear are not taken as seriously by the reader; when enough of these scenes pile up, the entire story has lost its impact.

The stereotype is a bit more insidious. Underdeveloping a character is usually an oversight; stereotyping is laziness, the beginning of a bad habit that can infect all your writing. Most writers—like most of their audience—have literally thousands of storylines and character types swirling about in their memories. In the early drafts of a story, a writer often just sketches the character types for minor characters, dipping into this vast reservoir of collective "central casting" characters. The mistake is to not go back and spend as much effort in polishing those characters out of their familiarity. It's very much like going to Disneyland. People always ooh and aah over the attention to every minor effect that goes into creating the fantasy of the Indiana Jones or Pirates of the Caribbean rides. "Look at the detail work," they exclaim. Same thing in writing: It's all in the detail work.

## Treatment

So, how do you stop cardboard characters from bleeding the life out of your story? Imagine what the character's life was like before events of the story. Think about what they're doing when they aren't on stage. Identify the one hope that each minor character has for making her life happier, and what the obstacles in her way are. If you do all that, then you will populate your stories with the kind of minor characters who enhance your fictional world rather than cripple it.

There are three areas of character development, for minor or major characters: (1) background, (2) internal conflict and (3) personality. By adjusting how much of each of these ingredients you inject into each of your characters, you form the kind of characters they are and the kind of presence they will have in the story.

**Background.** This is the characters' history, how they were raised, influential events from their past. Because they are not major characters, it is not necessary to give much information, if any, about their past. Two exceptions: (1) if their past is somehow linked with that of the protagonist and/or the plot of the story, and (2) if you can provide one event that defines who they are. The mistake some writers make is to provide too much background, give the complete history of each character—mostly because that's fun to write rather than because it helps the story. Be selective. The story of how a minor character got a crescent-shaped scar over her eye may be all the background you need to tell, as long as that story (1) defines the kind of person she is, (2) explains her motivation or (3) foreshadows a choice she may make later in the story.

**1. Defines the person.** The story of how she saved a dog trapped in mud, even though she knew she'd get a beating for being muddy when she got home, defines her as a compassionate, self-sacrificing character. That way you don't have to keep showing it in the story; the reader already looks at her that way.

**2. Explains motivation.** In college she had an affair with her English professor who, when his job was threatened, accused her openly of coming on to him to improve her grade. She got kicked out of the school. This might explain a certain lack of trust she has about men with power over her.

**3. Foreshadows.** Both of the above examples might foreshadow a choice the character must make later in the story. However, it doesn't necessarily tell us what she'll decide to do. In fact, this can be used as a suspense device. A traumatic past event in a minor character is described; a parallel event occurs in the current plot. Will she make the same choice she did in the past, knowing those results?

One of my students begins chapter nine of her novel by introducing a new but minor character, Harry Armbrewster:

> Harry Armbrewster looked at the two agents seated in front of his desk. God, they're young, he thought. Was I ever that young?

There is nothing unusual with Harry making this observation. People make it all the time, which is also the problem with it. Because people make it all the time, it has no meaning in and of itself. Those lines require something to go with them if they are going to distinguish Harry as a character. The detail work here would focus on what exactly he sees when he looks at them. Is it their youthful arrogance in how they slouch disrespectfully in front of him? Is it the too-loud tie one is wearing because he considers himself a ladies' man? What if he saw them more like his own children?

Harry Armbrewster didn't look at the agents as they silently entered his office and sat in front of his desk. Instead, he stared at the cracked plaster ashtray his son had once made for him. He had never smoked nor allowed anyone to put so much as a single ash in it, yet the colors were faded, all merged into a dirty beige. The only color was the yellowed glue he'd used to fix it when an earthquake had knocked it onto the floor. Afterward, it was the first thing he'd looked for. He looked up at the two agents sitting rigidly in the chairs and thought of his son, now older than these two men, with an ashtray from his own son sitting on his desk. These two were too neat, smelled too good to have children of their own, to be sentimental over chipped plaster ashtrays.

This version gives a little background by focusing on a single object: the ashtray. The character is now more real because the original interior monologue (his observation about the agents' youth) has context that develops his own character.

**Internal conflict.** While the major fuel for the plot of a story is the internal conflict of the protagonists, it is wise to give selected minor and peripheral characters internal conflicts of their own. It makes them more human and therefore real. For example, you have a scene in which the protagonist is a teacher lecturing a class. The minor character of the department's new secretary, Ms. Denver, delivers an important paper to the teacher. Typically, the beginning writer would have her enter the classroom, and then merely describe her physically:

Ms. Denver marched across the room on long, thin legs, her short, black skirt snapping like a flag with each step. Her blonde hair was ratcheted to her head in a tight lacquered bun. She handed Professor Connors the paper, pivoted sharply on one high heel, then exited with a brisk snap snap snap of her skirt.

There's nothing wrong with that description of Ms. Denver. It delivers a vivid physical image of her as well as suggesting a personality type. However, she's also an easy stereotype: the tight-bunned, humorless office worker. We see her, but easily dismiss her. This emphasizes to the reader that she exists merely to serve a function, in this case to deliver a paper. What if we also suggested inner conflict within the charcater?

> The knock was so faint that, at first, Professor Connors thought some student was impatiently tapping a pencil on the desk. But as he looked around for the culprit, the knocking grew louder and he shouted toward the door, "Come in!"
>
> The door opened slowly and Ms. Denver entered, her arms full of papers that were stacked at random angles. The stack was so high, she rested her chin on the top of the pile. Her eyes darted out at the students, then quickly away again. "I'm sorry, Prof. Connors," she said, "they told me to give this to you immediately."
>
> "No problem, Ms. Denver. Can I give you a hand?"
>
> "Yes, thank you. It's this one." She shuffled around so the corner of the paper that stuck out pointed at Professor Connors. He reached for it, but as he did, she took a helpful step toward him and tripped on the worn classroom carpet, sending the papers flying. Instantly, she dropped to her knees and began gathering papers. Students helped and she took their neatly stacked offerings with a quiet "thank you" without ever looking at them. As she moved across the carpet on her knees, she kept tugging the hem of her skirt down, even though it already covered her knees.

Yes, this is longer, but it has the advantage of introducing a character who appears to have an inner conflict. She's shy, but there seems to be more to it than that. She especially avoids looking at the students, which implies a specific reason. Perhaps she wishes she were one of them, or she's embarrassed about her job and worries that they see her as menial, etc. We don't have to know why. We just know that the paper has been delivered by a real person, not just a stereotype defined by physical characteristics.

**Personality.** One can downplay, or even ignore, background and internal conflict and concentrate on presenting a defining personality. This is done through various methods: point of view, action, interior monologue, dialogue or a combination of any of these. Ms. Denver walks into the same room:

> The classroom door flew open startling Professor Connors.
>
> "Professor Connors?" Ms. Denver said, walking across the room with a stack of papers tucked neatly under one arm. She looked out at the classroom full of twentyish-year-old students and smiled. "Hi there, boys and girls. Professor Connors boring your ears off with more of that *Bearwolf-Cranberry Tales* stuff where people talk gibberish? Personally, I don't get why you have to read anything where you need teeny footnotes to understand what they're saying."
>
> Several students laughed and one in the back said, "Me neither." Then they all laughed.
>
> "Damn straight," Ms. Denver said, handed Professor Connors the paper, winked at him, and left with a beauty queen wave to the classroom. Several students applauded.

This version presents Ms. Denver entirely in dialogue, revealing her to be confident, humorous, personable, and unintimidated. Even though she says *Bearwolf* and *Cranberry Tales* instead of *Beowulf* and *The Canterbury Tales*, we don't think less of her. In fact, that makes her endearing. The force of her personality mesmerizes us. Of course, the personality doesn't always have to be overpowering, it must just be compelling.

By adjusting these three components, you can make the minor characters *inhabit* your story rather than walk through it.


## PERIPHERAL CHARACTERS

Before deciding on which of the above components to emphasize, it is important to first distinguish between minor and peripheral characters. Minor characters play important roles in individual scenes and may reappear through the entire story. Peripheral characters—sometimes called "spear carriers" because that was their only function in ancient plays—pass through without greatly impacting the characters or overall story. A peripheral character may bump into a main character on the street, but then passes on without any further interaction. In essence, a peripheral character appears for only a moment, to provide texture and tone for the scene. However, peripheral characters should not be underdeveloped any more than minor characters; the difference is that they can usually be summarized by one or two characteristics or a single line of dialogue. For example, in the following excerpt from Martin Amis's novel *The Rachel Papers*, the narrator sits down to eat and describes the person next to him:

> To my right, dentures clicking like castanets, an old man chopped through a hot-dog at insect speed.

The character never appears again, but the single line does two things: (1) makes it clear to the reader that the setting is uncomfortable for the narrator, and (2) establishes the narrator as a bit sarcastically judgmental. This next example is a bit more developed, but the character is still peripheral:

> When the subway lurched suddenly, Jane's *People* magazine slipped from her hand and slid across the aisle against the polished black wingtips of a teenage boy about her age. Except he was dressed in a dark business suit with a white carnation pinned to the lapel. He picked up the magazine and handed it back to her.
> "Thanks," Jane said.
> "I get them free," he said.
> "What?"
> "The flowers. You were staring."
> "I'm sorry, I didn't—"
> "I get them free. My sister works at a florist. I'm on a job interview and she thought I'd look more professional. What do you think?"

Jane didn't want the responsibility of affecting his job interview in any way. After all, what did she know of the world of suits and polished shoes? She was wearing flip-flops and a tie-dyed skirt she'd bought at a thrift store for $1.75. She shrugged at him.

The subway train jolted to a stop. He stood up, plucked the carnation from his lapel, dropped it on the seat. "Yeah, me too." He exited.

The boy never appears again, but his presence has impact because he helps define the kind of person Jane is. Unlike the character in the Amis novel, she's not judgmental, in fact, recoils from the responsibility of communicating an opinion. But the scene is about how, even though she tries not to affect others, she does. People don't live in a vacuum, and even the smallest interaction with another has consequences. All this is implied without having to be stated. Shown, not told.

What makes this peripheral character work is the feeling that the young man in the suit has a life outside his role in the scene. The reader knows that his sister works at a florist; that it was her idea to wear the flower; that he is unsure of himself on job interviews or he wouldn't have allowed himself to be talked into wearing the flower, which obviously makes him feel self-conscious in the first place; that he's off to interview for a job he seems to need but probably won't get.

The following excerpt from Roddy Doyle's novel *A Star Called Henry* (see also the sidebar on page 63) introduces a peripheral character at a wedding:

The bridesmaid was a scrawny girl called Faye Cantrell who scratched so much and so loudly that the priest told her to stop it or he wouldn't let her friend get married. So she put her hands to her sides and concentrated so hard on keeping them there that she wet herself.

Doyle accomplishes so much through this peripheral character: (1) Placed in context with the previous pages, the scratching emphasizes the physical condition of the girl caused by hopeless poverty;

(2) the priest's shortness with her indicates his patriarchal condescension toward her and lack of sympathy (which is part of a motif about the negative influence of the Catholic Church on the Irish); and (3) when she wets herself, it demonstrates the level of obedience and lack of self-worth of women in this cultural setting.

☠ **Where peripheral characters usually go wrong is when the author has them doing exactly what we expect them to do, in a way that we've seen before.**

For example, in almost every mystery novel manuscript I read in workshops, there is a cop who, upon discovering the corpse, pukes his guts out (or as the most recent story put it, "emptied his roiling stomach on the pier"). This vomiting-cop character is so clichéd that *Saturday Night Live* did a skit in which every cop who comes upon the scene of the crime begins projectile vomiting, climaxing with ten or so cast members spewing all over the stage. The point of a peripheral character who hurls at the scene of the crime is to tell the reader just how gritty the scene is and thereby to raise the stakes. However, when you use a clichéd character, you actually achieve the opposite effect: The scene loses credibility, and the stakes are lowered. This excerpt from a student manuscript introduces a peripheral character:

> When the doors closed at the back of the hall, a man of slight build wearing a solid grey suit and a wide black tie stepped up to the podium.

The character then speaks, and the scene ends without any more information about the character. The author chose to give us a visual of the character, which is good, but nothing that helps define his tone or attitude. The visual is not striking enough to be memorable, so it doesn't really help to define the character. There are two choices here:

1. Give the character a more striking physical trait than just a nondescript suit:

> When the doors closed at the back of the hall, a man in a modest grey suit limped toward the podium. From the tightness of his lips, it was evident

that each step caused him considerable pain, but the ease with which he moved indicated he'd been enduring that pain for many years.

**2.** Give him an action that helps define him:

When the doors closed at the back of the hall, a man in an expensive grey suit strolled up to the podium. He smiled out at the crowd who quieted down to hear him speak about the union. But when the hall was silent, he suddenly lifted the podium over his head and hurled it against the wall, smashing it into chunks of splintered wood. "That, my friends," he bellowed, "is what your bosses think of your union!"

Either of these choices will enhance the character so that he becomes a presence in your story, rather than just a passing shadow.

**Minor characters** usually inhabit the entire story or play a major role in affecting the lives of the major characters. Best friends, parents, co-workers, neighbors and so forth are often the minor characters whose presence helps define the major characters' lives and conflicts. This is pretty much how it is in real life: People can be defined by the people they spend their time with. In the following example from A.L. Kennedy's novel *So I Am Glad*, we meet a minor character, Liz, who is the roommate of the narrator, Jennifer. All we know so far about Liz is that she's hardly ever around.

I often wonder why and how I know her at all. We share the same house, that's been true for a long time, but she has developed being absent into her principal character trait. This can give her an air of changeability— between sightings she may gain or lose weight, develop a suntan, earrings. To be brief, Liz is the kind of person you talk about because she is so consistently unavailable for talking to.

Kennedy establishes that Liz is removed from the lives of her roommates, but she also implies that Liz has *a life that goes on outside*

83

*the confines of the story*. This is a crucial element in establishing successful minor and peripheral characters.

Notice how in the example above there is very little physical description. Beginning writers often overload their minor characters with excessive physical description, hoping that this visual snapshot will be burned into the readers' minds, reappearing on the backs of their eyelids each time the character's name is mentioned. In fact, even the most poetic and vivid physical descriptions are more quickly forgotten than a more active identifying tag such as a defining action or dialogue exchange. Right now, when you think back on minor characters in stories you've read, it's rarely the physical attributes you recall, but rather what they said or did. For example, in the Kennedy novel, immediately after the above paragraph describing her character, Liz has a conversation with the narrator, Jennifer, that defines who Liz is. Liz has just asked Jennifer if she's spoken to one of the roommates, Martin, about his overdue rent. Jennifer is the first speaker, Liz the second. (Note: Kennedy is a Scottish writer, so the dialogue isn't "American.")

> "I was going to ask him, but then he was ill. Well, not ill exactly—a bit agoraphobic."
> "There's nothing wrong with him, though?"
> "No, I don't think so—he's just a bit sensitive."
> "Gay, you mean."
> "Sensitive. It's allowed for straight men to be sensitive now, I've read it in magazines. Not that I know what Martin is, either way. It's not very obvious and it's none of my business."
> "Sensitive."
> "Sensitive. But don't worry, it's not infectious."
> "If you're implying that I'm insensitive, you can fuck off. I'm in love, of course I'm sensitive."

This dialogue exchange defines Liz as direct to the point of rudeness, lacking humor (Jennifer has the wry comic lines; Liz's are unintentionally funny), with a relationship that is rocky and which she probably is in charge of. All this and more is revealed without one author or narrator intrusion telling us this. She is actively revealed, which is more compelling, and so many aspects of her are implied that we can imagine a character with a life outside the scenes she appears in.

Even villainous minor characters can be clearly shown with just a few brush strokes, as in the exchange in Graham Green's novel and script *The Third Man* between protagonist Holly Martin and the seedy Dr. Winkel. An obviously concerned Martin keeps asking questions about his recently killed friend. The doctor was present at the supposed accident and Martin suspects it might not have been an accident. But each time Martin asks another question ("Was there much pain, Dr. Winkel?"), he mispronounces the doctor's name, calling him Dr. Winkel (instead of the Austrian pronounciation Vinkel). The doctor continues to correct Martin's pronunciation after each question. Finally, Martin asks, "Could he have been pushed, Dr. Winkel?" The doctor pauses for a long beat, then says, "Vinkel." The doctor never says anything sinister, but his obsession with the correct pronunciation of his name during Martin's grief tells us he's egotistical.

Some minor characters are archetypal, which means they aren't meant to be fully developed, but rather representational. (See page 223 in chapter five for the difference between archetype and stereotype.) When an archetypal character appears, the author makes it clear that this is not your usual character, that we are meant to perk up and recognize that the character represents something bigger in the story, such as the archetype of the ferryman Charon who, in Greek mythology, ferried the dead across the river from the land of the living to the land of the dead. This archetype is used in stories to tell the reader that the protagonist is moving from a land he is familiar with and appears to have some control over into a world that is more chaotic and less under his control. The gondolier in Thomas Mann's novella, *Death in Venice*, who silently chants, "The signoir will pay." The cab driver in Martin Scorsese's *After Hours*, who takes the protagonist from his familiar world of the button-downed business district to the dark, sinister world of emotional artists, sleazy bars and random violence. Another archetype is that of Cassandra, another Greek myth, who was cursed to always be accurate in prophecies, but to have no one believe her. Shakespeare often used the archetype of the wise fool or clown to be a Cassandra-like character. Pip in Herman Melville's *Moby Dick*, is an oracle of the sailors' doom, though no one listens. In her short story, "Heavy Weather," British writer Helen Simpson tells the story of a couple in emotional turmoil as they try to cope with the demands of their two young children, baby Matthew and two-year-old Lorna. Husband Jonathan puts his shoe on, only to discover a reservoir of baby vomit in it.

> He bent to put on his shoes, stuck his right foot in first then pulled it out as though bitten.
> "What's *that*," he said in tones of profound disgust. He held the shoe in front of Frances's face.
> "It looks like baby sick," she said. "Don't look at me. It's not my fault.
> "It's all so bloody *basic*," said Jonathan, breathing hard, hopping off towards the kitchen.
> "If you think that's basic, try being me," muttered Frances. "You don't know what basic *means*."
> "Daddy put his foot in Matthew's sick," commented Lorna, laughing heartily.

End of scene. Throughout the story, little Lorna's appearances are always like this, always doing or saying something that underscores the building tension between the couple. As such, she's not a "real" character who is developed with subtle nuance; her role is to annoy and irritate. But these moments of irritation are contrasted with passages describing her physical beauty, again as a sharp contrast to how the parents feel about themselves. In the following passage from the same story (which appears earlier than the above passage), the couple lies in bed with their sleeping children.

> The smoothness and sweet smell of their children, the baby's densely packed pearly limbs, the freshness of the little girl's breath when she yawned, these combined to accentuate the grossness of their own bodies. They eyed each other's mooching bulk with mutual lack of enthusiasm, and fell asleep.

The children are archetypes of pure innocence, their bodies and minds uncorrupted. That's fairly predictable. But what makes this work is two things: (1) the remarkable prose style ("densely packed pearly limbs" "mooching bulk") and (2) the contrast of this image with the piercing, wounding comments that innocent Lorna makes throughout the story. The reader sees the damage, though Lorna does not.

### Physical Therapy

First, go through your story and put a "P" beside peripheral characters and an "M" beside minor characters. For minor characters, just concentrate on the first few scenes in which they appear. Draw a box around the passage in which a peripheral or minor character appears. Now read just those boxed parts of the scenes, not with any thought about the rest of the story. Read it as if each of these passages were a story in itself. Give the characters an identifying moment—either in an action, an exchange of dialogue, a physical description—that justifies their existence in the story as well as implies some sort of life outside the scene they're in. The waitress whose only function is to bring the main characters coffee, might be limping from banging her shin struggling to get her toddler dressed for daycare while he hid under the bed. Don't overdo it.

You must maintain some sort of rhythmic balance between characters; too much attention on minor characters can distract the readers from the main characters.

Second, use the character chart at the end of this chapter (page 114) for your minor (not peripheral) characters. Beginning writers too often use such devices only for the main characters. This results in the main characters being so well developed that they make the minor characters seem even more insubstantial. Treat each character as a major character; it's just that some aren't major in this particular story.

Third, there are little tricks that are used to create instant recognition of minor characters. A physical ailment can be memorable. A character on crutches, in a wheelchair, a cast, a lisp, thick glasses, etc.—if it's used in the scene and not just described—can be an effective visual tag. It's even more thematically effective if the ailment is a manifestation of the character's personality conflicts. For example, a character with thick glasses sometimes reflects a character who has no insight into his own life or sees people as he wants to see them rather than how they really are. Or the story of how a character got the cast on her arm can imply a lot about who she is: She fell training for the Olympic basketball team; she chased a purse snatcher and broke it when she caught up with him and they struggled over the purse; she fell out of a tree trying to retrieve one of her two dozen cats. In the film *The Big Fix* (based on the Roger Simon novel), Richard Dreyfuss has an arm cast the entire movie. The actor had broken his arm before filming, and the filmmakers decided to incorporate that into the film. Dreyfuss is a private detective who spends the movie interviewing various people. Each time someone asks him how he broke his arm, he tells a different story so people will relate better to him (e.g., he tells some farmworker activists he broke it picketing with Cesar Chavez). After hearing a dozen different stories, we discover at the end how he really broke it: skateboarding with his young son.

Another quick way to create identifiable minor characters is to give them a specific problem that they are trying to solve during the course of the story. The problem might not be related to the main conflict of the story; it doesn't really matter. This "problem" serves two purposes: (1) It creates a misdirection opportunity. While the readers are distracted by this character's problem, you can subtlely inject information about the main character or conflict; (2) It presents minor characters in an active and suspenseful situation, which allows us to experience them in a more compelling and defining way than just getting a passive description. Here's how it works: In the film *Getting Straight*, set in the late 1960s during campus protests, the main character, Harry (Elliott Gould), has returned to graduate school to become a teacher after a tour in Vietnam. He has a best friend, Nick, who keeps popping up, trying to get Harry to do drugs, chase girls and generally drop out. While Harry is racing to make it to a class he's already late for, Nick accosts him, reminding him of the good old days of smoking dope and chasing girls. This reveals Harry's past as a hippie protest leader; however, we soon find out that Nick gets his draft notice. This is his "problem," which keeps recurring during the film to affect and further define the kind of man Harry is. A protagonist with a friend who is going through an acrimonious divorce now has the opportunity to be defined by how he behaves as a friend; plus, we have the suspense hook of what will happen to this minor character.

This same technique can be used with other tag objects, such as the character's unusual name or the kind of car he drives. If the character is named Sagittarius or Valentine or Manifesto, there's usually a good (but mercifully brief) story that goes with it that helps the reader remember the character. The same with the bizarre car he drives (a wheezing Gremlin with zebra stripes bought from the local zoo), the unusual home he lives in (a loft above a slaughter house), or the strange job he has (assembling prosthetic limbs).

 ## Symptoms: Low stakes, bland personality

### Ailment: Uninvolving Protagonist

The protagonist isn't likable or compelling enough that we care what happens to him or her. Despite a robust plot, dramatic conflict and/or poetic style, reader involvement in the story remains minimal.

Nearly everyone has begun reading a book that they immediately liked, only to one day put it down—with every intention of picking it up—but somehow never getting back to it. It's not that the book was bad or offensive or incomprehensible, it's just that you somehow never got around to it. A good book should *compel* you to return to it. During the day when you're engaged in your usual activities, you should every once in a while get that anxious feeling that you can't wait to get back to your book to see what happens next. Obviously, there are many reasons a story can go bad, but perhaps the most serious and common defect is the uninvolving protagonist. When this happens, the reader begins to feel a sort of homesickness, as if she were traveling in an exotic foreign land that she can't enjoy due to loneliness. This loneliness is the result of not having a compelling protagonist as a traveling companion.

Healthy characterization of a protagonist is identifiable by the reader's commitment to finding out what happens next to that character, not merely because of a suspenseful plot, but because the

89

consequences of the plot matter due to how much the reader cares about the characters.

## Diagnosis

Reader involvement is often based on the stakes of the story: the intensity of the consequences that impact the protagonist. In other words, if the protagonist doesn't resolve the conflict, how serious is the damage to her life? But the intensity of those stakes for the reader is totally dependent on how much we care about the protagonist. And how much we care is often dependent on how developed the protagonist's personality is.

Personality isn't just about protagonists' circumstances (job, friends, conflict with boss, mother, lover) or their background (born on a mountaintop in Tennessee where he killed a bear when he was only three; his resultant fear of furry animals conflicts with his desire to become a pediatrician). Personality is about the character's tone, attitude, wit, charm, intelligence and wisdom. A compelling protagonist doesn't have to have all these characteristics, but some combination of them is necessary if we're going to be traveling with him through a story. It's what makes us care about him and therefore creates suspense about what happens to him.

"Care" does not necessarily mean "like." It's possible we don't like the protagonist; we may even be repelled. But if we don't like the protagonist, we at least need to find him somehow fascinating and compelling—so dynamic that we can't take our eyes off of him. Hannibal Lecter went from antagonist (villain) in Thomas Harris's *Silence of the Lambs* to co-protagonist in *Hannibal*. He's still a homicidal cannibal, but in the sequel his victims are all deserving of their fates, thereby making him, by comparison, more likable. However, this technique resulted in problems for the sequel—both in the novel and the film—that made it much less effective. (For more detailed analysis, see "Five Things That Went Wrong With Hannibal" on page 50).

In many stories we need to like the protagonist. This is especially true in genre literature, which often contains a template for plot structure. Therefore, for many readers the main attraction that distinguishes one novel from another is the protagonist. For example, mystery novels have a simple plot structure: There's a crime (usually murder) and a detective (amateur or professional) who must solve the case. The plot follows this detective as she interrogates reluctant people, many of whom are suspects. Given the familiarity of the plot, what keeps bringing the customers back to the bookstore for more? The personality of the detective. The cold analytical brilliance of Sherlock Holmes; the boozy disillusioned righteousness of Philip Marlowe, the indulgent and indignant couch potato Nero Wolfe. The list goes on to include every sort of physically and emotionally challenged detective type possible (blind, armless, legless, dwarf, Tourette's Syndrome, oft divorced, amnesiac, old, young, etc.). Since the plot format is fairly rigid, reader involvement will involve variations of dressing up the protagonist.

In *Annie Hall*, Woody Allen describes a romantic relationship as being like a shark: It has to constantly keep moving or it dies. Although that's not true about sharks, it's definitely true of protagonists in fiction: she must constantly be moving, meaning changing and developing. Sometimes a reader is propelled into the story by the promise of the character. The opening pages create an intriguing protagonist we want to get to know better. We expect that reading the story will do just that: let us know the character more and more intimately. It's like a first date: You are intrigued by a person and hope that on subsequent dates you will get to know more. But that presupposes there is more to get to know. If there is no more to get to know, then you'll quickly lose interest.

## Treatment

A protagonist must be *at least* one of the following: likable, compelling, redeemable.

**Likable** is obvious but not easy to accomplish. At a recent writing conference, I was asked to evaluate the opening chapters of seven student novels. Of the seven, two contained protagonists whom we all agreed (even the authors) that we didn't care about. The authors had written five hundred-page novels, yet we still didn't care about their protagonists, despite fast-paced plots in which their lives and the fate of the world hung in the balance. The reason their protagonists weren't likable was because they revealed no attractive personality traits. They weren't witty, charming or wise—they weren't entertaining. They were morally good, smart, brave and dedicated. While that's the kind of person you want to live next door, he's not necessarily someone you want to read about. One need not look further than elections to see that people prefer candidates with charisma even over candidates who are better qualified and maybe even better human beings. There are several ways to make a character likable:

1. **Give him a sense of humor.** This is a character trait, often shown through dialogue or internal monologue. We tend to like people who make us laugh. Sometimes the humor is directed at him instead of emanating from him. For example, in *Moby Dick*, protagonist Ishmael starts the novel as a humorless young lad who is going off to sea because he's depressed and a bit suicidal. His earnestness makes him easy prey for the innkeeper's joke of renting him a bed with Queequeg, the tattooed native who, in a parody of the shy-bride-on-the-honeymoon-night, climbs into bed with the horrified Ishmael. It's a funny scene that reveals Ishmael's naïveté and makes him endearing.

2. **Give him a seemingly impossible task to overcome.** This is a plot device, which may involve competition (in the novel and film *Vision Quest*, Louden must drop two weight classes to wrestle the undefeated champion; in the movie *Rocky*, underachieving pug Rocky must get in shape to give the champ a decent fight), or beating a deadline (dismantle a bomb before it explodes as in *Speed*), or completing a project (building a bridge in *The Bridge Over the River Kwai*) or facing overwhelming odds (hundreds of bandits in *The Magnificent Seven* and *The Wild Bunch*).

3. **Give him an emotional motive for his actions.** This is a character trait and plot device because it both defines the character and motivates the action. This would include *justifiable* revenge (e.g., murdering a family member as in the films *The Patriot*, *Braveheart*, *Gladiator* and *Get Carter* and the film and Brian Garfield novel *Death Wish*); attempted reconciliation with a loved one after a period of estrangement (Bobby in the film *Five Easy Pieces*,

Molly Giles's novel *Iron Shoes,* my own novel *Lessons in Survival,* written as Laramie Dunaway).

**4. Give him intelligence that promises insight.** This is a character trait usually demonstrated through internal monlogue. This is especially important because it's used for both likable and unlikable characters. If the story is "mainstream" or "literary," it means it has some aspirations toward giving us insight into the characters and the conflicts they face. With likable protagonists, these insights merely accentuate our affection for the characters. With unlikable protagonists, these insightful commentaries are our major link with caring about what happens to them. The hope of a payoff in the currency of wisdom is what keeps us tagging along with a character we may not like.

**Compelling** does not require likable. There's a crucial difference between "unlikable" (not yet displaying any likable qualities) and "dislikable"( not finding any reason to stay in this character's company). We may not like a character, but still find him riveting. In fact, Sherlock Holmes and Nero Wolfe, mentioned earlier in the chapter, are not likable: Holmes is arrogant, a drug addict and emotionally remote. Wolfe is also not warm and cuddly: He's arrogant, fussy and a food and wine addict. Yet, they are compelling by sheer force of their intellect. Writers overcome the problem of the unlikable protagonist by three methods: likable narrator, unlikable world and the car-crash factor.

**1. Likable narrator.** When faced with an unlikable protagonist, writers sometimes choose to have a first-person POV narrator who is very likable. These sidekicks, such as Dr. Watson for Holmes and Archie Goodwin for Wolfe, serve three functions: (1) They are likable, so we're more involved in the story; (2) they like the protagonist, despite their unlikable exterior, so we tend to be more forgiving; and (3) they provide an intellectual contrast: We like the narrator because he's like the reader, but we admire the protagonist because he's so much more brilliant than the narrator (and therefore the reader).

2. Unlikable world. Sometimes we read about truly awful characters, yet we are still compelled by them. We even find ourselves caring about them. This is achieved by giving the protagonists forceful personalities and by making them the lesser evil. Alex, in Anthony Burgess's novel *A Clockwork Orange*, is a young thug who ruthlessly preys on anyone he can. In the first half, we loathe him for his cruelty; we loathe ourselves for laughing when he's being funny. But we can't help ourselves. Eventually, when he's trying to go straight, we come to care about him because we see that, compared to all the other characters, he's not so bad. So, when characters are unlikable because of their crappy environment, such as in Irvine Welsh's novel *Trainspotting*, we are more tolerant and sympathetic of their bad traits. In Muriel Spark's novel *The Prime of Miss Jean Brodie*, protagonist Brodie is instantly pegged as an arrogant, manipulative and dangerous teacher. But she is also dedicated and, in her own way, very caring. The unforgiving moralistic powers that are trying to destroy her—represented by the dour Miss Mackay—are certainly much less attractive. Even though the reader sees the necessity of firing her, the triumph is tempered by realizing who the victors are. The world of the girls at Marcia Blaine School will be much drabber and less fun without Jean Brodie.

3. Car-crash factor. You know the cliché: you pass a car crash and slow down to gawk. Can't help yourself. You're compelled. This same principle applies in writing: Sometimes a protagonist is so relentlessly evil that we can't help but stare to see just how far he will go. Brett Easton Ellis's *American Psycho* and the movie *Henry: Portrait of a Serial Killer* feature irredeemably evil protagonists who compel the audience.

Redeemable means that there is something about the protagonist, even if it's just a glimmer of a hope, that indicates she might change her unlikable ways. The movie *La Femme Nikita* (as well as the American remake, *Point of No Return*) features a truly despicable protagonist, a young woman who deliberately shoots a policeman trying to help her. It is because of this ruthlessness that she's inducted into a government assassination squad, where she becomes the least unlikable in an unlikable world. As we see her falling in love with her supervisor, we see a hope for redemption and we now want her to survive and complete the process. Westerns like *3:10 to Yuma, Shane, The Magnificent Seven, The Wild Bunch* and *The Quick and the Dead* all present outlaws who do something decent in an effort to redeem themselves. The sign that they are redeemable is usually demonstrated through something that gives them pleasure, something that the audience can identify with. For Alex in *A Clockwork Orange*, it's his love of Beethoven. The reader's impression is that anyone who is this passionate about Beethoven has some spark of goodness in him.

To achieve these above-mentioned traits, you must manipulate two ingredients: vulnerability and admirability.

**1. Vulnerability.** It's the flaws in a character, not the strengths, that make us care most. The more vulnerable the character, the more we identify with her and therefore like her. There's a wonderful scene in an episode of the old TV series *The Mary Tyler Moore Show*. Mary's been promoted and given the task of hiring someone to fill her vacated job. Compulsively efficient Mary staggers under responsibility of selecting the perfect person. Finally, her boss, Lou Grant, calls her into his office and tells her why he'd first hired her. Not because of her qualifications, he reveals, but because during the interview he'd noticed she had a small run in her stocking and she'd kept tugging the hem of her skirt down to cover it. He was moved by that gesture and hired her. That is one of the best demonstrations in literature of *showing* vulnerability.

Revealing this trait is especially important with protagonists who seem otherwise indestructible: In *Raiders of the Lost Ark*, Indiana Jones is instantly admirable because he's so bold and daring; but he's instantly *likable* when he hops into the plane and cowers at the sight of a snake. ("I *hate* snakes!") Mel Gibson in *Lethal Weapon* reveals his vulnerability early when he sits alone and places a gun to his head over his despair at the death of his wife.

The danger is that too much vulnerabilty may seem like whining. It's best if the protagonist isn't too self-aware or obsessive about her flaws; the less she talks about it, the better. (Tip: Remember that the flaws in a character don't just make for a vulnerable and therefore likable character, they also create plot suspense. A character's particular vulnerability calls into question whether or not she will be able to survive the ordeal of the plot, whether it's a dangerous adventure or an emotional confrontation with other people. Without the possibility of kryptonite, there's no story.)

**2. Admirability.** Protagonists are admirable either for who they are or for what they can do. Yes, we admire people for who they are—Gandhi, T.E. Lawrence, Malcolm X—but in a story we admire them only when we see those *good qualities in conflict.* If the person is good, show her demonstrating that goodness when faced with opposition. With characters who aren't admirable for who they are, show some admirable quality. Fast Eddie in Walter Tevis's novel *The Hustler* is not a nice guy; as his nemesis Burt points out, "You've got no character." It's true: He cares only about himself and winning. But his skill at pool and his passion for it (see "Redeemable" on page 94) make him somewhat admirable. Peachy and Danny in Rudyard Kipling's *The Man Who Would Be King* are not admirable human beings, but their admirable quality is their fierce loyalty to each other.

Think of these traits as hot and cold water faucets: you adjust them to get the proper temperature that suits your story. In some cases, the admirability may be low, but it's gushing vulnerability. Other times it may be reversed or balanced.

It's easy to mistake giving a protagonist characteristics with giving them character. Characteristics by themselves create a character-type's mood rather than defining his specific personality. For example, the following excerpt from a student manuscript by Jeannette Encinias introduces us to her protagonist:

> Chelsea got a job answering phones and developed a quiet disgust for the receiver. She worked a couple days a week and always came straight home. She lived alone but was not terribly lonely. She kept canvases for friends, paint instead of lovers, and hung her artwork on one single wall to avoid confusion. She yielded to the Muse and worked in the hours of possession becoming

nocturnal, realizing that her most intimate moments with her craft rushed in just before dawn. Chelsea did have her dark moments, as all humans do. She would weep in the bathtub, wailing above the hiss of the faucet. . . . She dwindled in her isolation. . . .

Although the style is clearly very good, the resultant protagonist is not involving for several reasons: (1) We never know why she feels these bouts of depression. This is crucial, especially since the next scene involves her going to a bar to drink and smoke and act cynical and belligerent.

**Beginning writers often use smoking and drinking as major means to identify their character's angst. But without anything of substance to go with those habits, that's all they are: habits in search of a character conflict.**

(2) Chelsea's artistic drive seems to have something to do with her being a loner, but it's not clear. She could just as easily be self-indulgent, more interested in creating a persona of an artist rather than actually passionate about art.

**Suggestion for improvement:** Attribute her depression and isolation to something specific. Most beginning writers immediately shove in a flashback scene or internal monologue about something traumatic that happened when the character was a child. That can be effective, as long as it's not too obvious or clichéd. And even if there was a childhood trauma, what steps has she taken to overcome the negative effects it had on her life? Why does it still affect her after all this time? These questions also must be addressed if we are to elevate the motivating factor out of the "mommy was mean" level.

If you choose not to do the childhood trauma, you can look to the heart of the character herself. Perhaps she is disillusioned based on her experiences as an adult, either with events that personally happened to her, or because of her observations of how we all treat each other. If that is the choice, then it must be articulated in such a way (either by internal monologue or in dialogue with another) that doesn't sound trite and childish (unless that is how you want the character to come across to the reader). The better the passage that explains her malaise, the more depth the character and the story will have.

In Martin Amis's *Rachel Papers*, used in an earlier example, teen protagonist Charles Highway is insufferably sarcastic, exploits every girl he meets, and seems to have no respect for himself or anyone else. But he's compelling because (1) he has outrageous wit, a droll tone and exceptional intelligence; (2) the style is dazzlingly rich and poetic; (3) he's self-deprecating; (4) he displays redeemable personality. For example, when he's visiting the ex-nanny of the next girl he hopes to seduce, he notices how run-down the old woman's apartment is and feels guilty when she offers him a spread of food she's prepared:

> I noticed that Nan wasn't eating, so, after a couple of sandwiches for politeness's sake, I laid off the food, claiming a heavy lunch whenever she pressed more on me: "Have some more of next Wednesday's breakfast. Do try tomorrow's dinner."

A few lines later Charles leaves, but he stops to look back.

> . . . I looked back to give Nan a final wave, conceitedly indicating that I, in a mere two hours' acquaintance, had perhaps learned more about this sad indictment of our society than Rachel probably ever would.

Yes, he's a selfish little worm—as he readily admits—but we care about him because he exhibits (1) humor ("Have some more of next Wednesday's breakfast. Do try tomorrow's dinner."); (2) concern (refusing to eat the food he thinks she can't afford to spare makes us see a spark of humanity and therefore the potential for redemption); (3) self-awareness (he recognizes that he's conceited and is sarcastic about his superior attitude and therefore, again, has the potential for redemption).

There's a fine line between using humor to enhance the likability of a character and creating a repulsively sarcastic character. In the film *Love and Sex*, the protagonists (played by Jon Favreau and Famke Janssen) go through a rocky romance for which the audience is supposed to root for them to stay together. However, the scene that introduces them to each other uses humor to make us like them, but actually establishes an insurmountable problem. Famke is on a date at an art showing. Her date is a stand-up comedian still living with his parents whom, we learn through her voice-over confession, she's just dating to get out of the house. She finds him boring. While he's talking to her about the art, she looks around, sees Jon, and is attracted to him. The comedian goes off to get them drinks. Jon sidles up to her, they discuss the art, she says it's basically shock value without any meaning, he defends the art, she realizes he's the artist. The comedian returns with the drinks and Jon takes them both from him and says something like, "Oh, thank you, you're such a sweetheart." He then tells the comedian that Famke is not his girlfriend, she's now *Jon's* girlfriend. She instantly denies it. "Is this a joke?" the comedian says. "No, this is a joke," Jon says. "Two men walk into a bar, one of them is a stand-up comedian who lives at home with his parents." The comedian looks shocked, then hurt. "We'd better go," he says to Famke. But she doesn't budge. The comedian leaves, and the audience is supposed to feel good about her and Jon as a couple.

Here are the problems: (1) The comedian's not that boring. If we're meant to think she's better off with someone else—especially Jon— he'd have to be mean or inattentive or dismissive. (2) Their banter about the art, capped with the revelation that he's the artist, has been done before—often. (3) Jon's not funny with the comedian, he's cruel. And the fact that she just stands there while this nice guy is treated so meanly makes her equally guilty. Why would we care if this couple gets together or stays together? It's possible that this would work if this were a teen flick, but these characters are in their thirties. This scene establishes the character of the protagonists—whom we now don't like enough to care about the progress of their relationship, thereby sabotaging the rest of the movie.

 ## Physical Therapy

Author Molly Giles (*Iron Shoes*) has a very clever and effective exercise for exploring character. Adopting the point of view of her protagonist, she completes the following prompts:

My mother always . . .
My father never . . .

She encourages her writing students to use stream of consciousness while completing those phrases. Just let whatever comes out come out. Those two lines can be crucial keys to understanding who the protagonist is and therefore developing that dimension. (Note: Molly says that this exercise is quite successful with students, but that when she tries to reverse the phrases—"My mother never . . .; My father always . . ."—it doesn't work. That in itself says something about the way we think about people, let alone characters.)

Another technique that will help you think about all the aspects of your protagonist is to use a character development worksheet (see page 114). This is effective for two reasons: (1) It helps you ask certain questions about your characters that force you to think about them with more depth; (2) it provides a handy and time-saving reference to consult during the course of your story, script or novel. It's guaranteed that you will forget something about the character (color of eyes, height, car model, place of birth, etc.) and looking at this sheet is a lot easier than searching through the rest of the novel.

## Symptom: One-dimensional antagonist, overly evil antagonist

### Ailment: Stereotypical Antagonist/Villain

The antagonist or villain (not necessarily the same thing) is so stereotypical that most of what she does or says is predictable or, if not predictable, boring. Because the antagonist is the source of plot and character conflict in the story, a weak one immediately reduces the stakes and damages reader involvement.

The moustache-twirling villain. The harsh, ever-critical mother or father. The racist, sexist boss. The sexy, brainless blonde. We've seen them each a thousand times. When we see any one of them swagger onto the screen or page, we instantly release an internal sigh of disappointment. We know that if the writer wasn't able to come up with anything better than this for such a crucial character, then it is unlikely that the rest of the story will hold any surprises or insights. Antagonists can indeed have some of the traits that appear in the above list, but that can't be all that defines them. The harsh, ever-critical mother or father is a legitimate antagonist, but not if every time they appear in the story that is his or her dominant characteristic.

With a healthy antagonist, every scene in which she appears must be especially dynamic. This doesn't mean it must have sensational action or overheated dialogue, just that these scenes must have a heightened impact. The reader anticipates those scenes and expects a greater payoff. The well-developed antagonist must have wit, charm, intelligence and/or unwavering malevolence.

## Diagnosis

Even the best writers sometimes have a lapse when it comes to the antagonist. This is partially due to the realization that the stakes of the story depend so much on the antagonist's presence power (the amount of energy generated into the scene by the presence of that character). It's easier to generate this presence power by depicting a one-note antagonist who is always laughing maniacally and rubbing his hands with an evil smirk. The theory is that by concentrating on the one sinister characteristic each time the antagonist appears, you don't dilute the character's presence power. While this may be true of the worst examples of genre fiction, it isn't true of the best genre and literary fiction. Yes, in a good revenge story (in which the protagonist hunts down those responsible for ruining his life, killing his family, etc.), the antagonist must be truly evil. It is the audience's desire to participate in the protagonist's revenge that fuels the story. However, good writers realize that evil is even more disturbing and threatening when it isn't so easily recognized and strives to make the character more complex. When the protagonist disposes of the one-note antagonist, the story's impact is over, instantly out of the audience's minds. But with more complex antagonists, the end of the story is only the beginning of our thinking about it and being affected by it.

One major cause of a weak antagonist is not understanding exactly what his function in the story is. Although the antagonist can be viewed as the villain because he may be the superficial source of much of the conflict, he is not always unlikable or "villainous." In genre fiction, he is more likely to be a villain; in mainstream and literary fiction, he is more likely to be somewhat benign and even have a lot of similarities with the protagonist. Also, there may be more than one antagonist. In *Moby Dick* there are three antagonists: Captain Ahab, Moby Dick and the sea. Each is portrayed as a specific, individual character. None is inherently evil—in fact, Moby Dick and the sea are indifferent. Ahab is not evil—he starts out as a decent man who is religious and an asset to his community. What is evil is how his obsession with Moby Dick destroys his decency. This novel could just as easily have been told from Ahab's point of view with just the whale as the antagonist, but then the stakes would have been reduced because we would not have had an innocent victim (Ishmael), whose life hangs in the balance, to worry over.

The most important thing is to make the antagonist as fully developed as the protagonist, or there's no believable conflict. In many stories, the antagonist must start off seeming much stronger than the protagonist to create suspense about whether he will be overcome. In the case of genre novels where it's inevitable that he'll be overcome, the suspense is about how he'll be defeated. On a more subtle, psychological level, the villain is a manifestation of the obstacles the protagonist puts in her own path. For example, in William Goldman's remarkable suspense novel *Marathon Man* (see the case study on page 34), protagonist Babe is following in his father's exact footprints: attending the same graduate school, studying the same courses, etc., in an effort to vindicate his father's suicide. The problem is that by adopting his father's life, Babe is killing any kind of life he may have chosen for himself (a type of personality suicide). This is a suspense thriller, so there are a lot of nasty antagonists—government assassins, ex-Nazis and rogue agents— running around trying to kill each other and Babe. He overcomes them all and saves his own life. But he also saves his life from the most persistent and sinister antagonist—himself. He overcomes his obsession with his father's death, his rage at those who caused it, his own guilt that he'd been a powerless boy at the time, unable to help.

In James Dickey's novel *Deliverance*, there are three antagonists: the hillbillies, the land, and the protagonists' own arrogance in thinking they were in control of Nature rather than a part of it. The evil hillbillies who rape and terrorize them are a manifestation of an uncaring Natural Order. The canoeists think that the world is a good place, they are good men and there is is a watchful God who will protect them; what they discover is an indifferent natural world where they are not in any way "chosen." This same theme comes through in Thomas Harris's *Red Dragon*, when at the end the protagonist ruminates over the Green Machine, meaning the indifferent natural order. The serial killers that he hunts are just manifestations of that indifferent, morally chaotic universe. Once you've identified all the potential antagonists in your story, it will be easier to give them all appropriate characters and thereby not have to dump all the responsibility on one stereotypical character who will inevitably break under the weight.

At this point you may be saying, "What the hell is he yammering about? I just want a nice simple bad guy who commits the murders." Absolutely right. What I have explained is not how every antagonist must be written, but the range of how they might be written, from the most basic to the more sophisticated.

## Treatment

There are three basic types of antagonist:
1. Love to hate
2. Hate to hate
3. Have to cringe

**1. Love to hate.** This is the character that the reader loathes, who has no redeemable qualities and must be destroyed by the ending. In general, we will find this antagonist in genre fiction such as thrillers, men's adventure, suspense, espionage, romance, romantic comedy, etc. While in such a case it is perfectly acceptable to create a character toward whom we feel nothing but hate, the danger is in focusing only on the reason we hate him.

My screenwriting students will often include Nazis as villains, and it's remarkable how similar the descriptions are: pockmarked, hollow-faced, scarred and so forth. In addition, these dastardly Nazis are almost always sexually perverted, usually sadists and enjoy the occasional kicking of dogs and small children.

This kind of clichéd writing is not for students alone; I was watching the BBC production of *The Scarlet Pimpernel* in which antagonist Robspierre is introduced stroking the painting of the death of Marquis de Sade. The same problem occurs in numerous courtroom dramas such as *The Rainmaker*, in which Jon Voight plays a smug, corrupt attorney for the smug, corrupt insurance company. This is the one-dimensional antagonist whom we are anxious to see brought down by the end.

Yet in *A Civil Action*, the antagonist attorney played by Robert Duvall is much more interesting as a character and more menacing, not because he's willing to pull dirty tricks, but because he's intelligent and competent. The difference is that, with antagonists like Voight's in *The Rainmaker*, there will be less suspense as to the outcome—we know Voight must be punished at the end. With more complex antagonists, the outcome is not certain. We don't crave the antagonist's destruction as much, so therefore we're left with the merits of the case and the ability of the protagonist.

Abusive parents/spouses have to be dealt with in a subtle way as well. If the abusive character is stereotypical, the story becomes a melodrama in which we only care about seeing revenge. But if there is nuance to the character, as in Russell Banks's novel *Affliction* (as well as the film adaptation), the story becomes a richer and deeper exploration into the relationship between the abused and the abuser. So, feel free to create a deplorable antagonist, but provide him with sufficiently developed characteristics that make him interesting first as a character—even if we didn't know anything about his evil side.

In some cases, the mindless antagonist who is pure evil can be an appropriate and compelling character: zombies, the great white shark in *Jaws*, killers in most slasher films.

**2. Hate to hate.** This antagonist is presented with enough compassion that, though we may deplore his actions, we don't necessarily deplore the person. We may even like him. The motivation for this antagonist's actions are understandable, perhaps even noble. It's just that we have more emotional attachment to the protagonist.

Examples include the wife in Anne Tyler's novel *The Accidental Tourist*; Robert Shaw's Sheriff of Nottingham in *Robin and Marion*; Clint Eastwood's lawman character in *A Perfect World*; Rutger Hauer's Christlike artficial man in *Blade Runner*; the Irish vampire in the Preacher graphic novels; and Robert Ryan's ex-outlaw in *The Wild Bunch*. Each of these antagonists is portrayed as sympathetic, though in some cases they kill the protagonist.

**3. Have to cringe.** Here the antagonist is often played for comic effect. She doesn't do evil as much as she provides a constant source of embarrassment and humiliation for the protagonist. Rather than shooting bullets, she fires barbs. This character is often one of authority, usually a parent. Whenever this antagonist appears, the reader or audience cringes in anticipation of the next bizzare thing she will do or say. Examples include the mother in Larry McMurtry's novels *Terms of Endearment* and *Evening Star*; the mother in Carrie Fisher's novel, *Postcards from the Edge*; the mother in Molly Giles's novel *Iron Shoes*; the mother in Albert Brooks's film *Mother*; the aunt in Graham Greene's novel *Travels With My Aunt*. This type of antagonist is not one that must be overcome (such as the abusive father and husband in *Affliction* and in Richard Price's novel *The Wanderers*), but one which must be embraced. She usually is an obstacle only because the protagonist *perceives* her as one. Once the protagonist comes to accept that character's eccentricities and acknowledges their similarities, she no longer has to fight her.

In some cases the relationship between the protagonist and the antagonist is so symbiotic that it's unclear which is which. This is especially true of stories that are narrated by one character but are about another. Nick Carroway narrates F. Scott Fitzgerald's novel *The Great Gatsby*; Al Mannheim narrates *What Makes Sammy Run*; much of Muriel Spark's novel *The Prime of Miss Jean Brodie* is from Sandy's POV. The title characters are actually antagonists to the narrators' protagonists; the focus of each story is how those title characters affect the narrators, how they change *them*. It's also true of stories in which we clearly recognize who is good and who is bad early on, only to have the author gradually reverse the roles: Stanley Elkin's story "A Poetics for Bullies" introduces a narrator who describes his technique for bullying the other kids, and a Christ-like character who tries to help the kids. Eventually we come to see that the helpful kid is actually a greater bully and the narrator is actually the kids' savior.

Above we deal with three types of antagonist. But there are also four main categories of archetypes: boss, family, criminal, land.

1. **Boss.** Someone who controls the protagonist's life, such as the various officers in Joseph Heller's novel *Catch-22* and Sigourney Weaver in *Working Girl*.

2. **Family.** Someone who controls the protagonist's emotional life. See the examples from "Have to cringe," on page 105.

3. **Criminal.** Someone who can be overcome by force. Most popular in genre fiction.

4. **Land.** Setting can embody what the protagonist must face within herself, such as in James Dickey's *Deliverance*, Joseph Conrad's *Typhoon* and *Heart of Darkness* and Paul Theroux's *Mosquito Coast*.

Many suspense stories will involve two antagonists: Mr. Big and his Evil Henchman. This is done for two very practical reasons: Mr. Big is evil because he's the planner; Evil Henchman is evil because of the method of carrying out the plan. This allows for more flexibility in not having to show the same antagonist each time. Also, it allows the story to be stretched out because, to show the protagonist is making progress, he'll have to dispose of the minor antagonist. This heightens the final climactic confrontation.

There are three specific areas that the writer can adjust to improve the characterization of the antagonist: (1) unique personality, (2) unpredictable actions and (3) empathetic motivation.

**1. Unique personality.** Give the antagonist a personality that is distinguishable from all other antagonists. Determine what makes this character different than every other bitchy mother, aggressive father, power-hungry wannabe, smug serial killer, etc. that's been done before. One effective way to do this is to take away the "evil factor" (the thing the antagonist does that hurts the protagonist) and figure out who that character is without it.

**2. Unpredictable actions.** Antagonists often have a certain list of "evil acts" in common. Sometimes they steal the protagonist's lover; sometimes they kill the protagonist's family; sometimes they try to rule the world. To create a unique, nonstereotypical antagonist, break out of the familiar pattern of how he does these actions, or at least how these actions are revealed to the reader. This is crucial because (1) it's more interesting to the reader to be surprised; (2) it makes the antagonist seem more powerful and clever because it gives him superior knowledge (the audience can't figure out the greater plan, which gives the antagonist a godlike presence); (3) the antagonist often symbolizes the concept of chaos, an influence causing the protagonist's life to move out of her control. (This is the mythic power of a character like Satan, who represents our passions—hence the red and fire, symbols for emotions. When we allow our emotions to govern our actions, we feel out of control, in a state of chaos.) The more unpredictable the actions, the more the antagonist fulfills this symbolic role.

**3. Empathetic motivation.** To make the reader like the antagonist more, you must spend more time developing the motivation for his actions. Even the early Superman comics gave arch-villain Lex Luthor a reason to hate Superman: While they were boys and best friends, Lex was caught in a chemical fire in his lab; Superboy blew out the fire, but the chemicals caused the teenage Luthor to go bald. He blamed Superboy. This is actually pretty solid motivation: Lex is just a teen who's now bald. He feels freakish, no longer attractive to girls (a form of impotence). To overcome this perceived impotence, he overcompensates by developing his genius, but misuses it because he obsesses on the perceived cause of his impotence.

While we're with comics, examine the *X-men* movie. It opens with a little boy and his parents being dragged off to a concentration camp. When the Nazi's separate the boy from his family, the boy's screams of rage and loss echo in the ears and hearts of the audience. This boy becomes the villain of the story. His motivation for his villainy is to prevent the world from becoming like Nazi Germany. This opening makes us understand him, even wonder if he isn't right in his assessment. But we deplore him because of his methods and his gang; we recognize that he's become the very thing he's trying to stop.

In the end, the antagonist is often overcome by the protagonist. How he is overcome is just as significant as the development of his character. There are two major methods of overcoming the antagonist: (1) direct confrontation or (2) overcoming the need to defeat the antagonist at all.

**1. Direct confrontation.** This involves the protagonist taking direct action to remove the antagonist from her life (divorce, lawsuit, capturing, killing, turning in to the police, arguing, refusing to see or speak to the character, etc.). The climax of the story will usually be this confrontation. If it's a genre story, this will probably be an action scene: a life-threatening chase. If it's a drama, it will more likely be a conversation, followed by a dramatic gesture (such as packing the car and leaving). For example, in *An Officer and a Gentleman*, Richard Gere's character has a breakthrough, not when he physically fights his antagonist, Louis Gossett, Jr., but when he tearfully admits *in conversation* that he needs the military because he has nowhere else to go. The grand gesture then is sweeping Debra Winger off her feet and out of the factory.

**2. Overcoming the need to defeat the antagonist at all.** Here the protagonist comes to the realization that the antagonist is not the terrible enemy she thought he was. Instead of changing the conflicting situation, she changes her perception of the situation (and the antagonist, who probably symbolizes her situation), embraces this new vision and is happy. Going back to *An Officer and a Gentleman*, Richard Gere's antagonist is the unrelentingly tough drill sergeant, Louis Gossett, Jr.; however, he comes to change that perception and see the sergeant as his friend. The real antagonist in this kind of story is the protagonist's own pride, which *causes* his misperception of the world. He distracts himself from the reality of his self-created conflict by projecting the conflict on an imagined antagonist.

## THE DEFINING SCENE

In most stories, the antagonist has a defining scene: the scene that defines the scope of his character, both sympathetic and unsympathetic (usually the one that introduces him to the reader). In the film *The Third Man*, Harry Lime (played by Orson Welles) is as evil as one can be: He murders innocent people, is responsible for the agonizing deaths of many children, turns in his former girlfriend in exchange for his own freedom, attempts to murder his best friend. Yet his wit and charm are so compelling that audiences of the movie wanted to see more of him. Despite the fact that he was killed at the end of the movie, he was brought back in a radio series as well as a television series. Harry Lime is the perfect antagonist: charming, witty, intelligent, articulate, ruthless, yet oddly sympathetic. Of course, it helps that the famed British novelist Graham Greene wrote the script. His defining scene is one of the most famous in literature, film and fiction. He meets his old friend Holly Martin on a giant Ferris wheel in which the compartments are the size of elevators. Harry takes them to the top, and when Holly argues with him about the evil that Harry is doing, Harry grins and replies:

"Don't be so gloomy . . . after all, it's not that awful— you know what the fellow said . . . In Italy for thirty years under the Borgias they had warfare, terror, murder, bloodshed—they produced Michelangelo, Leonardo da Vinci and the Renaissance. In Switzerland they had brotherly love, five hundred years of democracy and peace, and what did that produce? The cuckoo clock."

In *Silence of the Lambs*, Hannibal Lecter's defining moment is his toying with Clarise Starling while she interviews him in prison, capped with his famous, "I ate his liver with some fava beans and a fine Chianti," followed by his tongue slurping. In *Three Days of the Condor*, the enigmatic assassin played by Max Von Sydow is defined in the first scene in which he systematically and efficiently murders every person in a CIA office. When he is faced by the unarmed woman who is Robert Redford's girlfriend, she realizes he is about to kill her and says calmly, "I won't scream." He nods his head in a sympathetic, grandfatherly way and says, "I know." Then he kills her. Though his action is ruthless, he is also portrayed as a professional who represses his own emotions to complete the assignment.

In my own suspense novel *Assassin's Apprentice*, the chief antagonist, Kit, is introduced while in bed with his mother-in-law. The reader is not informed of the circumstances yet because I want the reader to immediately recoil from the man. But I soften the reader's initial judgment in two ways: (1) His name is Kit, which is a pleasant name, and (2) he's playing the guitar while his mother-in-law sleeps beside him. Having him playing the guitar also softens his character. In the following passage, several pages into the scene, the real nature of Kit's relationship with his mother-in-law is revealed.

> Kit pulled the covers off her and slid his hand across her hip, just as he used to with Jodie. Jodie's mother's body was startlingly similar in proportion, though a bit lumpier here and there. His hand came to an automatic rest at the small hollow at the base of her spine, just as it always had with Jodie. He let it rest there, fingers stroking the older slightly drier skin, imagining Jodie's face. She had been dead three years now, and sometimes Kit had trouble remembering exactly what she looked like. Not the features, he had plenty of photographs and portraits around his twelve-bedroom mansion to remind him of that. No, it was the expressions he missed. The goofy faces she'd make when imitating their friends, the serious ones when she was frustrated that her painting wasn't going well. What she had looked like the first time they'd had sex at her studio, the day they got married at a Tokyo Buddhist temple, while screaming at him during childbirth that their next kid was coming out of him, even if she had to create an orifice herself. Now he could only recall scraps of her face when he exhumed another memory. An eye, the mouth, the flip of hair around her ear. And he was running out of memories to conjure

up, ones that weren't corrupted by overuse. If he used the same memory too often, her face was replaced with one from the photo albums, with a frozen expression, as cold and waxy as her corpse.

He wondered if Margaret had the same problem remembering her dead husband, Bert. Both father and daughter had been killed together while riding in a taxi, a freak accident with a moving van. Kit envied his father-in-law having died with Jodie. How often Kit had imagined himself and Jodie dying together, usually going down in a plummeting plane while he held her hand and calmly told her how much he loved her. Only then could she have no doubt of his love, and he'd wanted her to know the certainty of it.

Kit let his hand slide further down his mother-in-law's hip while he clenched his eyes and concentrated on Jodie. It was working, there she was, smashing a tennis ball past him, laughing, blowing across the top of her racket as if it were a gun she'd just outdrawn him with. And then it was gone, the image receded into darkness like a pickpocket stepping back into a dark doorway and that old familiar pain of loss gnawed through his stomach. He squeezed Margaret's buttock, as if he could wring out another memory of Jodie. But it was hopeless.

This occasional sex with his mother-in-law had begun a year ago, the second anniversary of their spouses' deaths. He couldn't even remember how it first happened, just that they'd had dinner together to commiserate and somehow, after several bottles of obscenely expensive wine, had ended up in bed. They never talked about it. But every three or four months Margaret would come over in the middle of the day looking lost and disheveled like an amnesiac and they would have sex and lie in bed for an hour or so. Then each would arise and go their separate way without speaking of it.

This passage is designed to achieve the following effects on the reader:

• It is at this point that I want the reader to feel sympathy for Kit, to recognize that what at first may seem like a perversion is a desperate act of love for his dead wife, and of compassion for his mourning mother-in-law. In fact, I wanted the very act that readers would find perverse (sleeping with his mother-in-law) to be the act that they would see as redemptive (he sleeps with her out of grief for his dead wife and compassion for her suffering). This is meant to keep the reader slightly off balance and reluctant to jump to conclusions about the morality of any of the characters. This enhances the suspense: Since we can't know the morality of the characters, we can't be sure how they'll act in the key scenes. It also establishes a thematic subtext about the nature of morality blah, blah, blah, which I want to be an important, but subtle, part of the novel.

• It establishes the potential for redemption. Part of the suspense of the novel is the possibility that Kit will alter the course for all the destruction he's causing.

• Finally, I like toying with the concept of "the banality of evil," as Hannah Ardent put it. That evil is a gradual process that occurs when one assumes the right to commit it, and that the people who assume that right are often those whom we'd find most unassuming: those who see themselves as embodying society's moral values. This makes the evil all the more menacing since we can recognize ourselves in him.

 **Physical Therapy**

When I was just starting out as a writer, I read an interview with a famous actor who was asked how he made his villains so believable and with such depth. He responded that when he took on the role of an antagonist, such as Iago in Shakespeare's *Othello*, he sat down and wrote a brief biography of that character, detailing everything in that character's life before the events of the play. In that way he understood the reasons the character was the way he was and why he did what he did. It was important for him, he explained, to like the character, no matter what evil he wrought. This technique applies equally to writers seeking to create memorable antagonists. Here are some key questions to answer from the antagonist's POV:

- What do I want most out of life?
- What do I most fear losing?
- What will I stop short of doing? (What line would it be morally wrong to pass?)
- Why am I like this?
- Am I comfortable with who I am?

## Character Development Worksheet

### Physical Description

| | | | |
|---|---|---|---|
| age: | height: | weight: | voice: |
| eyes: | hair: | build: | |
| health: | | scars, marks: | |
| clothing: | | | |

### Living Situation

| | |
|---|---|
| occupation: | car: |
| home: | pets: |

### Personal Characteristics

goals:

attitude:

habits/mannerisms:

sports:

peeves:

hobbies:

magazines/books:

movies:

music:

motives:

### Background

birthplace:

parents:

spouse/lover:

children:

military:

education:

CHAPTER THREE

# Setting

### Symptom: Underdescription/overdescription
*Common Ailment*
**Wallpaper Settings.** Misused setting that is either (1) bland wallpaper that just lies passively in the background, not actively contributing to the story; or (2) gaudy wallpaper that screams for attention and distracts the reader from the story.

### Symptom: Description overload
*Common Ailment*
**Clumping.** Chunks of description thrown into a scene slow readers down and detract from the overall effect. Readers may skip these sections to get back to the story.

### Symptom: Low-impact settings, off-beat pacing
*Common Ailment*
**Wrong-Address Settings.** Settings that aren't the best possible choice to heighten all the elements of that particular scene. Conventional, predictable scenes qualify too.

## FAQs Frequently Asked Questions
? How much setting description does my story need? pages 118–120
? How can I describe setting effectively without slowing down the story? pages 120, 131–132
? How can I use setting to control pacing? pages 134–135
? How can I use setting to underscore theme? pages 119, 124–126
? What if a compelling but unusual setting isn't realistic for a scene? page 137

## Symptom: Underdescription/overdescription

### Ailment: Wallpaper Settings

The two most common mistakes writers make with setting is to (1) underdescribe (bland wallpaper) or (2) overdescribe (gaudy wallpaper). The setting, whether it be the city where the story takes place or the various locations of each scene, must emit some degree of lurking presence. How intense that presence should be depends on how significant a role the author wants the setting to play in the tone, atmosphere and motivation, or even theme, of the story.

When the setting is sketchy, the entire story can falter because it seems less realistic, as if the author has not done her homework. The setting is **underdescribed** if you're reading a story and feel as if each scene is dimly lit and you're squinting at blotchy shadows instead of distinct objects. You know the characters are sitting in some kind of restaurant, or they're driving through some sort of countryside—but you just can't visualize any of it. This gives you an uneasy feeling, like you're an uninvited guest to the party and are being ignored by the other revelers.

The setting is **overdescribed** if you're reading a story and feel as if you're at the same party, but you have to keep bobbing your head around all the other guests to get a glimpse of the fleeing protagonists. Every time you approach the protagonists to hear what they're saying, another stranger intercepts you to engage in annoying conversation about the history of this chair, or how vivid the colors are in this painting, or how the clouds outside resemble the Beatles, with that fifth cloud off by itself giving off the sad, isolated look of Pete Best, the Beatle before Ringo. And so forth. This distracts the reader from any emotional core of the scene, thereby reducing involvement, suspense and how much we care about the characters.

A healthy setting *enhances* the story the way a flattering frame enhances a painting. The size, shape and color of the chosen frame depend on the nature of the painting itself. A frame doesn't hide in the shadows, nor does it overwhelm.

116

## Diagnosis

There are three main ingredients to any story: character, plot and setting. The balance among these three is delicate; increasing or decreasing the amount of any one of these ingredients changes the "taste" of the story, thereby shifting the reader's attention. Although most of the attention is given to the two flashier elements of character (including dialogue) and plot (including suspense), setting can be the most difficult of the three to make work. That's why it so often doesn't.

The underdescriber is usually just negligent. He can't be bothered with the nuances of description because he's in a hurry to stoke the plot and keep the story chugging along. Or he's so enamored with his own characters that he enjoys the sound of their dialogue and doesn't want to interrupt them with details that he considers distracting or mundane. Sometimes he's right; sometimes merely suggesting the setting is enough for a scene and any extra description would cripple the rhythm. We'll discuss that option in "Minimal Description" on page 122. For now, the important distinction is between the writer who deliberately withholds setting description for a specific purpose and the writer who doesn't recognize when more detail is helpful.

The overdescriber is too enthusiastic—or else just showing off. One reason for this problem is Writing Workshop Syndrome, which occurs when writers critique each other's manuscripts without skilled guidance (like deciding to perform brain surgery on yourself). When the class critiques a manuscript in one of my workshops, there's usually someone who cries out, "I can't smell the salt in the air, taste the sweat on their lips, feel the rustle of nose hairs in the breeze." The short answer to that complaint is, "You're not supposed to." If the writer continuously assaults a reader's senses, it's as if the reader walked onto a car lot, only to have five different salespersons simultaneously pitch five different cars. The reader becomes so disoriented that she leaves without buying anything. Which is exactly how she'll leave your story, without buying into it. Description of setting is a tool to achieve a goal, not the goal itself.

## Treatment

First, determine the role that setting plays in your story. To do this, you need to answer the *Big Picture* question:

*How significant is setting to the development of the characters' personalities and/or to the plot conflicts?*

## THE BIG PICTURE DESCRIPTION

With the Big Picture, setting is a major character in that it influences what the characters do and how they feel. For example, the film *3:10 to Yuma* (based on Elmore Leonard's short story) opens with a shot of the dry, cracked desert ground, which has obviously gone a long, long time without water. This shot of the desert is held for a long time. Why? There is nothing inherently visually interesting about dry, cracked ground. But the movie is trying to tell us something: The parched ground is not just the condition of the land, it's also the moral condition of the people who live here. They are not deserving of rain. They have been tested by the land—and have been found spiritually lacking.

Here's why: The drought has left small-time rancher, Van Heflin, without enough water to save his ranch. His relationship with his wife is equally parched (he intimates that if they had water, maybe he and his wife wouldn't always be "too tired"—meaning they'd have sex). Outlaw Glenn Ford and his gang rob a stagecoach. Ford is caught, but the townspeople, fearing retaliation by his gang, will not take him to the next city to put him on the train to Yuma, where there's a jail. Heflin volunteers because he wants the reward money to buy water rights. What we see so far is that no one does anything because it is the right thing to do for the community; the people operate only out of selfish motives. Eventually, Heflin rejects an even larger sum offered by Ford to let him go. Heflin risks his life no longer for the money, but because he wants to do what's right for the community. Once he makes this choice, the rain falls. A baptism from above. In this case, the setting is constantly emphasized: every movement by every character causes a whirlwind of dust, because they live in a hell caused by their own selfishness.

Another example of setting as a substantial character is in what Hollywood refers to as "fish-out-of-water" stories. In such scenarios, a person leaves his comfortable surroundings and journeys to a place where everything is different; these differences become the core settings of each scene. Examples include *Splash* (mermaid on

118

land), *Witness* (tough cop among peaceful Amish) and *Lord of the Flies* (proper private schoolboys on a tropical island). The popularity of this formula is so great because it allows for instant conflict in a clash of cultures that, let's face it, is just plain fun. However, this contrast can also be used to create a richer thematic layer as well. In these stories, description of the setting is used selectively as a contrast to what the protagonist is used to. There's no need to describe every detail; concentrate only on those elements that cause conflict with the protagonist. If you describe too many setting elements, you lessen the impact of those things that cause conflict.

Certainly in many works, the nature of the landscape is a major influence on why characters do what they do: the roiling sea in Herman Melville's *Moby Dick*, the Southwest desert in Barbara Kingsolver's *Animal Dreams*, the dust bowl Midwest in John Steinbeck's *Grapes of Wrath*, the dense jungle in Joseph Conrad's *Heart of Darkness* and Paul Theroux's *Mosquito Coast*, and so on. In each of these stories, the setting isn't just a place where the events of the story happen, it's a motivating factor in why people do what they do.

Setting can also be used as a symbol for the nature of the universe's attitude toward humanity: Is it benevolent, malevolent or indifferent? (See the Crash Symbols ailment on page 177). For example, in literature, the sea is often symbolic of the indifference of nature toward humans. On land, humans have more control over their environment and therefore base beliefs about their own roles in the universe on this sense of order. But the sea can't be controlled. (Jungles also often symbolize the same loss of control, as with the Conrad and Theroux stories mentioned above.) So once the characters are on the sea, or in the jungle, they reexamine their beliefs about a universe that has moral order and is benevolent toward humanity.

## BIG PICTURE TREATMENT

*If setting is meant to be a motivating factor or a reflection of the conflicts within the characters, then more description is possibly necessary.* You want to make sure that you've sufficiently described the setting so the reader understands how important it is. However, be sure you emphasize what it is about the setting that is significant. For example, if the setting is meant to be a symbolic Garden of Eden, then you want to stress those aspects of the setting, such as in Paul Theroux's *Mosquito Coast.* In this novel and in the subsequent film starring Harrison Ford, the setting starts out as a paradise. But because the protagonist commits murder, albeit for a good cause, he sets himself up as godlike and is therefore punished. Instead of being kicked out of the Garden, he goes mad and becomes a threat to his family, which leaves him. In the last part of the story, the setting is threatening and wild.

*If setting is not significant to the story, avoid excessive description.* If you want to show us a filthy, disgusting alley, don't feel compelled to drag us through each slimy puddle, toss us into an overflowing trash dumpster, then rub our noses in the dried vomit. As with most things in life, sometimes less is more. Use one metaphor, one adjective or one defining characteristic of a room, rather than two or three. Think of fiction setting the same way you might a play's set. Most of the time a stage play uses set design to *imply* the larger setting. The false fronts of buildings, even the elaborate interiors may be realistic, but the audience never mistakes them for real. For example, if you want the reader to experience how depressing a hospital ward is, you only have to *imply* it by describing a few aspects that suggest the larger image.

> The hallways seemed narrower and darker than other hospitals I'd been in, but that could have been because of the artwork on the walls: oversized prints of small ships being tossed on stormy seas. As I walked down the hall, the ships seemed to get smaller and the storms more violent. Though I saw no one else in the hall, the constant sound of slippers scuffing across linoleum accompanied me like a harsh ocean wind.

There is no attempt to describe the usual suspects: antiseptic smells, drab paint jobs, indifferent faces of the staff, or the defeated expressions of the patients that are usually used. Instead, the sinister artwork on the walls and the unseen scuffing of slippers creates the ominous mood without slowing the pace down so we forget why we're even there.

A more advanced technique to establish setting is to merge setting with character. Instead of describing the physical setting you describe an ethereal property of the setting from a character's POV. In the following excerpt from the short story "Over," Rose Tremain describes the room of the protagonist, who is bedridden and watched over by a nurse.

> His curtains are drawn back and light floods into the room. To him, light is time. Until nightfall, it lies on his skin, seeping just a little into the pores yet never penetrating inside him, neither into his brain nor heart nor into any crevice of him. Light and time, time and light lie on him as weightless as a sheet. He is somewhere else.

Tremain focuses only on the light coming into the room and the character's relationship with that light. We understand from this description that the light can't penetrate into his brain or heart—that he is already removed from life, waiting in a private place to die.

Sometimes all that is needed is one descriptive detail to imply the rest. In the opening of the student story, "Inhale," by Cathy Wakamatsu, one image is presented that defines the family we are about to meet:

> Our house is the only house on the street that still has its trashcans out on Fridays—they collect it on Wednesdays but none of us bothers to bring them in. That's how you can tell us apart from the other houses. There are a couple of other stragglers, brown bins marked with red tape, black ones spray-painted 9602 so they don't get confused with its neighbors, but they all return to the side of the house, if not the backyard, by Thursday nights. Of course, we didn't used to be like this.

What the author does well here is select one image—the trash cans no one bothers to retrieve after trash day—to announce that there is some conflict amidst the family that lives in the house.

I'll leave the subject of overdescription with some words of advice Anton Chekhov gave a young writer: "Descriptions of nature should be extremely brief and offered by the way, as it were. Give up commonplaces, such as: 'the setting sun, bathing in the waves of the darkening sea, flooded with purple gold,' and so on. Or 'Swallows flying over the surface of the water chirped gaily.' In descriptions of nature one should seize upon minutiae, grouping them so that when, having read the passage, you close your eyes, a picture is formed. For example, you will evoke a moonlit night by writing that on the mill dam the glass fragments of a broken bottle flashed like a bright little star, and that the black shadow of a dog or wolf rolled along like a ball. . . ."

## Minimal Description

Many writers deliberately just sketch the details of setting in order to create a mood, rather than a vivid picture. When mood is the dominating impact the author wishes to achieve, highlighting a specific setting detail is more effective than presenting many details or using stylistic flourishes like metaphors or similes. By not distracting the reader with unnecessary details, the author can emphasize a single setting detail, thereby supercharging that detail to provide more impact. In Jhumpa Lahiri's short story "A Temporary Matter," the husband and wife protagonists are in their kitchen, discussing a notice they just got in the mail announcing a planned power shutdown. There have been no details about the appearance of the kitchen.

"It says March nineteenth. Is today the nineteenth?" Shoba walked over to the framed corkboard that hung on the wall by the fridge, bare except for a calendar of William Morris wallpaper patterns. She looked at it as if for the first time, studying the wallpaper pattern carefully on the top half before allowing her eyes to fall to the numbered grid on the bottom. A friend had sent the calendar in the mail as a Christmas gift, even though Shoba and Shukumar hadn't celebrated Christmas that year.

Since this is the only description given of the kitchen, our eyes focus on it and from that detail, we are meant to extrapolate more about the characters. It's as if someone went into a dark bedroom and had to decide which item in there to shine a flashlight on—a single object that would reveal most about the person who lived there. In this case, the corkboard is bare except for the calendar; there are no notes, coupons or messages. It implies a certain stagnation in their lives. The calendar itself is a misdirection. Notice the dialogue that opens the paragraph: Shoba is uncertain of the date, which suggests some disorientation about her life. She goes there to check on a date, but what the author wants us to know is that they didn't celebrate Christmas. Why not? What happened that has left them stagnant and disoriented? Any additional description would distract the reader from the larger feel of the setting, which is one of barrenness.

Several authors are famous for this "minimalist" technique, including Raymond Carver, Tobias Wolff and Ann Beattie. In the following passage from Carver's short story "A Small, Good Thing" (which is incorporated with other Carver stories into the Robert Altman movie *Short Cuts*), a father arrives at the hospital, where his son lies in a coma. His wife, Ann, is already there.

> He arrived back at the hospital a little after midnight. Ann still sat in the chair beside the bed. She looked up at Howard, and then she looked back at the child. The child's eyes stayed closed, the head was still wrapped in bandages. His breathing was quiet and regular. From an apparatus over the bed hung a bottle of glucose with a tube running from the bottle to the boy's arm.

Hospitals and patients are favorite subjects of overdescribers. They like to describe every anguished expression of the parents, each moan of pain of the patient. Here Carver deliberately avoids such details in an effort to avoid melodrama (which elicits emotion for the sake of emotion, while drama elicits emotion in an effort to gain insight into the nature of our feelings.) He doesn't even refer to the boy by name here, though we know his name is Scotty. Carver doesn't want us to indulge ourselves in the cheap, easy emotion of seeing a little boy in this situation. Rather, he wants us to feel the helplessness and disorientation the parents feel about the situation, as well as the alienation they feel toward each other, even though they don't yet realize that's how they feel. There's no description of smells, drabness of the room or hospital sounds. There's only the boy, his bandaged head and a bottle of glucose. But the mood couldn't be more emotionally intense or suspenseful.

**Mood in Action**

In James Hawes's novel *A White Merc With Fins*, chapter two opens with a description of London:

> It was Saturday night, about 9:45, close orange sky and damp warmish streets. London was on the move, re-grouping its molecules for night running, morphing itself along the neural paths of seven million phone books and filofaxes; a hundred thousand tribes, each with its own territory, rules, traditions, leaders, heroes, enemies and court jesters, gathering themselves in cars, buses, taxis and tubes. The whole world had finished working and shopping and eating, the early-evening films were emptying out, everyone was just waiting to party, raring to kick it into gear and keep running late, this is what the city lived for and worked for Monday to Friday, nine to five, this long night that would go on until the week was buried and Sunday half dead.

Based on this paragraph, what is your impression of London and Londoners? (Take time to look at it again before reading on.)

Here's my impression: a busy but desperate throng of people trapped in a near-feudal environment, anxious for some relief from unfulfilled lives. This is how I arrived at that conclusion: (1) The first sentence describes a clammy, uncomfortable setting: ". . . close orange sky and damp warmish streets." *Close* and *damp warmth* make it feel claustrophobic and sweaty—a version of hell. (2) "London was on the move . . ." makes the city seem like a living creature, a beast with a will beyond that of any of the individuals. Again, this makes it seem like an unpleasant place for people. (3) The reference to phone books and filofaxes makes it seem like an impersonal place populated by people too busy to enjoy themselves. (4) The references to tribes and all things tribal "each with its own territory, rules, traditions, leaders, heroes, enemies and court jesters" gives it the feel of a medieval castle, a feudal system in which people are locked into their thoughts and attitudes based on the influences of environment rather than free will. (5) The final sentence catalogs a bustling, desperate populace in a frenzy to find some relief from their usual lives. The run-on sentence creates a downhill, out-of-control rush that slams into the grim passage: ". . . this long night that would go on until the week was buried and Sunday half dead." That last image of death enforces the vision of people caught in a whirlpool of repetition with no hope of escape.

The reason Hawes presents such a grim vision of London is that it provides the motivation for the criminal act the protagonists are about to perform. Notice that he hasn't selected one of the slums of London, with its trash and drugs and criminals. Had he done that, the motivation would have been a desperation and frustration with the daily horrors of survival. But Hawes makes it clear here and elsewhere that his protagonists—all college-educated, lower middle-class members—are responding, not to the trials of the slums, but to the numbing, deadening routine of lives measured by telephones and filofaxes.

Similar works that use setting as a major influence and/or symbol include Thomas Mann's *Death in Venice* (also the movie version), the movie, *Don't Look Now,* based on a Daphne du Maurier novel also uses Venice as a symbol of death and misperception, in the same way Woody Allen's *Manhattan* uses that city, as does D.H. Lawrence's *Women in Love* (also the movie version). Both A.L. Kennedy's *So I Am Glad* and Muriel Spark's *The Prime of Miss Jean Brodie* use Scotland as a dominating influence of why the characters act as they do.

David Guterson's novel *Snow Falling on Cedars* uses a lot of description of the land and weather to show that setting is important, not just as a backdrop, but as an active influence on the characters and action in this scene. A writer can further emphasize this notion by beginning a scene with setting description, as Guterson does here:

> Outside the wind blew steadily from the north, driving snow against the courthouse. By noon three inches had settled on the town, a snow so ethereal it could hardly be said to have settled at all; instead it swirled like some icy fog, like the breath of ghosts, up and down Amity Harbor's streets—powdery dust devils, frosted puffs of ivory cloud, spiraling tendrils of white smoke. By noon the smell of the sea was eviscerated, the sight of it mistily depleted, too; one's field of vision narrowed in close, went blurry and snowbound, fuzzy and opaque, the sharp scent of frost burned in the nostrils of those who ventured out of doors. The snow flew up from their boots as they struggled, heads down, toward Peterson's Grocery. When they looked out into the whiteness of the world the wind flung it sharply at their narrowed eyes and foreshortened their view of everything.

Why this rich and lengthy description of snow? Because Guterson wants the reader to understand that the snow isn't just frozen water, it's a cosmic force that puts in perspective the people in the community he's writing about, as well as the murder trial the novel is about. The snow, which is described as "ghosts" and "devils," suggests an indifferent universe that doesn't care about human notions of right and wrong. Therefore, the only justice in the world is that which the people provide. The key phrase here is ". . . the whiteness of the world the wind flung it sharply at their narrowed eyes and foreshortened their view of everything," which describes the effect of the natural world on the people involved in the trial: it blinds them. In this way, setting is used to do more than establish the weather, but also to underscore the theme of the book.

To achieve a more intimate portrayal of setting, and emphasize its connection to the character's conflict, concentrate on one aspect of the setting, as A.S. Byatt does in her short story "Medusa's Ankles," which begins with setting description:

She had walked in one day because she had seen the *Rosy Nude* though the plate glass. That was odd, she thought, to have that lavish and complex creature stretched voluptuously above the coat rack, where one might have expected the stare, silver and supercilious or jetty and frenzied, of the model girl. They were all girls now, not women. The *Rosy Nude* was pure flat colour, but suggested mass. She had huge haunches and a monumental knee, lazily propped high. She had round breasts, contemplations of the circle, reflections on flesh and its fall.

The narrator walks into a hair salon because of the Matisse print she sees through the window. What is it about the painting that compels her to enter this particular salon? When we answer that, we will know that, because she is revealing this information to us as motivation, it goes to the heart of the protagonist's interior conflict, the one that will propel the plot. The feature that catches her eye is the ripeness of the model's figure, that it is not the skinny, bony, airbrushed-to-perfect-shape body that is the icon for contemporary women. The painting suggests to her a place to enhance her own beauty that isn't a slave to popular fashion. In fact, the story is about the middle-aged protagonist's fear of aging, loss of sexuality, and therefore her increasing marginalization by society. All this is revealed by having her describe a painting—which symbolizes the salon and what sort of salvation she hopes to find in it.

Another technique to create the big picture setting is to weave the details in within the flow of the narrative and action, as in the opening of Leonard Michaels's short story "Mackerel":

She didn't want to move in because there had been a rape on the third floor. I said, "The guy was a wounded veteran, under observation at Bellevue. We'll live on the fifth floor." It was a Victorian office building converted to apartments. Seven stories, skinny, filigreed face. No elevators. We climbed an iron stairway. "Wounded veteran," I said. "Predictable." My voice echoed in dingy halls. Linoleum cracked as we walked. Beneath the linoleum was older, drier linoleum. The apartments had wooden office doors with smoked-glass windows. The hall toilets were padlocked; through gaps we could see the bowl, overhead tanks, bare bulb dangling. "The stairway is good for the heart and legs," I said. . . .

Michaels is establishing the story's main conflict by contrasting what the narrator says with the way the setting is described. The narrator is trying to convince his girlfriend to move into a building she considers dangerous. He tries to reason with her by saying, "The guy was a wounded veteran, under observation at Bellevue. We'll live on the fifth floor." But immediately following his rationale, we are presented with a grim description of the building. The setting details are arranged so that each is worse than the one before it, until we're left with the image of the padlocked toilets with the "bare bulb dangling." By doing this, Michaels shows the reader that the narrator is an unfeeling lout. Even if he were right about the place—which he clearly isn't—the point isn't who is right but that someone he loves wouldn't feel safe there and he wants her to move in anyway. Michaels reveals this all within the first few sentences merely by interweaving the dialogue with the setting description.

 ### Physical Therapy

Director John Ford was a pioneer with his Westerns in that he used the actual settings of the West to help audiences experience the rugged and unforgiving environment that helped shape the morals and character of the people exposed to it. His characters weren't just wandering around the backlots of Tarzana pretending to be in Arizona, they were actually there, often dwarfed by the canyons and deserts and pastures where the real people lived and died. It helps when a writer understands the connection between character, plot and setting. Sometimes, the setting is just window dressing to add spice to the scene, but the core settings—just like the main sets of a play—carry a greater weight. So give careful thought to the three main ingredients of your story:

1. Describe the characteristics of the setting.
2. List how the setting affects the character(s).
3. List how the setting affects the plot.

This can be done both on the grand scale of the general setting of the story and the small setting of an individual scene.

**General setting:** Orange County, California (the setting of T. Jefferson Parker's novel *Laguna Heat*, among others). A sprawling suburban cluster of many smaller cities that seem to overlap each other, each connected by always-jammed freeways. Includes a large spectrum of socioeconomic classes, from the wealthy socialites of Newport Beach, to the surf-and-party beach communities of Huntington Beach, to the gang-infested neighborhoods of Santa Ana and the strict planned communities of Irvine. Also includes one of the largest Vietnamese communities in the country. Every strata of society is here, generally comingling at the supermalls of South Coast Plaza and Fashion Island.

**Specific setting:** Rain Forest Cafe at South Coast Plaza. Theme restaurant with jungle sounds and live exotic birds. Always busy, especially with mothers and their children. The entrance is usually filled with dozens of empty strollers. Perfect scene for a heated emotional discussion, because the characters might feel restricted about what they can say—and what language they can use—because of all the kids.

## Symptom: Description overload

### Ailment: Clumping

Clumping, a form of overdescription, occurs when a writer unloads the entire description in one section of the scene. The momentum of the scene grinds to a halt while the reader must endure paragraph after paragraph of descriptions of the scenery, the weather, the car, a history of the bugs splatting against the windshield.

### Diagnosis

A writer must choose the right places in a scene to give descriptions. Following is an excerpt from a student manuscript, a Western, in which the author provides setting description:

129

Leaving the rock-lined irrigation ditch that flowed from Montezuma Well, they followed Beaver Creek north. Three miles after leaving their campsite they veered northwest when Beaver Creek swung east. They dipped down into Rarick Canyon, where they watered the cayuses at the creek in the bottom of the canyon. Changing saddles to fresh horses, they wound their way up the steep wall on the west side of the canyon.

After riding over tall hills, they followed a slender pathway down a cliff and struck Dry Beaver Creek. Moving north, they stuck with the dry watercourse until they found the junction of Jack's Canyon and Woods Canyon.

This description continues for another full paragraph. The author is generally a good writer, but this passage doesn't work for several reasons: (1) There are too many names of places. The reader gets confused, starts to wonder if the names are important and may even try to memorize them. The result: The reader is pulled out of the story. (2) The scene shouldn't start with this description because it's so passive. This would be better if he had started with some specific action, such as the riders trying to cross a stream. Or if they were having a conversation. Then the dialogue would serve as a misdirection while he painlessly injects a few setting details. (3) The POV is omniscient, which makes the description even blander. However, if the author had written the description from one of the riders' POVs, the reader would be more compelled to read it. (4) Most important, we don't really need all this information. It's irrelevant to the plot, doesn't enhance the characters, and adds nothing to the mood.

Remember, you don't have to give everything at once. As David Guterson, mentioned earlier in the chapter, advises, "[Y]ou may get bogged down in a sentence that's descriptive detail about landscape, spend a lot of time on it, then realize that the entire paragraph, maybe the entire page, maybe two or three pages of descriptive detail are doing nothing . . . and it's time to remove them. But there's a lot of satisfaction in tearing away, and allowing something really clear to emerge as a result."

**Treatment**

Decide whether all that information is crucial to the scene: Does it enhance the scene, or are you just showing off? It is usually better to dole out these descriptive moments throughout a scene, between more active moments. In Elizabeth Tallent's "No One's a Mystery," the eighteen-year-old narrator is driving in a truck with her older, married lover. He has bought her a diary for her birthday and is telling her that life is too predictable—so predictable that he knows what she will write in it that night.

> "How do you know?"
> "I just know," he said. "Like I know I'm going to get meat loaf for supper. It's in the air. Like I know what you'll be writing in that diary."
> "What will I be writing?" I knelt on my side of the seat and craned around to look at the butterfly of dust printed on my jeans. Outside the window Wyoming was dazzling in the heat. The wheat was fawn and yellow and parted smoothly by the thin dirt road. I could smell the water in the irrigation ditches hidden in the wheat.

The cleverness of this technique is that a character poses a question ("What will I be writing?") and then the writer injects setting description between the question and the answer. This ensures that readers pay more attention to the description because you have already heightened their awareness by asking an important question. They are more focused on the setting description. Plus, you've heightened suspense about the answer to the question because you've delayed giving it.

There's more going on in Tallent's description than just details about the setting. Start with the narrator's reference to the dust splotch on her pants as a "butterfly." She uses this word because she is a romantic kid who thinks this is the love of her life, even though he's telling her it's nothing more than another in a long mundane string of affairs. The rest of the description of Wyoming is very concise: bright, wheat fields, dirt roads, the smell of irrigation water. It may seem a little desolate to the reader—suggesting why she's with him in the first place (limited opportunities)—but her word choices echo her romanticism even here. She calls Wyoming "dazzling" instead of blistering. She uses "fawn" to describe the color. The road parts the wheat field "smoothly." Without overdoing the description, the reader not only gets a snapshot of the scenery the characters are driving through—and that defines their existence and choices—but also gets a peek at the kind of girl she is.

This technique dilutes clumping, and it highlights the descriptive passages to give them more impact.

### Physical Therapy

Take ten minutes to expand on a scene you've written, a turning point in a story. Include as many pertinent details as necessary: smells, sounds, people in the background, backstory of objects central to the scene. Then read the scene twice and contemplate what it should accomplish. Cut description that intrudes on the narrative and doesn't in some way complement the plot or characters. The goal: to bind characters, plot and setting descriptions so seamlessly that you can't remove the description without diminishing the scene.

### Symptom: Low-impact settings, off-beat pacing

### Ailment: Wrong-Address Settings

Choosing the proper location is often crucial to the success of a scene. Emotional involvement, humor and suspense can all be heightened, or destroyed, depending on where a scene takes place. For example, a company trying to win the business of a large corporation would take the people they're trying to woo out to dine at a fancy restaurant to sip vintage wine, rather than to chow burgers and slurp shakes at a Jack-in-the-Box. The location of that all-important first date tells a lot about the person who chose it—and may determine whether there is a second date.

The wrong setting can make a scene sluggish, whereas the right one can intensify and energize a scene. Whether or not a particular scene has the wrong setting may be difficult to determine because it is a subtle problem. You might write a scene that has all the elements to make it work: The characterization is rich, the plot is involving, the dialogue is pithy and moving, the descriptive passages clear and poetic. Yet, it somehow doesn't have the snap it should. A certain element that powers the scene is missing, like reading a good book in light that is too dim and strains your eyes.

## Diagnosis

A healthy setting choice resonates beneath the surface of whatever is happening in a scene. Filmmaker Orson Welles was especially masterful in using settings to heighten all the elements of his films. In *Lady From Shanghai*, the lovers meet secretly at a public aquarium. As they embrace in the semidarkness, sensually illuminated by the enormous fish tanks, their barely pent passion is enhanced. Plus, there is also the danger of exposure because they're in a public place—as we see when a group of schoolchildren giggle when they discover the couple kissing. How much different the scene would have been if it had been set in a restaurant over nachos!

Later in the film, Welles has all the principal characters shooting at each other in a fun-house with mirrors (a scene that has been duplicated in movies from Bruce Lee's *Enter the Dragon* to Woody Allen's *Manhattan Murder Mystery*). Not only does this create suspense as they mistakenly shoot at the various mirrors, but it emphasizes the thematic motif of conniving people who deliberately present deceptive personas to each other. A good way to understand the importance of setting to particular scenes is to list a few of your favorite story, novel and film scenes, and imagine them set elsewhere.

Beginning writers are sometimes lax in taking advantage of setting choice because they focus their attention on the more dynamic elements of plot, character and dialogue. While it's true that those elements are crucial to the story's success, it's also true that selecting the right setting can significantly enhance their impact. Choosing where a scene takes place can add thematic dimension to a scene or make it more suspenseful. While working on my own novels, I have often rewritten scenes that seemed flat by transporting them to an entirely new setting that suddenly made the scene more exciting, intense or comic, depending on what I was trying to achieve.

As with most elements of writing, one major cause of poor scene selection is the reliance on what you've read or seen before. Your mind is filled with certain types of scenes that usually take place in the same setting. For example, in a Western, the hero and the villain might confront each other in a saloon, which will likely be followed by a brawl. Even though there are many good, realistic reasons for such a scene to take place there, the fact that we've seen this scene set there so many times suggests it might be a good idea to move it elsewhere. Be on guard against the familiar and the comfortable in making writing choices, especially scene settings.

 **Treatment**

Treatment starts with this basic question: Is each scene set in the best location to enhance whatever the scene is about? Be flexible. A setting you love may not be the best choice for a particular scene. A setting might be too dominant, or too bland, for what you need in the scene. If that's so, jettison it and select a new, more compatible setting.

One aspect to consider is that the choice of setting can control the pace of the story in two ways: (1) It controls the pace within a particular scene (which we've already discussed), or (2) the scene itself is used to control the pace of a larger story or novel. For example, a suspense novel generally involves chasing after someone. But if every scene is a wild chase, the reader loses interest. So the suspense novel must include sedentary scenes to separate the faster-paced chase scenes. A scene at a Paris café might be followed by a chase scene up the Eiffel Tower, but the effectiveness of the chase is dependent on the contrast between it and the calm café scene. Without the sedentary café scene, the chase is not as exciting.

To most effectively use setting to control pace in a larger work, make a list of all the scenes and where they are set. Then by looking at the neighboring scenes, determine whether the pace of each scene needs to be slower, faster or the same. Those that need to be slower or faster can be transposed into a different setting that will automatically achieve this. The discussion that occurred while the couple shopped at an overcrowded Macy's, thus giving it a hectic tone and therefore faster pace, could take place on the cab ride to Macy's.

One major cause of poor setting selection is that writers within genres sometimes become intimidated by the conventions of the genre. Rather than approach these conventions with creativity and originality, they merely imitate what they've read before. For example, most detective novels follow the same pattern: There's a crime, after which the detective must interview a bunch of people to find out who committed the crime. These interviews are there not only to gather information, but also to introduce suspects. The problem each detective novel writer faces is how to make this round of interviews interesting. One way is to hamper the detective. Rex Stout's Nero Wolfe chooses never to leave his home; instead he sends his sidekick (the first-person narrator), Archie Goodwin, to do the legwork. The reader now knows that for the mystery to be solved, the suspects must show up at Wolfe's door, a setting so familiar and comfortable to the readers it's like their own home. Jeffrey Deaver's quadriplegic forensic expert in *The Bone Collector* also cannot leave his home, so the settings are a continuous juxtaposition of his bedroom, the crimes in progress and his sidekick, who is trying to solve the murders.

Another technique is to make each interview like its own mininovel. The person being interviewed is such a compelling character that the readers can't take their eyes off the character. In addition to the riveting character, an unusual setting helps misdirect the reader from the fact that the writer is just following a pattern. For example, it's popular to interview a character at work, which gives the author an opportunity to describe the workplace and details of the job. Let's say the character trains dolphins for Sea World. The reader gets all sorts of interesting information about how that's done. Of course, this involves research. I once decided to have a suspect pilot a skywriting plane. In order to give the scene as much authentic texture as possible, I went to a local skywriting company and interviewed a pilot. At their core, such scenes are the same: Introduce suspect and give reader information toward the solving of the mystery. The author's expertise at characterization and setting are what distinguish the good from the bad.

You must push yourself to think beyond the familiar. I recently asked my scriptwriting class where they would set a scene in which a couple with children discusses getting divorced. Two-thirds said the kitchen. While there's nothing inherently wrong with setting this scene in a kitchen, the fact that so many *expect* the scene to be there tells us it may be too familiar, too predictable. This in turn could reduce the tension of the scene because the reader, already alerted to a generic setting, may also reduce the drama of the emotions to mere generic melodrama. Instead, the writer might want to come up with a setting that catches the reader off-guard, forcing her to pay attention to every detail of what's going on and what's being said. For example, what if, instead of setting this scene in the kitchen, we set it at Disneyland? Specifically, the teacup ride. Now instead of a discussion in a familiar kitchen, the couple is in a spinning teacup talking about their divorce while their children ride the teacup next to them. The contrast of their children laughing in the "happiest place on earth" while the parents discuss visitation adds impact to the scene. Also, the sensation of spinning while they dismantle the stability of their lives and the lives of their children can make the reader experience the physical emotions that the characters might be going through. Plus, you have the thematic irony of the children being thrilled at the controlled chaos of spinning just as they are about to experience the wrenching pain of the uncontrolled real thing.

Changing setting can enhance the action. In the romantic comedy film *Speechless*, Michael Keaton and Geena Davis are speechwriters for opposing political candidates. One of the conventions of the romantic comedy genre is a scene in which the intended lovers fight with each other to indicate they don't like each other. This film cleverly sets this scene in a public school, with Keaton and Davis there to tell the children what they do. However, as each describes his or her job, they start to take potshots at the other. But because they're in front of children, they have to be clever, despite their rising anger. This choice of setting makes the scene funnier while at the same time revealing more about the wit and intelligence of the characters.

Most of the time, appropriate settings will reveal themselves naturally as part of the characters' daily lives. We will see them at home, at work, in the car, etc. You don't want to strain the scene by forcing a setting that might seem contrived and thereby detract from the content of the scene. When the characters would ordinarily be home, set the scene at home, not on a rollercoaster. But even within the mundane world of "home," the writer has many choices. For example, you want to write a scene in which the father wants to have a talk with his son (about school, sex, behavior or whatever). I've seen several movies and TV shows, and read many novels where such a scene takes place, each time in the garage with the father working on some sort of machine (car, motorcycle, lawnmower). The idea is to have them do some bonding during the talk. The father can ask for a wrench or show the kid how to do something. But because we've seen this scene in this setting so often, the setting is a cliché and is just as damaging to the scene as if you were using clichés in the narrative or dialogue.

You don't have to move it out of the home, nor do you have to resort to machine substitutes such as throwing a baseball, football or basketball while they chat. You could still have an activity—which is in essence the setting, regardless of where this doctoring takes place—but it might be one that both surprises us and still enhances the relationship. For example, the father cuts himself somehow on his back; the son has to help bandage it because the father can't reach it. While bandaging, the father begins the discussion. You have the misdirection of the wound and bandaging, while also presenting the irony of the father trying to heal the son's internal wounds as the son cleanses the dad's external wounds. There are variations of this reverse-rescue setting: father caught in tree needs son to saw off branch while they talk. Or the setting could be the bathroom where the father is giving his infant son a bath while talking to the older son. The contrast of the two sons can add emotional impact to the scene.

I was recently hired to rewrite a comedy screenplay. One of the first things I did was look at where each scene was set to see if that same scene couldn't take place in a setting that was more conducive to comedy. The original writers set a climactic scene at a bluegrass music festival. The problem with that is that bluegrass appeals to a smaller audience and offers very little visual humor. So I changed the setting to a Tribute to Music Legends festival, in which all the acts impersonated their favorite music performers. That allowed us to have more visual gags of people dressed up like Willie Nelson or Meat Loaf. It also allowed us to add humor by poking fun at some of the stars being impersonated (there's a gag about Chris Isaak's hair) and to take advantage of the fact that people are in makeup to exploit mistaken identities for humor. (See also chapter one for why the screenwriter for *Chocolat* changed the time period.)

 **Physical Therapy**

Make a list of all the scenes you've already written in your story or novel. Grade each according to how effective the scene is (A, B, C, etc.). Take the scenes that are less than an A and list three alternative settings. Choose possible settings, not necessarily based on the content of the scene, but just on a compelling location. Now imagine that scene in each of these new settings. If any of these alternatives energize the scene, try rewriting the scene in that particular new setting. Don't be afraid to let the change in setting alter your original scene; the dialogue may change, the characters' actions may change, but you may even get to know them better.

CHAPTER FOUR

# *Style*

**Symptoms: Bland phrasing; writing that echoes published writers but is less effective**
*Common Ailments*
**No Style.** Writer is not experienced enough to have developed a style.

**Clichéd or Imitative Style.** Writer lacks voice to distinguish his style.

**Symptoms: Monotonous phrasing; overwritten and confusing passages; muddled details**
*Common Ailment*
**Inappropriate Style.** Style is inappropriate for the effect it's supposed to achieve.

**Symptoms: Oversimplified, emotionally shallow characters; major cross-gender characters who seem minor; inaccurate gender-specific details**
*Common Ailment*
**Unconvincing Cross-Gender POVs.** Difficulty capturing the voice of characters who are not the same gender as the author.

## FAQs Frequently Asked Questions
? How do you know what your style is? page 141
? How do you develop your style? pages 141–142
? How do I know what style is right for a particular story? pages 148–157
? What is voice? pages 143–144
? How does POV affect style? pages 148–151

## Symptoms: Bland phrasing; writing that echoes published writers but is less effective

### Ailment: No Style

The author's overall style lacks any distinguishing characteristics. It isn't strong enough to reveal a unique voice that compels the story.

### Diagnosis

When English teachers give a student a separate grade for style and for content, they're telling students that the two aren't the same. They're related, yes, but not the same. Style is to content what fingers are to a hand. Without compelling, alluring style, content is just a clumsy fist, a shadow of its potential. On the other hand, lyrical style without content is like painting fingernails on that same closed fist. Useless. But careful reading can teach writers how to improve both of these areas in their own writing.

### Treatment

There are two main areas of style: (1) overall and (2) specific.

**Overall.** This relates to your general style that occurs throughout a story. The overall style establishes the story's voice. Each writer, like each singer or athlete, has her own style. When you read Lorrie Moore or Philip Roth or Barbara Kingsolver or Stephen King, you usually recognize their individual styles, even if the book is being narrated by different characters with different voices. An author's overall style is usually established by the kinds of elements she emphasizes in her writing. For example, Stephen King's style is usually distinguished by a casual yet intimate tone, lots of references to pop culture, graphic descriptions of bodily functions, rich characterization and smartass teen humor (which he does exceptionally well). These aren't the only characteristics of his style—he has an impressive range—but this characterizes his general style, and what many of his imitators emphasize. However, Lorrie Moore's style is recognizable by the poetic similes, the world-weary wit in both narrative and dialogue, and the richly textured descriptions. No matter what story of hers you read, these elements will stand out. With Raymond Carver you will get much less description, particularly in emotional scenes. And so it is with our best writers, each playing to her specific strengths.

**Specific.** Whereas the "overall" style is a shotgun approach—blasting out the key characteristics of the author's voice—the "specific" style refers to a sniper's approach: finding the right style for certain scenes. Writers recognize that some scenes require that they emphasize certain characteristics of their overall style and pull back on others. If a scene is meant to be emotional, including too much setting description can defuse the emotional buildup. If a scene is meant to be tense, too much humor might lessen the tension. If a scene is meant to be suspenseful, not enough description could rush the scene and dilute the suspense.

First, you need to establish your own overall style. Second, you need to know which of the tools that compose your style should be used in specific scenes to enhance whatever the goal of that scene is.

## HOW DO YOU KNOW WHAT YOUR OVERALL STYLE IS?

It's not always easy to know what your style is. When I finish a novel, I usually wait a few months before I begin another. Yet, when I sit down to start my new novel, I find that I've forgotten my style. It's embarrassing, like forgetting your children's names. I sometimes read the first few pages of my previous novels to remind myself of my style. After I get going, it all comes back to me again. Nevertheless, my style has to be shaped and refined by judicious editing and polishing. Plus, my style evolves with each new book as I take on new characteristics and abandon others.

## HOW DO YOU DEVELOP YOUR OVERALL STYLE?

You don't necessarily consciously choose your style. It develops over a period of time as you experiment with various techniques. Most writers discover their style by imitating the writers who made them want to write. For me as a teenager, those writers included Larry

McMurtry, J.D. Salinger, Donald Westlake, Ross Thomas and S.E. Hinton. Over the years my style has changed significantly as I've matured and as my reading habits have changed. Elmore Leonard and David Mamet greatly influenced me in changing the rhythm of my dialogue, even though my dialogue is nothing like theirs. Lorrie Moore and Deborah Eisenberg inspired me to work more on word choices and similes.

 ### Physical Therapy

Writers, like painters, start as imitators. They read books they enjoy and want to write a work just like the one that gave them so much pleasure. By copying the eyes of a painting, the artist learns to duplicate the proper strokes. In fact, it is helpful sometimes to use tracing paper and simply trace the drawing, learning proportions and the relationship of eye to eyebrow, etc.

Take a first chapter from a book you particularly admire and retype it. This is an excellent method for learning a specific writer's techniques. The mere act of typing another writer's words slows the reading process and magnifies the individual words. It's like looking into an electron microscope where you can see those tiny microscopic creatures stalking around on your skin like dinosaurs. You see what you couldn't see just reading the words. It teaches you their rhythms, forces you to examine their effects. It's like having a tennis pro stand behind you, his hand gripped over yours on the racquet, and going through the proper backhand motion. When he lets go and steps away, your muscle memory should take over and perform the same stroke. That's what you're doing by retyping a published chapter, developing your muscle memory for writing.

If you've ever had to retype your own story or chapter over a couple of dozen times, you know you start treating your manuscript with annoyance, as if you were an overworked editor. You begin to question your choices. Do I really need this next paragraph? What purpose does it serve? Is it just description for the sake of it? Do I want to type it all if it's just filler? These are healthy questions, which is why, even though I work on a word processor, I often retype entire chapters from scratch several times. The physical act of typing it over forces me to examine the words with more objectivity.

### Ailment: Clichéd or Imitative Style
Inevitably writers first sound like the authors they read, and that's OK. That's how you learn. But if a writer's style doesn't advance beyond that point, it risks becoming derivative or clichéd.

### Diagnosis
There are plenty of articles and books that discuss the pros and cons and techniques of the various points of view. But we're going to look a step beyond that to show how to produce the most important element of style: **voice.**

Voice is the one component of a work that is unique to the individual author. It is like Aristotle's definition of "essence": The essence of something is that special quality without which that something would no longer be what it is. Uh, let's rephrase that. Though there are many possible ways to describe a horse (e.g., an animal with four legs, an animal that can be ridden), these descriptions aren't exclusive to a horse. A cow or even some dogs will fit. But there is something about a horse, its essence, that makes it uniquely a horse and not any other animal. Without that essence, it would cease being a horse.

Voice is like that.

### Treatment
Voice is what every writer strives to develop. Anyone can write a detective novel, but a Raymond Chandler novel is uniquely his. Dashiell Hammett also wrote detective novels, but though Chandler and Hammett are often lumped together, their styles are quite different.

Let's examine a couple of opening paragraphs from each author and see what clues are offered. This is how Chandler's *The Big Sleep* starts:

> It was about eleven o'clock in the morning, mid October, with the sun not shining and a look of hard wet rain

143

in the clearness of the foothills. I was wearing my powder-blue suit, with dark blue shirt, tie, and display handkerchief, black brogues, black wool socks with dark blue clocks on them. I was neat, clean, shaved and sober, and I didn't care who knew it. I was everything the well-dressed private detective ought to be. I was calling on four million dollars.

Now compare that with Hammett's first paragraph for *Red Harvest*:

I first heard Personville called Poisonville by a red-haired mucker named Hickey Dewey in the Big Ship in Butte. He also called his shirt a shoit. I didn't think anything of what he had done to the city's name. Later I heard men who could manage their r's give it the same pronunciation. I still didn't see anything in it but the meaningless sort of humor that used to make a richardsnary the thieves' word for dictionary. A few years later I went to Personville and learned better.

Both stories are in first-person point of view, both narrator's are private detectives, both settings are the same era. So where are the differences that define each author's voice?

Let's start with Chandler. The first sentence is descriptive—a crisp, cool single sentence that gives a picture of the setting. Hammett does not do this. If you read the first paragraphs of other Chandler novels, you'll find that he almost always starts with a descriptive sentence or two concerning setting. Hammett does not. The second sentence lists what the narrator is wearing. The tone is a bit jaunty, humorless, with a twinge of self-contempt, like someone dressing up for a party he doesn't want to attend, but doesn't have the nerve to refuse. What particularly in that sentence shows the humor? The black wool socks with the dark blue clocks. The next sentence, though once again delivered with a jaunty humor and bravado, also displays a little self-contempt. He refers to himself as shaved and sober as if this was not his usual condition (indeed, between cases, it is not). The fourth sentence amplifies his attitude by saying he is everything the well-dressed p.i. *ought* to be, emphasizing his appearance over what he really is. The last sentence is the plot hook. When four million dollars calls on a run-down character like Philip Marlowe, something must be terribly wrong.

In other words: A slightly seedy detective whose opinion of himself is not the greatest has been summoned by a multimillionaire who can afford a much more reputable detective. That in itself is quite a hook. But more than plot, what makes the reader want to keep reading about this slightly seedy detective is his wry humor, the stinging comments that seem to peel back the edges of peoples' veneer, even his own.

How is Hammett different? Notice how his opening paragraph reveals very little about the narrator. We learn only that he spends a lot of time around a certain underworld element, as revealed by the use of the word "mucker" and the fact that he has heard all these references to Personville from the various shady sources. He is also familiar with thieves' language. Basically, it is a paragraph of plot hook, with the narrator maintaining a lower profile. In fact, we never even learn his name in the novel.

Further comparisons using more text of each novel will show that Chandler likes longer, descriptive sentences with snappy metaphors and similes. Hammett prefers the sharper, crisper sentences.

 ## Physical Therapy

**1. Read poetry.** Poet Samuel Taylor Coleridge once said, "Prose consists of words in their best order. Poetry consists of the best words in the best order." Your style can be vastly improved by reading good poetry. This will make you very aware of how powerful correct word choices can be. Avoid the gushy, feel-good poets whose work seems like Hallmark cards. Some of my favorites include Ann Sexton, W.D. Snodgrass, Richard Wilbur, Stephen Dobyns, Marilyn Hacker and Sharon Olds. But there are literally hundreds of others just as good.

Now go through a draft and highlight every word that could be stronger, clearer, more active. Beginning writers often make the mistake of including several descriptive words rather than the single right word. Whenever I do this mine-sweep of my own manuscripts, I precede the task by reading poetry. Good poetry reminds you to focus on the words, not the story.

**2. Customize fiction reading.** While working on your fiction, read writers who are exceptional in the areas you are trying to improve. As I mentioned, when polishing my dialogue, I would read Elmore Leonard, Ross Thomas and playwright David Mamet. In fact, reading plays is especially helpful for learning how to write effective dialogue. As a beginning writer, I used to read a new play every night. The key, though, is to not continue reading. Stop after a few pages, just when you get the hang of it, and immediately go back to your own writing.

## Symptom: Monotonous phrasing; overwritten and confusing passages; muddled details

### Ailment: Inappropriate Style

Style is inappropriate for the effect it's supposed to achieve. The style fails to contribute to the readers' enjoyment or understanding of the story; it may even distract the readers from maintaining suspension of disbelief.

### Diagnosis

There are three major types of inappropriate style:

**1. Monotonous style.** Flat, lifeless style that saps the energy out of the story. For example, if you use a repetitious sentence structure, the style will intrude by lulling the reader out of the story.

> We walked toward the house. We saw that the lights were on. So we knocked on the door.

Those simple declarative sentences are each fine on their own, but put them all together and they can deaden the impact of a scene. The characters seem like they're sleepwalking through it. However, if that's the effect you want to achieve, then this would be one method of doing so. But there are many opportunities here to make this more visually vivid. "Walked" could be changed to "ambled," "hurried," "shuffled," etc. "House" could use an adjective: "big," "yellow," "run-down," etc. Look at the next two sentences and see where you might have added or changed words to make this more visual.

Be careful of overwriting (see number two) by loading this down with more words than necessary. Sometimes "walked" is the perfect word.

**2. Overwritten and confusing style.** An overly ornate style interferes with the story. The trick is to select the right words to evoke the proper reader response, whether it be emotional or visual or intellectual, without yanking the reader out of the story.

> The hot, arid wind blew across the coal-black asphalt like the devil's own fetid breath.

Huh? There's so much crap in there I'm no longer standing on the asphalt. Instead, I'm transported to the author's study, watching him gloat over his prose. Yes, poetic imagery is a wonderful addition to your prose style, but it must be subordinate to the greater cause: affecting the reader by drawing her deeper into the story. If she stops, even to admire your genius, she is now out of the story thinking about your genius and not the characters.

**3. Blown moments.** Certain moments need special attention to style but don't always get it. At these moments, it is crucial that every word be the right one, clichés be avoided at all costs, and the reader be startled by the accuracy of the moment. Rose Tremain does a good job of delivering at such a crucial moment with dead-on word choice in her short story "Over." She describes an aging man's morning routine:

> The nurse opens his mouth, which tastes of seed and fills it with teeth. "These teeth have got too big for me," he sometimes remarks, but neither the nurse nor his wife laughs when from some part of his ancient self he brings out a joke.

This moment is important because it establishes the old man's relationship with his wife as well as the hopelessness of his situation (which relates to the central conflict). She does it subtly but powerfully with this phrase: "tastes of seed and fills it with teeth." Tasting of seed surprises us, but seems somehow perfect. Filling his mouth with teeth also takes us by surprise because it's not how we're used to describing putting in dentures, yet the simple phrase makes him seem all the more helpless and pathetic.

 **Treatment**

Although there are many subtle elements that combine to create a writer's style, you can greatly enhance your own style by focusing on these two crucial areas: narrative voice and descriptive texture.

## NARRATIVE VOICE: HITTING THE HIGH NOTES

You meet someone for the first time and she starts speaking: instantly you like or dislike her. If someone asked you what that person said that made you like or dislike her, you might answer, "It isn't what she said, it's the way she said it." That's the narrative voice. The way we say something establishes the instant relationship with the reader.

**First-person POV.** If the story is written in the first-person point of view (POV), the relationship you're developing is between the narrator and the reader. Whether you want the reader to like, dislike, admire or loathe the narrator, most important is getting the reader to be compelled by him. This is achieved by creating a very specific narrative voice through the tone. For example, look at the opening lines of Tim Gautreaux's short story "Welding with Children":

> Tuesday was about typical. My four daughters—not one of them married, you understand—brought over their kids, one each, and explained to my wife how much fun she was going to have looking after them. But Tuesday was her day to go to the casino, so guess who got to tend the four babies. My oldest daughter also brought

over a bed rail that the end broke off of. She wanted me
to weld it. Now, what the hell you can do in a bed
that'll cause the end of a iron rail to break off is beyond
me, but she can't afford another one on her burger-
flipping salary, she said, so I got to fix it with four little
kids hanging on my coveralls.

The plot information revealed here is simple: man has to babysit
his four grandchildren while welding a bed rail. That's an interesting enough plot conflict, but what makes the story one you want
to read is the personality that comes through the narrator's voice.
Here's how the writer achieved that: (1) His attitude is that he's
being put-upon. But his sarcasm ("and explained to my wife how
much fun she was going to have looking after them") reveals that
he's also good-natured about it, not mean or bitter. Your basic
grumpy old man. (2) Notice the intimacy he develops with the readers by directly addressing them ("you understand" and "so guess
who got to tend"). (3) He has a sense of humor ("her burger-
flipping salary"), which immediately makes us like him; we know
that his tone will be entertaining. (4) The fact that his grammar is
not perfect ("a iron rail") makes him more human; a highly educated man in this situation who was also grumpy would have
seemed much less lovable and more prickly. Without all these
elements, the story might have opened like this:

On Tuesday my four daughters showed up each with
her child in tow and asked my wife to babysit. Since it
was my wife's day at the casino, I ended up with the kids.
In addition, my oldest daughter asked me to weld a
bed rail that had somehow broken off.

**Third-person-limited POV.** Third-person limited POV, in
which we're focused only on one character's perspective, is
trickier because we're not inside a character's head, thereby removing some of the confessional intimacy. Then why use it?
you might ask. Because first-person can be too intimate, its effect
sometimes achieved by contrasting how the narrator thinks
about the world with the world described as it really is. Third-

person-limited gives us just enough distance that we can trust the narrator's perspective more. The following opening of Frederick Busch's novel *Harry and Catherine* demonstrates how to still achieve intimacy despite the distance:

> Her son was studying Catherine as she stood at their kitchen window. She felt him. He'd been doing it more and more often, idly and with no special intensity, she thought, but with a kind of dreamy stare. She knew that sort of study, when you sit with your chin on your palms, your elbows on the kitchen table, looking at something, at the thing itself, for certain, and also looking through it. She tipped the roasting chicken and looked down, considering her son behind her, the way he must have been looking at and into and past his mother. He's looking at the rest of his life, she thought. I'm a ghost at the center of the prospect.

This is a wonderful example of creating many effects through narrative voice: (1) The focus is on the connection between Catherine and her son. ("She felt him.") (2) The conflict is her awareness of how his attitude toward her is changing, evolving. ("He'd been doing it more and more often . . .") Such a change can be frightening, which establishes the stakes: mother losing the comforting intimacy of her relationship with her maturing son. (3) It indicates that what he's doing is something she's done herself ("She knew that sort of study . . ."), either in a past relationship or more recently. (4) She is an insightful and articulate woman. ("He's looking at the rest of his life, she thought. I'm a ghost at the center of the prospect.") That phrase—"a ghost at the center of the prospect"—is poetic, a rich, yet scary image that distills her apprehension. A major conflict is revealed in that simple yet elegant phrase.

**Third-person-omniscient POV.** This POV has no restrictions regarding the perspective from which we will view the fictional world. It could go back and forth between characters, or it could be an omniscient know-it-all voice outside the specific time of the story. The narration of John Irving's novel *The World According to Garp* often reveals information about the future of various characters that is outside the time frame of the novel's events. A clear example of this god-like narrative voice is the opening of Charles Dickens's novel *A Tale of Two Cities*:

It was the best of times, it was the worst of times, it was the age of wisdom, it was the age of foolishness, it was the epoch of belief, it was the epoch of incredulity, it was the season of Light, it was the season of darkness, it was the spring of hope, it was the winter of despair, we had everything before us, we had nothing before us, we were all going direct to Heaven, we were all going direct the other way—in short, the period was so far like the present period, that some of its noisiest authorities insisted upon being received, for good or evil, in the superlative degree of comparison only.

Here we have a narrative voice that has a wisdom about the world, and the readers trust that this voice will continue to comment on events and put them in perspective. In this POV, the intimacy is formed with a narrator who isn't really part of the story, but whom we trust. Here's an example of how we might use this POV in a contemporary story:

Jenny and Aaron had been in love with each other their whole lives without ever admitting it to the other. Every time one of them was free, the other, tired of waiting, jumped into another relationship. But that was about to change. All because of a dead hamster, a jar of marbles, and an ugly rumor that no one wanted to disbelieve.

The narrative voice here is informational, telling us details that are outside the knowledge of the characters as well as outside linear time itself. This creates a sense of purpose to the events, while at the same time creating suspense (what about the dead hamster, the jar of marbles, and that ugly rumor?).

## DESCRIPTIVE TEXTURE: THE EMPEROR'S NEW AND IMPROVED CLOTHES

Descriptive texture is what tranforms mere information into a multidimensional world. It's the difference between telling the reader about an event, and creating the world so that the reader experiences the event for himself. There are different kinds of styles: Some writers (such as Raymond Carver and Ann Beattie) prefer minimalism (which is highly selective about which details are to be included), and other writers (such as Stanley Elkin and Lorrie Moore) favor a rich, denser style (which uses sensual descriptions and lots of metaphors). Most writers fall somewhere between this spectrum. The important thing to remember is to select the style that you most enjoy reading yourself. This will probably be the one you'll be most successful writing.

Beginning writers often make the mistake of either overdescribing or underdescribing. Overdescribing sometimes occurs because the writer sees a descriptive passage as an opportunity to show off her talent, to dazzle the reader. However, the actual effect is to stop the story dead by distracting the reader from the characters. Description is a tool to enhance the story, the same as a frame enhances a painting. If the frame is too ornate or large, it overshadows the painting. What do you think of the following description:

> The craggy, mist-shrouded mountains erupted out of the fetid jungle like the jagged tail of a slumbering dragon guarding the tropical paradise as if it were Eden itself.

If that made you gag, you have good instincts. There are so many adjectives in that description that the average reader can't hold on to them all when he finally stumbles, gasping for air, past the final period of that sentence.

Underdescribing can also be detrimental to the story. Although Ernest Hemingway is known for his spare prose style, there's a difference between spare and nonexistent. Here's nonexistent:

> Big mountains were on the other side of the jungle.

Snooze. Words like big are relative, so the reader doesn't have anything to compare the size of the mountains to. Therefore, "big"
is meaningless. The verb "were" is passive, making the mountains
seem bland and diminutive.

How do you know when to elaborate a description? When the
thing being described has impact on the characters, affects them,
or affects how the reader is meant to perceive them, then you elaborate. For example, if the mountains described above are mentioned merely as a passing landmark and have no further role in
the story, just tell us they're there and move on. But if they appear
as a means of showing how insignificant the characters are in the
larger natural world so that they gain a new perspective on their
lives, then elaborate. Make the mountains a character.

Describing characters is another opportunity to define your style.
But the same rules apply: Develop description only to achieve the
desired impact. It's like stepping on the gas pedal of your car; only
do so in relation to how fast you want the car to go. In his short
story "A Poetics for Bullies," Elkin has the narrator, Push the Bully,
describe a new kid in the neighborhood.

> He was tall, tall even sitting down. His long legs comfort-
> able in expensive wool, the trousers of a boy who had
> been on ships, jets; who owned a horse, perhaps; who
> knew Latin—what didn't he know?—somebody made
> up, like a kid in a play with a beautiful mother and a
> handsome father, who took his breakfast from a side-
> board, and picked, even at fourteen and fifteen and six-
> teen, his mail from a silver plate. He would have
> hobbies—stamps, stars, things lovely dead. He wore a
> sport coat, brown as wood, thick as heavy bark. The
> buttons were leather buds. His shoes seemed carved from
> horses' saddles, gunstocks. His clothes had grown once
> in nature. . . . His eyes had skies in them. His yellow hair
> swirled on his head like a crayoned sun.

What makes this descriptive passage so effective is not just the image of the boy being described. Those actual details are few: He's
tall and has expensive clothes, blue eyes and blond hair. The rest

is Push's projection. He sees the boy as some sort of god-figure and so the description is filled with imagined characteristics to imply that. Elkin overwhelms the reader with detail, most of it imagined by Push, to demonstrate how overwhelmed Push feels at that moment. But the precision of the language has another effect: It reveals Push to be highly intelligent and articulate, two attributes that make us side with him.

**Descriptive Texure Checklist**

• **Be selective.** Not everything needs to be described. However, don't edit yourself on the first few drafts. You feel like describing the setting sun for five pages, then do it. But when you're doing your final editing, think of the big picture. The hardest part of editing is not cutting out the bad stuff, but cutting out the good stuff that otherwise diminishes the story as a whole.

• **Similes and metaphors.** A good simile instantly elevates the style because it reveals the level of the writer's craft and intelligence. It announces to the reader that he can relax, he's in good hands. Go ahead, suspend disbelief, it says, you can trust that the story will be rewarding. Beginning writers are too fond of clichéd similes; "She moved as gracefully as a cat," appeared in a student manuscript yesterday. In this excerpt from Elkin's story, Push comments on the effect the new kid is having on the girls at school.

> Gradually his name began to appear on all their notebooks, in the margins of their texts. . . . The big canvas books, with their careful, elborate "J's" and "W's" took on the appearance of ancient, illuminated fables. It was the unconscious embroidery of love, hope's bright doodle.

Here Push is showing how the new kid has become mythologized, has become the icon for Hope. What phrase better reveals style than "hope's bright doodle"? If I ever write a metaphor so simple and powerful, I will feel satisfied as a writer.

## Using Descriptive Texture in Key Scenes

In this excerpt from student Shiloh Godshall, the rock-climbing protagonist, after a suspenseful struggle to reach the top, has a moment of reflection on what she sees.

> I reached the top with euphoria coursing through my veins. I swept my arm across my brow and looked out over the desert. The life that exists and thrives in this exacting world humbles my own. Tiny purple flowers collide magnificently with the pale sand. They stand proud, taunting the wind to test the strength of their loosely anchored roots.

Shiloh's instincts are excellent. She wants her character to reflect on what she sees, comparing it with her own life, which we've learned is coming loose at the roots. Great idea, but not quite there yet. Certain phrases weaken the impact. (1) "with euphoria coursing through my veins": This is too clichéd and passive. It is better to make the reader share the euphoria rather than tell them that you're euphoric. Her euphoria is the payoff for her struggle up the mountain; it's also the reader's, which is why they need to experience it and not just be told about it. (2) "The life that exists and thrives in this exacting world humbles my own": Too direct. This is telling rather than showing. The line might work as dialogue, but as internal monologue it seems too self-conscious and precious. (3) "Tiny purple flowers collide magnificently with the pale sand": This is pretty good, except for the word "magnificently," which again is too intrusive. (4) "They stand proud, taunting the wind to test the strength of their loosely anchored roots": This is

*continued*

a terrific idea that is compromised by two words, "proud, taunting," which is too preachy. The result of all these little moments is that it makes the character seem a bit melodramatic and self-consciously "poetic."

A few pages later in Shiloh's novel, the protagonist and her husband have sex on the rough rocks. This scene is also a "moment" in that its goal is to define their relationship. We already know they have problems, but now we need to know if there's enough passion there for the reader to want them to fix those problems and stay together. The intensity of this scene must indicate that to us.

> His fingers slipped effortlessly up my moist body leaving tingly prickles behind. I pulled him to me; our bodies hot, tired, and energized, melded together perfectly. His callused hand cupped my face and we kissed.
>
> His lips caressed mine. They followed my nose, to my eyes, to ears, neck. I held my breath and looked out at those fiercely tiny wildflowers.
>
> The hardness of the rock seemed to yield momentarily. Our bodies explored and mingled. Craig's lips moved from my neck to my breasts, from my stomach, to my thighs. My fingers left trails through his dark hair. I touched his firm body in all its hidden places.

For this scene to be effective, it must match the euphoria she described a few pages earlier when she reached the top of the mountain. Anything less would tell us that there's not sufficient passion here. The description of their sex is mostly mechanical, detailing what's being done, but without any emotional impact. Plus, the description is a little "romancy" in that it uses too many familiar sex scene phrases: "melded together perfectly";

"lips caressed mine"; "Our bodies explored and mingled"; "I touched his firm body in all its hidden places." Those phrases need to be replaced with more original and evocative phrases that make this moment special to them and unique to the reader.

 **Physical Therapy**

**1.** Determine what POV is best for your story. Don't be afraid to experiment by changing back and forth. In at least half the novels I've written, I changed POV several times until I found the one that was most comfortable. In one novel, I had written ninety pages in first-person POV before changing to third-person-limited.

**2.** Ask yourself what it is about the narrator that the reader is supposed to like, care about, or be compelled by. Pick one characteristic that will make us want to sit next to this person at a dinner party—then emphasize that in the opening. Is the narrator witty? Then show her wit. Is she insightful? Work in some insight. Is she compassionate? Show it right away. For example, Lorrie Moore begins her short story, "Vissi D'Arte," by introducing the POV character's dominating characteristic:

> Harry lived near Times Square, above the sex pavilion that advertised 25 CENT GIRLS. He had lived there for five years and had never gone in, a fact of which he was proud. In the land of perversities he had maintained the perversity of refusal.

That last line has a certain witty wisdom that distinguishes Moore's style.

**3.** Beginning writers often establish the narrative tone in the opening pages, then forget to maintain that tone throughout.

Once you've established this dominating characteristic, be sure to continue to develop it throughout. Look for opportunities to reaffirm her personality. For example, if the narrator has a sarcastic attitude, when she describes someone as having oily skin, she might think: "Someone should take a squeegee to his forehead."

## Symptoms: Oversimplified, emotionally shallow characters; major cross-gender characters who seem minor; inaccurate gender-specific details

### Ailment: Unconvincing Cross-Gender POVs

When writing in the point of view of characters who are of the opposite sex, the author is unable to create authentic voices. Instead, those characters seem stereotypical. The contrast of strong POV development with characters of one sex with weak POV development with characters of the opposite sex results in the reader losing faith in the author. Consequently, the reader cares less about even the well-drawn characters.

### Diagnosis

Beginning writers often make the mistake of treating characters of the opposite sex as if they were minor characters by sheer virtue of their gender. The writer will think of the character as a mere catalyst to the protagonist's emotions, thoughts and actions, rather than as an interactive character. In other words, the writer sees these opposite-sex characters as serving a function and nothing more. Lip service is given these characters by dressing them up with some background, emotions and thoughts, but those often come across as tacky accessories rather than believable parts of the character.

### Treatment

In my fiction workshops over the years, I've noticed a consistent problem among many beginning writers: Some who have no problem writing from the point of view of a precocious young child, a hundred-year-old grandpa, or even a slobbering werewolf with chronic mange, suddenly freeze up when writing from the point of view of the opposite sex. Men writing from a woman's viewpoint present a cardboard selection from the Female Stereotype Hall of Fame: Tank-Topped Ditz, Tough-but-Sexy With H.O.G. (Heart-of-Gold), Cranky Professional Who Really Needs a Man, Stepford-Drone and Fem-Nazi. Women writing from a male point of view dust off the too-familiar male menagerie: Can't-Commit Yuppie; Testosterone Hun in Baseball Cap; Tough-but-Sexy B.O.S. (Buns-of-Steel) and Sensitive Doe-Eyed Nurturer. Sometimes they mix and match a few characteristics, but the effect is usually the same: a predictable character whose every action, thought and dialogue we know a page or two before we read it.

The result: readers who are bored and editors who reach for the "Reject" basket.

Cross-gender writing is nothing new. Authors around the world have been successfully writing from the point of view of the opposite sex for centuries, including contemporary genre writers such as Stephen King to mainstream writers such as Philip Roth. Wally Lamb's *She's Come Undone* was a national best-seller thanks to being an Oprah's Book Club selection and a gritty, ultra-realistic cross-gender perspective. David Guterson was able to write in both gender points of view in his wonderfully touching *Snow Falling on Cedars*. Imagine how less powerful John Irving's *The World According to Garp* would be without Garp's mother's viewpoint. How effective would Elmore Leonard's *Out of Sight* be without the point of view of his female agent?

A writer unable to present the point of view of a character of the opposite sex limits his options as a writer. It's like a basketball player only able to dribble with one hand or a tennis player with no backhand. Worse, the avoidance of doing so could signal a lack of ability in creating characters of the opposite sex, even when not in their point of view.

F. Scott Fitzgerald once said, "Begin with an individual and you find that you have created a type; begin with a type and you find you have created—nothing." Writing from the point of view of the opposite sex can be vastly rewarding to you as a writer as well as to the quality of your story. But how can the conscientious writer developing characters of the opposite sex avoid creating "nothing"? Start with some of the following tips on cross-gender writing.

## How I Became a Woman (Writer)

One day a few years ago, after having published more than twenty hard-boiled mystery, suspense, western and adventure novels, I decided to become a woman. No surgery required.

Rather, it was a creative and career choice. After years of toiling in the bountiful fields of various genres, I wanted to return to my writing roots from college and graduate school: "serious" literary fiction. First, I knew I would have to reinvent myself. After all, who would take me seriously as a "literary" writer after looking at what I'd written before: a mystery series about a bumbling con man, spy thrillers, and, under pseudonyms, Westerns (the "Diamondback" series as Pike Bishop); futuristic adventures (the "Warlord" series as Jason Frost); and the international investigative reporter (the "Dagger" series as Carl Stevens). Somewhere in there I also wrote several of Don Pendleton's Executioner books. Manly men doing manly things.

Before starting my new novel, I had to first remove myself from my old writing self. That is, I didn't want any of my old voice coming through. Let's face it, though the names and genres changed, the protagonist was always male—a fantasy extension of myself, just wittier, smarter and better looking. To avoid that pushy guy elbowing his way into my new novel, I decided to write from a woman's point of view. But after completing eighty pages, I was scared. What had I been thinking? Who was I to suddenly try something like this? I always thought that the female characters in my other novels were strong creations, but I had never written strictly from their point of view before.

In an effort to discover whether I was fooling myself, I made up a woman's name—Laramie Dunaway—and sent my eighty pages to my female agent pretending to be a first-time woman writer. I figured if I could fool my agent—a woman the same age as my four women characters—I could relax.

A month later I received an enthusiastic letter from her offering to represent Laramie Dunaway. I immediately called my agent and gleefully told her the truth. A long silence followed, then amazement at my new direction. When I told her why I'd tricked her, we both agreed that I should maintain my anonymity when we sent the book to publishers. Shortly thereafter Warner Books bought the novel, but under the belief that I was a reclusive woman. I never spoke directly with my woman editor, not for that book or the following two (*Borrowed Lives* and *Lessons in Survival*) I wrote as Laramie.

Ironically, I had my greatest critical and financial success with those novels. They have been published in many countries and were best-sellers in England. All three have been optioned for films. I received plenty of mail from women readers and many excellent reviews, including some from *Cosmopolitan* and other women's magazines. While a genre writer, most of the fan mail I had received came from young boys and prisoners.

More ironic, however, was that having distanced myself so far from myself, I felt like I was writing more about *the real me* for the first time. In *Tootsie*, Dustin Hoffman's character says, "Becoming a woman made me a better man." For me, becoming a woman made me a better writer.

## WHAT IS CROSS-GENDER WRITING?

The difference between cross-gender writing and merely presenting a character of the opposite sex can be seen in the following examples.

**1.** Not cross-gender writing:

Samantha walked into the bar and looked around for Pete. When she didn't see him, she glanced at her gold watch—a gift from Pete—then turned to the bartender. "Pete been in this morning?" He shook his head no. She shrugged, spun around and walked out, ignoring the appreciative glances that followed her.

**2.** Cross-gender writing:

Samantha walked into the bar and looked around for Pete. Where the hell was he? She glanced at her watch, rubbing her wrist where the worn band pinched. She should get a new watch, she knew, but this was the watch Pete gave her on their third date back in Carlton High. Right after the Harvest Moon dance, standing in the headlights of his father's new Thunderbird. Amid the fluttering moths that circled the headlights, he'd opened the small white box and nervously lifted the layer of cotton to reveal the gold watch. Nothing in her life had ever shone as bright before—or since.

One sample is not necessarily better than the other, just different. The first example presents a stark but clear action. We experience what happens but without emotional involvement. This would be effective writing to promote the pace of a story or even build suspense. The second example presents more of the character's reaction to the situation. We know she's angry (*Where the hell was he?*), and we also have some sense of her life with Pete: (1) possibly he doesn't love her as much as she loves him, which is why he's always late; (2) she still loves him—or has some unrealistically romantic hope for their relationship—because she refuses to get a new watch that would be more comfortable; (3) her life since receiving the watch may not have been as fulfilling as she'd hoped. (*Nothing in her life had ever shone as bright before—or since.* The "or since" implies this.)

Obviously that's a lot of speculation to make based on one paragraph—we'd have to see the context of the rest of story to be sure—but one can see that the second example is using Samantha's point of view to tell the story. The stakes in the first example involve Samantha's attitude of inconvenience; the second example suggests stakes involving her entire relationship with Pete, which impacts her memories of the past and hopes for the future.

## HOW CAN I KNOW WHAT "THEY" ARE THINKING?

In a movie I once saw, an angry artist complains about the old saying that a writer should always write from his or her own experiences. "If that were true," he hollers, "we'd never have *Peter Pan!*" Or *Alice in Wonderland, The Wizard of Oz*, fantasy or science fiction, historical novels or any of Shakespeare's plays. The problem is in interpreting the phrase "own experiences" too literally.

Experience doesn't have to mean actually having done the thing itself. Rather it can mean, "I've thought about this experience so thoroughly and with such intensity that it's as if I experienced it myself." Sure, on occasion Hemingway liked to get out there and mix it up with the bulls he wrote about, but he didn't drag a mast up a hill and die like Santiago in *Old Man and the Sea*. Rebecca Wells, author of *Divine Secrets of the Ya-Ya Sisterhood*, surprised at the intense popularity of her novel (Ya-Ya clubs have formed across the nation), commented, "I didn't write the book because I had a group of friends like the Ya-Yas. I think I wrote it because I wanted one."

For your writing to remain credible and involving, you have to create fully developed characters of both sexes, even if most of us have not had the opportunity to experience being both male and female. Because we must populate our fiction with a wide variety of characters who must then passionately interact, we are faced with the challenge of creating a broad spectrum of characters based purely on observation rather than personal experience. Each writer can't possibly have experienced every gender, race, age, profession and so forth of all the characters in their stories. We have to learn how to fake it, but in such a way that the reader never knows.

A few years ago a novel (*Famous All Over Town*) about a teenage Latino boy won a lot of acclaim for its author, Danny Sanchez. The Latin community bestowed an award on the novel. Eventually it was revealed that "Danny Sanchez" was not a young Latino man but the pseudonym of an elderly white man. He had done his job stepping outside the confines of his own life experiences.

## THREE TIPS TO IMPROVE YOUR CROSS-GENDER WRITING
### Tip #1: Observe

Observation of others is really the stock and trade of every writer. To flesh out our fictional characters, we borrow traits and experiences and backgrounds from friends and relatives and pretty much anybody who hasn't copyrighted his or her life. But we often avoid this same conscientiousness when creating characters of the opposite sex. Probably because most of us think, "Hey, I've been observing them all my life. I'm even married to one." If the existence of all those self-help books on relationships have taught us anything, it's that being near someone, even sharing our life with them, doesn't necessarily mean we "know" them. One way we get to know them is through observation.

The first step in observation is to do so in a nonjudgmental way. Otherwise you are tainting any information you gather and will inevitably use it only to "dress up" a stereotype. In fact, the very details you may deem worthy of including in your fictional creation may reflect a bias toward stereotyping. ("Ah ha, see how he sets the beer can on the coffee table without a coaster? Typical male." Or, "She wants to try on yet another pair of shoes? Just like a woman.") You have to keep your mind open or you'll miss the really good stuff. Don't interpret, just watch.

The fact that a person doesn't do something the same way you do doesn't make it less effective or valuable. For example, throughout history many prominent philosophers and "thinkers" have proclaimed that women were less able than men when it came to making moral choices. Sigmund Freud echoed many before him when he said: "One cannot resist the thought that the levels of normal morality are different for women. Their super-ego never becomes so unshakable, so impersonal, so independent of its effective origins, as we demand it of a man." The male conclusion that women were somehow morally inferior was reached because women make *different* moral choices than men. Psychologist Carol Gilligan's *In a Different Voice* presents a study of moral reasoning in men and women that refutes that biased concept. Her conclusion is that men reason from private-oriented ideas of individual rights and fair play, while women reason from private-oriented ideas of responsibility and caring for others. For example, a girl and a boy, aged 11, were both asked whether a poor man should steal a drug that would save his wife's life. The boy said yes, because the life was worth more than the property. But the girl said no, it would be better to borrow the money for the drug or work out some sort of payment with the druggist. She reasoned that if the man stole and got caught, the sick woman would be alone. Women may focus more on community needs while men focus more on personal achievement. One is not morally superior, but just understanding that difference—without judging—can help when creating a character's thoughts, motivations and actions.

The second step in observation is to amass plenty of material before reaching any conclusions, and then to look past the obvious interpretations to the more subtle ones. For example, the stereotypical man/woman relationship usually portrays the man as a slob and the woman as excessively neat. (Reversing this isn't really breaking the stereotypes, it's just shifting them.) The couple argues over why, after she's complained to him a hundred times about throwing his dirty clothes on the bedroom floor, she walks in to discover him doing it yet again. The quick interpretation is that they are arguing because they are different personality types. More likely, though, the argument isn't about clothes (or loose toothpaste caps, or raised toilet seats or drinking straight from the milk carton). The argument is about frustration that the one person doesn't respect the other. She's yelling because she's made it clear that not having dirty clothes thrown on the floor is important to her; so when he once again drops the clothes on the floor he's saying, "I don't really care what's important to you." From his perspective, he's saying, "I'm an adult and as such no longer want to hear my mother's voice telling me what to do. This is how I was when you married me, back when you laughed at it and thought it was gruffly charming." These, too, are simplistic interpretations, but they attempt to look past the observed detail to see beyond the obvious conclusion.

The third step in observation is the simplest. Look for the small details that define the demands of being the opposite sex. For example, what's wrong with the following:

> Helen adjusted her new clip-on gold seashell earrings, hoping Mr. Carlton would notice them. He should, they were big enough. Just then the phone rang and she snatched it up, pressed it to her ear, and said, "Carlton and Sons. How may I help you?"

Technically, there is nothing wrong here. However, some professional women wear clip-on earrings to work because they are easy to remove before talking on the phone, because pressing the receiver against the earring could hurt.

Now, switching sexes, what's wrong with the following?

> Albert stood at the last urinal in the row of a dozen shiny black urinals hoping the job interview went better than he thought. One of the senior partners who'd been at the session, though he hadn't spoken, entered the restroom. He wore an expensive suit that probably cost more than Albert's car; his silk tie alone equaled Albert's rent. The partner walked up to the urinal next to Albert and proceeded with his business. Albert felt ashamed at his own cheap suit, the frayed cuffs showing plain.

The problem: men's room etiquette. A man entering a restroom will rarely stand at the urinal next to one where another man is standing. He will leave at least one urinal space between them. Albert wouldn't think about his suit; he would feel uncomfortable because his space was invaded.

These are examples of simple details that should be addressed. Use enough of them and you've created a believable point of view.

Of course, these interpretations required gross simplification—not all women or men would react this way. But if your character doesn't, it's your job to make us believe the reason they wouldn't is because of the unique way you've presented them. Otherwise, we will just chalk it up to bad writing.

## Tip #2: Research

Years ago I was watching a TV interview with the author of a novel about Oklahoma. The interviewer, who'd grown up in Oklahoma, lavished enthusiastic praise on the author for his authentic descriptions of the state's scenery. When the author confessed he had never been to Oklahoma, the interviewer became visibly angry. "Of course, you have," he insisted. "Otherwise you couldn't have written such an accurate description." "Actually," the author said, "I got all that from reading books in the Beverly Hills Library." The interviewer glared.

Most writers know the importance of research when it comes to setting or police procedure or even fashion. But when it comes to a character's point of view, many of us get lazy. Yet, this is an area in which it is even more important, since it helps you better understand the character. The further the character's life experiences are from yours, the more important that research becomes. This would be particularly true in cross-gender points of view.

In *Heartbreak Ridge*, Clint Eastwood plays a tough marine sergeant intent on winning back his ex-wife. In an attempt to understand what he'd done wrong during their marriage, he constantly reads women's magazines. He hopes to find in those pages more about what women want. Actually, that's not a bad place for writers to start. Just remember, women's or men's magazines do not reflect the perspective of *all* women or men, so select the kinds of magazines your character might read. One of the best means of discovering this is to glance at the ads inside. What are the ages of the models? Are the articles concerned with being hip and trendy? Or are they geared toward professionals who already have achieved some level of success? *Cosmopolitan* appeals to a specific group of women, generally between twenty and thirty-five and in the beginning of their careers. Think *Ally McBeal*. However, *Vogue* attracts a slightly older, more sophisticated audience. For men,

*Maxim* targets the twenty to thirty-five group, while *Men's Health* and *Gentleman's Quarterly* want the 35-and-up group of professionals. By reading the magazines your opposite-sex character might read, you gain some insight into his or her concerns.

When I was writing spy novels, I read a lot of gun magazines. I learned the lingo and sprinkled it throughout my novels for authentic texture. The women whose points of view I use in my Laramie Dunaway novels are generally professionals who work in a business atmosphere, so I had to learn about makeup and clothing. What was applied when and where. What was the term for that kind of blouse collar? Now, guns and makeup aren't what define men or women, but they are examples of what has to be learned, depending upon the interests of your character and the genre of the novel.

Even more important than magazines, read novels written by and featuring a point of view of the opposite sex. This immersion in that point of view helps you focus on how your character perceives things. It's not unlike athletes viewing sports films before a game to conjure up their "game face." If you're really conscientious, you might also read novels by the opposite sex from other countries. This helps you filter out some of the male-female concerns that may just be cultural and look at what is more universal. What does each sex have in common with members from around the world, regardless of their cultural influences?

**Tip #3: Empathy**
To write convincingly from the point of view of the opposite sex, there are three key elements you need to determine.

**1. Determine what is likable.** An actor was once asked how he played villains so convincingly, made us loathe them, yet still care about them. He replied, "First, I find a way to like them." Once he found something sympathetic about the villain, he would write a brief biography of that character, detailing how he went from likable to evil.

Same principle applies here. When writing from the point of view of the opposite sex, first decide what it is about him or her you like most—and introduce that characteristic to the reader as quickly into the story as you can. What I like most about my women narrators is their off-beat wit, as demonstrated in the opening of *Lessons in Survival:*

> I was driving home still thinking about that dead grasshopper I'd just dissected for my class, its thorax as hard to crack as a tin thimble. Watching me struggle over it, my students had become restless and giddy, so I'd made some off-hand joke about the grasshopper being a typical male, afraid to open up to a woman.

**2. Determine what most causes the character to suffer.** One of the questions parents dread hearing from their children is, "Why is there so much pain and suffering in the world?" A popular answer is that every time we feel pain or we suffer, it makes us more empathetic to others. Our suffering allows us to imagine how others suffer and makes us want to stop their pain. In that way, pain and suffering are what bind a community together.

That same concept should be applied to your opposite-sex character. When you understand what most causes a character to suffer, you will know something essential about that person. For Season, my narrator in *Earth Angel*, it was guilt. Her fiancé, clinically depressed over some recent bad fortune, bursts into the medical center where she is a doctor and starts shooting, killing several people and himself. In shock, Season immediately blames herself for not seeing the signs, for not being enough of a doctor or a lover to have helped him. This guilt drives her to set off on a quest to secretly help relatives of the victims of the shooting, to become their "angel" and cause them to get what they most want in life. What she discovers along the way is that this misplaced guilt has been there her whole life, long before this incident.

**3. Determine what the character most wants.** Freud once lamented that despite his thirty years of research into the feminine soul, he had never been able to answer the question, "What does a woman want?" Indeed, the question of what a character wants is what we writers must ask about *all* our characters. But even more so when writing from a cross-gender point of view because we often mistakenly think that everyone else wants out of life exactly what we want. Perhaps in the grand scheme we all do want the same thing—to be happy. But what each of us imagines will make us happy, and what we're willing to do to achieve that vision, are the key points that separate us. Does a woman want the same things from her lover as a man? Does a man want the same things from his family as a woman? If you answered no, then you must next determine why not. If you answered genetics or upbringing, then you must ask why we are hardwired that way or why our society has raised us that way. Each question leads to a deeper understanding of that cross-gender character.

## DANGER—SLIPPERY ROAD AHEAD

The danger in cross-gender writing is in self-censoring ourselves into being too politically correct. Writing from the point of view of the opposite sex can make the writer nervous—she doesn't want to be accused of misrepresenting others, or seem as if she has some bitter grudge ("Couldn't get a date for the prom, huh?"). So she makes the opposite sex too perfect—and therefore too boring. Remember, you are creating a character, not an icon. A woman character doesn't have to represent all women; nor does a male character have to represent all men. They may strive to do so, the way each of us strives to be some notion of a good person. But we aren't always good, and we don't always do the right thing. Perhaps your otherwise model male character does something "piggish"; or the idealized woman character does something nasty. That's just making them human.

And that's why we want to read about them in the first place.

# CHAPTER FIVE

# *Theme*

**Symptoms: Melodrama; narrow, plot-centered focus**

*Common Ailment*

**Insufficient Intellectual Involvement.** Writer focuses on emotionally involving personal characters at the expense of intellectual involvement, which allows readers to contemplate universal truths and connections to their own lives.

**Symptom: Noticeable lack, or overbearing use, of symbols**

*Common Ailment*

**Crash Symbols.** The writer ignores symbols completely, leaving readers to draw their own conclusions (and leaving other thematic elements to pick up the slack), or puts them on center stage as the concert percussionist crashes the cymbals.

**Symptom: Imitative theme**

*Common Ailment*

**The Photocopy Effect.** Story has no substance. It seems imitative, like a pale photocopy of better stories.

## FAQs Frequently Asked Questions

? What is theme? pages 172-173

? What makes a theme effective? pages 174-176

? What templates does theme follow? pages 182-196, 203-217

? How can I use symbols to reinforce my theme? pages 178-180

? How does theme fit in with character, plot and other story elements? pages 197-203, a case study

? How are archetypes used in theme? pages 222-227

## THEME OVERVIEW

The first obstacle in developing theme is confusion: What the heck *is* theme? Nothing sends beginning writers screaming from the room faster than mentioning that obscene little word. You start cringing like a small-time hood in an interrogation room, bright lights glaring in your eyes and a sweaty Dennis Franz bellowing in your ear, "What's the theme, punk?" This reaction is usually caused by the fear that you don't know what the theme means, let alone how it applies to your writing. Well, relax, because your story already has a theme, you just might not know what it is yet. But once you learn how theme works, you will be able to use it as a tool to make plot choices that are more original and effective. This is true whether you are writing genre fiction or mainstream-literary fiction.

### What Theme Is

Tell someone you're writing a novel and his first response is, "What's it about?" That's when you probably launch into a detailed description of your plot: "A gruff retired cop and a spunky Vegas showgirl are on the run from the Mob because . . ." But a story is usually "about" much more than the plot activity, it's also about the *impact* of the plot on the lives of the characters—and the readers. That impact is what makes a story memorable, and exploring that impact is what theme is all about.

There's a wonderful episode of the old TV series *Northern Exposure* (syndicated on A&E) in which the Native American shaman, Leonard, comes to town to learn more about white culture. Because shamans use stories and myths to heal the sick, he figures this endeavor will make him a better healer. He proceeds by sitting at a table with a tape recorder and asking the town residents to come by and tell him their favorite stories. But everyone who comes by tells him about a different popular urban myth they've heard, such as, spiders in a beehive hairdo or Kentucky Fried rats.

Leonard asks, "What happened next?"

They shrug and say, "Nothing. That's it."

He then asks each individual, "What impact on your life did this story have? How did it change you?"

But the person just looks confused and says, "Huh?" Later he despairs that the stories have no point, they are just plots meant to shock.

The best fiction arouses the reader's curiosity in two areas: (1) While reading the story, the reader should be asking, "I wonder what will happen next?" (2) After reading the story, the reader should ask, "How did the story affect me and why?"

Here's a simple way to define the elements of a story:
- Plot is *what happens.*
- Character is *whom the plot happens to.*
- Theme is *why the plot happens.*

Understanding theme allows you to know why certain plot events are common and therefore how to make the most of them in an original, effective way. So, when we're discussing theme, we're examining
- why the events in the story took place
- how the characters were changed by what they went through
- what insight into the situation the reader gained as a result of experiencing the plot

### I Don't Need No Stinkin' Theme!

A lot of beginning writers will say, "Hey, I'm just writing a mystery novel. I want it to be a page-turner and nothing more. I don't need a theme for that." These writers are absolutely correct; a page-turner can be written without the author *consciously* incorporating theme, just as some self-taught tennis players can win a few amateur tournaments without formal lessons. But the best writers, just like the best athletes, learn to use *all* the tools of their trade if they wish to be successful professionals. Dashiell Hammett and Raymond Chandler not only were very conscious of themes in their work, they also wrote essays discussing them (see Chandler's essay "The Simple Art of Murder"). Plot choices in the best novels are based on themes, not mere whim. It's really a matter of who's in charge of the story: Is the writer using, or being used by, plot conventions that occur in all stories?

At its heart, theme is a close examination of the story's conflict. Author Joseph Campbell (see the Joseph Campbell Archetypal

Model on page 222) once quoted an Eskimo shaman who said that the only true wisdom "lives far from mankind, out in the great loneliness, and can be reached only through suffering. Privation and suffering alone open the mind to all that is hidden to others." Stories allow us to experience the suffering of others by proxy, to empathize with their pain, but to have just enough distance that we can better understand the reasons for that suffering, and take another step toward true wisdom. But be clear about this: It is not emotion and suffering alone that makes one wise, it is the exploration and understanding of that emotion and suffering. In other words, theme.

## Symptoms: Melodrama; narrow, plot-centered focus

### Ailment: Insufficient Intellectual Involvement

Theme is not the same as plot conflict. Plot conflict focuses mainly on the personal: the effects of the story on specific characters. Plot conflict affects our *emotional involvement*, which is how much we care about the outcome of the events. Theme focuses on the universal: how those personal effects reflect feelings and thoughts that all people share. The degree to which we are compelled to examine these emotions is the *intellectual involvement*. Many wonderful stories have been told that engage us merely on an emotional level. The best of literature, however, including the best of genre writing, engages us first on a personal, emotional level, then makes us examine those emotions to understand them better on a universal level.

### Diagnosis

All stories have the same basic theme: People want to be happier than they are. Once we recognize that, things get a little trickier. The writer has to figure out (1) what will make the characters happy (which may be different than what they *think* will make them happy), and (2) what's keeping them from getting what will make them happy.

Have you ever watched a movie and found yourself tearing up, yet resenting your own emotion because you realize that you're being manipulated? Stories that arouse only emotion are called melodramas. We may read or watch melodramatic stories or movies and find ourselves weeping, laughing and/or biting our nails with suspense. When it's over, we are satisfied that we had a good ride, but we never give the story or characters serious thought. Usually that's because the story engaged us only superficially; we allowed our emotions to be manipulated, and we were probably aware of the manipulation even as it was happening. Such stories don't really engage our deepest emotions, but rather trigger superficial emotional responses. We see a movie in which an evil antagonist kicks a dog; we have an emotional response: sympathy for the dog, loathing for the antagonist. When the writer is too obvious with this manipulation, you get reviews like this one, from *Book* magazine: "Complete with a smidgen of violence and a dab of romance, the book feels contrived, its ingredients carefully weighed to manipulate emotions."

### Treatment

With drama, we are touched in a way that isn't merely conditioned response. The true drama addresses the shared hopes and fears of all people. That's what makes it universal. The following examples illustrate the difference between the personal and universal levels:

**Personal.** The plot conflict involves successful career woman, thirty-three-year-old Beth preparing for her wedding. That situation itself presents plenty of stressful conflicts. Add to this two complications: (1) she has some doubts about her ability to commit fully to the relationship, and (2) her estranged mother, a recovering alcoholic, is coming to stay for two weeks before the wedding. Our emotional involvement with this story is based on how much we care about Beth and therefore want to see her resolve these conflicts.

**Universal.** The universal looks at the pattern of the plot to see what that pattern has in common with the reader. We don't have to be in the midst of planning a wedding or have a recovering alcoholic mother to identify with the characters or their anguish. The specific plot only represents the *idea* of the conflict: We all have to face questions about our emotional commitments and come to terms with past relationships. So, the plot choices in this scenario will reflect those universal concerns, which is the intellectual involvement.

The personal conflict focuses on Beth solving her immediate problems: planning the wedding and dealing with her mother. The universal conflict focuses on Beth being happy, her life in balance. (We also see this breakdown of plot and character conflict using this same example in chapter one on page 11.) To be happy, Beth must first reconcile with her estranged mother. That's a plot conflict, but the theme addresses, (1) why she needs to do this, and (2) what impact this conflict has already had on other aspects of her life. For example, Beth's estrangement from her mother is caused by her mother's previous drinking while Beth was a child; her mother did not protect and nurture Beth when it was needed. Here there might even be flashback scenes of Beth in a painful adolescent relationship, needing her mother's advice and comfort, but not getting it.

Now an adult, Beth is struggling to work things out in a rocky relationship with her husband-to-be, when Mom arrives, adding stress to the already troubled relationship. Beth must overcome her hatred of someone who doesn't exist anymore (the drunken mother, now sober). Beth's tie to the past, where she resents not being protected, may have manifested itself into her becoming either a person who now is distant because she trusts no one to protect her, or overly needy of protection. She sees neither in herself. To triumph she has to slay the angry Beth, the Beth whose ego still makes her seek revenge. Then she will be able to love her mother *and* her future husband.

Novelist Diane Johnson (*Le Divorce*) admits that the writer doesn't always know the story's theme at the beginning, that the act of writing is in fact the journey of discovering theme: "But novels are never about what they are about; that is, there is always deeper, or more general, significance. The author may not be aware of this till she is pretty far along with it. A novel's whole pattern is rarely apparent at the outset of writing, or even at the end; that is when the writer finds out what a novel is about, and the job becomes one of understanding and deepening or sharpening what is already written. That is finding the theme."

## Physical Therapy

Like playing a sport, analyzing literature is a skill developed over time through practice. Whenever I want to try to improve at a sport, I start by buying a book that tells me what to do. Same thing applies here. You will need to read a few books of literary criticism. Stay away from the theory books at first: They're much too confusing for most people. Instead, read essays that analyze specific literary works that you are familiar with or would like to read. Even reading Cliffs Notes or Monarch Notes about famous works will give you some insight into understanding themes. Better still, take a literature class, which gives you the advantage of a professor and other students to interact with while exploring themes. And finally, read interviews with writers. Avoid the glossy interviews in magazines like *People* and *Entertainment Weekly*. Instead, look for the *Paris Review* interview books and others like them (e.g., *Writers [on Writing]: Collected Essays From The New York Times, A Voice of One's Own: Conversations With America's Writing Women, Writing for Your Life*).

## Symptoms: Noticeable lack, or overbearing use, of symbolism

## Ailment: Crash Symbols

Writers failing to use symbols effectively in their work tend to fall under two extremes: they ignore them completely, leaving other elements of theme to pick up the slack, or, less commonly, they trot them out to center stage as the concert percussionist crashes the cymbals—just to make sure you noticed. In the first instance, writers are forsaking good opportunities to imbue their stories with nuance and texture. In the latter, readers may feel intellectually insulted and cease to take the writing seriously. Overbearing symbolism, while less common, can be particularly disastrous, because modern readers are wary of didactic themes. A hundred years ago spoon-feeding readers a moral to the story was acceptable.

## Diagnosis

Symbolism is a shorthand method for a writer to signal to the reader what the universal conflict, or theme, is.

This requires little to no additional *content*; it does mean arranging story elements to add *context* and contemplating how characters and objects in your story relate to the overall message. Symbols fall into two categories: *Universal symbols* recur in all types of fiction and generally represent similar ideas from story to story. Water and rivers, for example, translate into life (especially in cultures based in arid regions) or purification (especially in the Judeo-Christian tradition). Storms often symbolize chaos and disorder. *Situational symbols* are more personal and derive meaning from the context of a particular scene. They might hold no significance, or an entirely different one, in another scene.

Note that symbols, particularly situational symbols, are open to interpretation, sometimes an interpretation the author never intended. Symbols and other thematic elements contribute greatly to a story's depth and allow readers to draw new meanings and interpretations from it even after repeated readings.

 **Treatment**

Symbols come in five varieties: title, homage plot, character names, objects and setting.

**1. A title** may reference another literary work whose theme is so familiar that the reader knows this story will be dealing with the same theme. Many stories are titled after a quote from the Bible (for example, John Steinbeck's *East of Eden*).

**2. The homage plot** openly uses the same plot structure as a famous story or myth to signal a similarity between this story and the one being used. The Coen brothers' film *O Brother Where Art Thou?* takes its title from a fictional movie referred to in the classic movie *Sullivan's Travels*, thereby telling the audience this is about naive but good-intentioned people like the protagonist in *Sullivan's Travels*. But *O Brother*'s plot is based on Homer's *Odyssey*, which tells the audience that the adventures of the characters will be more mythical and symbolic than realistic.

**3. Character names** are also used to refer to others, thereby implying a connection. Sometimes the names are direct, sometimes variations of the original. Chris and Jesse are common when a writer wants to imply the character is modeled after Jesus Christ. Herman Melville's *Moby Dick* is filled with characters whose names come straight from the Bible, with each biblical name appropriate to its namesake's personality. Mary and variations of Job are popular, as are names from Greek and Roman mythology, the names referring to myths that parallel the story's universal conflict. Writers may also use names from other literary works to indicate a similarity in theme. For example, both the film *Apocalypse Now* and Stephen King's novel *Dreamcatcher* have a character named Kurtz, a reference to the doomed tragic hero (TH) in Joseph Conrad's "Heart of Darkness." (See Tragedy on page 189.) Did King know what he was doing? To make sure you get the connection, he has one of his characters observe that Kurtz's name is "simply a little too convenient."

**4. Objects** can also be used to indicate theme. For example, eyeglasses are popular to show that the universal conflict is about how a character is unable, or refuses, to see her situation clearly and therefore must suffer the consequences. Various crosses can be used to show a Christ-like character, such as the crossroads and photograph with the cross-like tear in the film, *Cool Hand Luke*. Even a character's age can be symbolic, the most popular being thirty-three, the age of Christ at his death. Apples and apple trees refer to the Biblical Garden of Eden story, as in Richard Wilbur's short story "A Game of Catch" and Robert Frost's poem "After Apple-Picking."

**5. Settings** can also be symbolic. Hospitals, libraries, universities, scientific laboratories and government buildings are often used as symbols of humanity's accumulated knowledge—and of the impotence of that knowledge. This means that, as much as we think we know, it's not nearly enough to understand our place in the universe. For example, in Joyce Carol Oates's story "Naked," the protagonist is jogging in the woods by the university where she works. She is attacked by a group of twelve-year-olds. She tries to make sense of what's happened to her, to find rational explanations. But the reader quickly sees that this constant rationalizing is why her life is so empty. The university represents this false vision of truth that prevents her from intuiting a deeper truth. Prisons are obvious symbols of oppression (see Tragedy). This oppression could be caused by society (meaning social conventions that imprison us, such as what makes one a "man" or "woman"). Or it could be more universal, demonstrating that we are all imprisoned by our brief time on Earth.

In stories that involve land and bodies of water, land generally represents the part of our lives we can control: in psychological terms, our conscious actions, our super-egos. Water usually represents the part of our lives we can't control; its vastness and depth dwarfs us, making us feel impotent to control our fates. In psychological terms, this is our unconscious minds, the part that we can't access with rational thinking. It's the part of our psyche that influences us in ways we struggle to control.

Weather is part of a setting and can be used to signal theme. Hot weather can show moral barrenness (Paul Bowles's novel *Sheltering Sky*); tropical weather in jungles can symbolize the Garden of Eden (Paul Theroux's *Mosquito Coast, Apocalypse Now*); rain can symbolize a moral cleansing (the end of the film *3:10 to Yuma*), or the need for moral cleansing, a symbol of the forty days and nights of rain to wash the world of its sins (the films *Blade Runner* and *Seven*).

Professions can also be used symbolically, though they are usually directly related to setting. A priest might represent righteousness, but so might a cop, whose duty it is to uphold the law (which are reflections of the SB's Rules). For example, Morgan Freeman's detective character in *Seven* is shown right at the beginning as living a monkish lifestyle. He's retiring because he's lost his faith in the Plan, the same way the young priest in William Peter Blatty's novel *The Exorcist* lost his faith in the plan.

 ## Physical Therapy

The ability to use symbolism requires some basic knowledge of the major sources of symbolism. So, you're going to have to do some reading, especially these basic texts: the Bible; Greek, Roman and Norse mythology; and art history books.

If you already have a general knowledge of these things, now you can start applying it. List the characters' names in your story, then rename them after characters in the Bible or mythology. Make sure that whomever they are named after embodies some aspect of who the character is or what her conflict is.

 **Symptom: Imitative theme**

**Ailment: The Photocopy Effect**

The story is too familiar, reads just like every other story in the same genre. This can be true even of literary stories based on events in the writer's own life. Continual exposure to plot patterns over a lifetime of reading, as well as movie and TV watching, has worn a well-trod path in your brain of how to tell a story. Now your story merely echoes those familiar plot patterns, without a clear understanding of why those events are part of the pattern. This results in writing a story that is a pale copy of other, better stories, like a third-generation photocopy.

Even the genre story designed to do nothing more than entertain will seem boring and predictable. Worse, the mainstream literary story, attempting to move the reader on some deeper level, will have the same cookie-cutter effect. The protagonist may be enduring life-changing and emotionally wrenching conflicts, yet readers are more curious than moved. They feel confusion at their own lack of involvement, given the apparent intensity of the situations; this confusion leads to resentment at the author for not engaging them on a deeper level.

**Diagnosis**

Writers having trouble with theme often don't understand how it contributes to plotting choices. Writers look at their plots and think because the events are dramatic and have a lot of conflict, they are automatically interesting. Not so. Conflict must be presented in such a way that readers recognize the connection between the characters' conflicts and their own.

A healthy theme creates a compelling drama rather than a forgettable melodrama. It does this by unifying the plot elements so that all events that occur in the story relate to one another, combining to affect the readers on both emotional and intellectual levels. As Margaret Atwood (*The Blind Assassin*) said, "The writer functions in his or her society as a kind of soothsayer, a truth teller, that writing is not mere self-expression but a view of a society and the world at large and that the novel is a moral instrument."

Now that we've reached some understanding of the elements of theme, we can see that it's not just some scary philosophical mumbo-jumbo to make us feel stupid, it's a practical tool to make us better writers. True, theme does act like a prosecuting attorney in that it lines up all this circumstantial evidence in front of the readers and asks them to reach some conclusions about the characters in the story. But that's how literature helps readers to better see their own lives. For me, that's the appeal of "reality" television shows like *Real World* and *Road Rules*, and even the game shows like *Love Connection* and *Blind Date*. These shows put people in situations, then allow them to comment on what's happening to them. For example, many times on *Blind Date*, a woman will be rejected by the man and then later comment to the camera, "He couldn't deal with the fact that I'm a strong woman with ideas of my own." What the audience saw was not a strong woman, but an obnoxious individual with no regard for the other person.

Or the man will say, "She's too conservative, doesn't like my wild personality." What the audience saw was a boring guy who acted up every time she tried to have an intelligent conversation, because he had nothing intelligent to say. This is a great example of the unreliable narrator, who is unable to see his life for the way it really is. At its root, all theme tries to do is show this to the readers in such a way that the readers examine their own lives more closely.

## Treatment

There are three popular approaches to applying theme: (1) the Six World Visions, (2) the Joseph Campbell Archetypal Model, and (3) the Psychological Model.

## SIX WORLD VISIONS IN SEARCH OF AN AUTHOR

The easiest way to approach theme is by examining the six major world visions.

The bulk of human thinking, as in philosophy, religion and art, is divided between two ways of seeing the world and our place in it: *Orthodox* and *Naturalism*. Orthodox presents a world governed by a Supreme Being (SB) looking out for the best interests of people; Naturalism presents a world governed by the natural process, which is indifferent to humans. Each of these world visions has two variations that offer plot templates related to that vision. The two variations of Orthodox are tragedy and comedy; the two variations of Naturalism are tragicomedy and satire.

Every story ever written will fall into one of these six categories. This is not a limitation of writers' creativity or originality, but rather an acknowledgment that there are only a handful of basic approaches to how we look at the world. In outline form, the world visions look something like this:

1. Orthodox
   a. Tragedy
   b. Comedy
2. Naturalism
   a. Tragicomedy
   b. Satire

Don't be too quick to think you know what they mean just because you've used the words before. We're going to examine these categories, not the way you studied them in high school English, but the way writers use them to better understand how to plot.

Consider the following paths of thought:

- We want to live a moral life, but what should those moral rules be—and why?
- How do we temper our gentle desire for morality with the harsh demands of daily survival?
- We examine the various forms of love in our lives—romantic, paternal, fraternal, etc.—and wonder what we need to do to be lovable and to show our love.
- We think about our place in the larger scope of existence, and wonder why bad things happen to good people.

Most of our other concerns are variations of these four questions. That means that all our stories, whether genre or literary, will revolve around these issues.

### Orthodox: People Who Need People

**The Template:** The word *orthodox* means to strictly keep to traditional doctrine, meaning the Orthodox story will contain the following elements:

• **Supreme Being (SB).** There is a powerful and caring being (or beings) responsible for what happens on earth.

• **The plan.** There is a plan for humanity, but only the SB knows the exact details of that plan. The plan will benefit humanity because it calls for good to be rewarded and evil to be punished— if not on earth, then later. Whatever happens on earth is for the eventual good of people. Everything on earth (including other animals, plants, natural resources) is here to serve the greater good of humanity.

• **Soul.** Humans have a soul, the essential, nonphysical part of themselves that lives beyond whatever happens to the physical body.

• **Faith.** Even though humans don't know what the plan is, they have faith that it is a good plan and that it is in their best interests. [Since faith means to believe in something for which there is no evidence, there doesn't have to be any evidence that the plan is good. So, pointing to massive disasters that have devastated humanity doesn't disprove the plan's beneficence. It only means that we, as humans, can't know the role that an event plays in the plan or how it ultimately will prove to benefit us. For example, you win $80 million in the lottery. Is that good? Yes, you say. But someone kidnaps your entire family and holds them for ransom. Things go wrong and the kidnappers slaughter your loved ones. Now was winning the money good? No, you say. But you then use the $80 million to build a hospital dedicated to saving the lives of otherwise destitute children. This hospital saves the life of two-year-old

Sammy, among many others, who would have died. Now is winning the money good? Yes, you say. But Sammy grows up to sadistically torture and murder dozens of children that he wouldn't have if you hadn't had the money to build that hospital. Now is winning the money good? And so on. The point is, humans can't see the big picture; only the SB can. Therefore, only the SB knows what is good and evil behavior, and we have to take the SB's word for it.]

• **Universal absolute moral values.** There are universal absolute moral values concerning what is right or wrong behavior. These rules are the same no matter what the circumstances or situation; they do not change based on culture or history. It doesn't matter where or how you were raised, these same rules apply to everyone. It's vital that individuals do not try to tailor or reinterpret these rules (see Tragedy).

• **Revelation.** The SB reveals to humans what these universal moral values are, usually through sacred texts such as the Bible, Koran, Book of Mormon, etc.

**How it works:** A compassionate SB has a master plan for the fate of humanity. In order to be happy, either in this life or the next, people need to follow the SB's moral teachings. Even when it appears that a special circumstance arises, making it reasonable to break the rules, don't. Reason is limited by restrictions of human knowledge, a limitation the SB doesn't have. If you follow the rules, and have faith that the plan is good, you will be happy. If you break the rules, or create your own rules to override the SB's rules, you will be punished, either with death or symbolic death (alienated from the community). The punishment might be directly from the SB (lightning bolt, or a curse, for example), or it might simply be a natural result of being the kind of person who arrogantly chooses his own morality above that of the community he lives in. This results in the person becoming an outcast, which brings unhappiness.

**Why bad things happen to good people:** Humans interpret that what's happened is bad because they can't see the larger plan.

Even the most horrible, distasteful, disgusting, heartbreaking event is for the eventual good. People shouldn't be distracted by the horrors of the material life, since that's only temporary; they need to concern themselves with the more permanent spiritual life. The main character conflict Orthodox stories face is coming to grips with what seems like an unfair world. They are raised with a fairytale view, then confront unexpected horrors. When the world doesn't meet their childish expectations, they lose faith in the SB and the plan. But Orthodox stories treat this crisis of faith as a natural part of the maturation process. By the end of the story, the protagonist regains his faith because he is able to see the world beyond the moral, and therefore illusionary, concepts of good and evil, fair and unfair, and recognize it on a much greater level. In the film, *The Legend of Bagger Vance*, angelic Will Smith coaches Matt Damon to look beyond the traps and hazards of the golf course, and see the bigger picture of all things as One. The ability to do this restores Damon's lost faith. British author Anita Brookner (*Hotel du Lac*) describes this conflict in her personal life: "I do envy those who can take life a little more easily. I am too handicapped by expectations. . . . The idea that right will triumph because this is England. It was implanted early by the novels of Dickens."

**How it works in plotting:** A vast majority of literature from the past 5,000 years has followed the Orthodox vision. The major reason for this is that literature originally evolved from the religious leaders of communities. They were the storytellers and their stories were designed to teach the community how to behave (as well as to explain the origin of material things like the planets, trees, etc.) Therefore, their stories are either about people who follow the rules and are rewarded (Orthodox, Comedy) or who break them and are punished (Orthodox, Tragedy). In an Orthodox story, the protagonist will confront a conflict and overcome it for the sake of the community. The character may enter the story as a loner and an outcast, used to doing things for selfish reasons, but comes to realize that there is a plan and chooses to have faith in the plan and the SB by doing what's right for others. The key plot convention here is the happy ending: good people are rewarded; evil people are punished. Often a coincidence allows the good people to triumph over the evil (see *deus ex machina* in Comedy).

Most sports stories are Orthodox because they use sports as a metaphor for "playing by the rules." The game of life has certain rules (given by the SB) and we play by them even if we don't agree or understand them. In *The Legend of Bagger Vance*, Damon plays a renowned golfer who comes back from WWI having "lost his swing" (his desire to play the game). He entered the war a golden boy whose life seemed charmed. But seeing the horrors of war caused him to believe the world was chaotic, not ruled by a caring force. Now, instead of a golden boy, he's a hard-drinking, poker-playing nonbeliever with no direction. Eventually, he overcomes his personal demons (rather than an evil enemy) with the aid of a supernatural helper, Smith. Smith plays an angelic being whose only role is to reinspire Damon's faith. A golf match involving two excellent golfers and a spiritually damaged Damon is arranged. Damon tries to run away, but he is met by cheers from the locals, who now see him as a local hero. He plays, but falls way behind because he lacks faith in the game and therefore doesn't play well. As Smith keeps telling him, "It's a game you can't win," (like life, since we all die) so you have to get your pleasures by embracing that. Under Smith's tutelage, Damon begins to come within reach of winning. But then his ego gets in the way—he starts playing to the crowd—and he plays to win. Again, he falters. And again Smith teaches him it's a spiritual game, not meant to be won. Damon even calls a stroke against himself for the most minor infraction (evidence that he's embraced the rules of the SB). Of course, he does win, for the benefit of his community, Savannah. His triumph at golf lifts all the locals' spirits during the Great Depression. As with other sports films, the fact that he wins the match contradicts the spiritual theme of the story (see also the case study on the ending of *Vision Quest* on page 14). This merely reflects America's ambivalent attitude toward themes of spiritual enlightenment. What good is it, our stories often ask, if we don't get some material reward to go with it?

The writer has to be careful not to contradict its own themes, which is why the more you understand the thematic patterns you're working with, the more consistent your plot choices will be. For example, the film *The Contender* is Orthodox, but it makes a plot choice that actually undermines its own vision. Joan Allen plays a vice-presidential nominee facing tough confirmation hearings. The opposition wishes to reject her by showing photographs and affidavits from witnesses that indicate she took part in group sex while in college. She refuses to answer their questions about the alleged incident, maintaining that whatever happened was personal and not the business of the committee or the American people. Her conviction on this point is such that she won't even discuss it with the president or his advisors—even at the risk of being withdrawn from contention. Had the movie ended with her silence intact, it would have been upholding the principles it was preaching through her character; it would have been about character. However, the filmmakers made a plot decision that undermined their own commitment: They included a scene in which she reveals to the president exactly what happened that night. Why? Because they were afraid the audience would lose sympathy for her if they believed the accusations? If they did, then they would be the kind of people the film was preaching against. There is no *character* or *plot* reason to tell us what happened at that party except to satisfy the audience's misplaced curiosity.

Another film that contradicts its Orthodox theme is *Air Force One*, in which Harrison Ford plays the president of the United States. After making a controversial speech in which he says the U.S. will have zero tolerance for terrorists, his plane is hijacked by terrorists. Instead of following protocol and escaping via the pod, he stays behind to fight the terrorists, eventually overcoming them and freeing the hostages, including his own wife and child. Audiences cheer and we all go home wishing Harrison Ford would run for president. Except for one thing. His character is a lousy President. Instead of escaping, which is his duty so he can't be held hostage over the U.S., he stays behind to rescue his own family. He puts his own personal needs above his sworn oath of office. If an Embassy guard left his post to attend his own family crisis, he'd be court-martialed and imprisoned. Even worse, after Ford's brave speech about not giving in to terrorist demands, he gives in to terrorist demands as soon as they put a gun to his daughter's head. He orders the release of a general who is responsible for the murder of thousands of innocent people, with full knowledge that this man will now continue his carnage. Each decision he makes as president is for the benefit of his family over the well-being of everyone else, despite his oath of office. The audience, of course, forgives all that because he kicks terrorist ass in act three, even though his success involves substantial *deus ex machina*.

Examples: Orthodox is most popular among genre stories, particularly romance, westerns, mysteries, adventure, and sci-fi. This does not mean all genre stories are Orthodox; in fact, there are many that deliberately are not (the novels *The Maltese Falcon* (though not the movie) and *Hannibal*). But most are because they basically tell the story of a good person who defeats an evil person for the sake of the community rather than for his own personal gain. The good person may even die, but if they die happily, this is the reward. Such is the case in *Gladiator*, which is basically a fancy revenge story: You killed my family, now I'll kill you. This is the same plot as *Braveheart*, *The Patriot*, *Get Carter*, *The Limey* and a thousand other stories. Other Orthodox stories include: *Star Wars*, *High Noon*, *Three Kings*, *Raiders of the Lost Ark* and *It's a Wonderful Life*. Most sports stories that involve an underdog winning, such as *Hoosiers*, *Rocky* and *Karate Kid* are Orthodox, as are the various tellings of the story of Jesus and other Savior archetypes.

### Tragedy: Good Person Goes Bad

The Template: People often mistakenly interchange sad with tragic. A newscaster will announce, "A tragic accident occurred this evening. . . ." However, in literature, tragic has a more specific definition and the Tragedy world vision has definite plot conventions.

• **Admirable Tragic Hero.** The Tragic Hero (TH) is on some level admirable. Often this is portrayed by having him be very successful: he's a rock star, famous writer, wealthy industrialist, king, prince, etc. This is a crucial element because he represents what the audience wants to become. We may not want to actually be a rock star or wealthy industrialist, but we do want what that symbolizes: someone who seems to have complete control over his life, someone who doesn't have to compromise to the whims of others.

We look at the TH in the beginning of the story and sigh, "Now that's the life."

However, in lieu of being materially successful, the TH may instead be admirable by sheer force of his charisma. He does what he wants to do, when he wants to do it, consequences be damned. He's funny, witty, intelligent and talented at something.

The main attribute of the TH is that he is constantly trying to expand the boundaries of self-determination. That means that, like a child, he's always pushing the limits as to what he can get away with. He's trying to determine how much control he has over his own life. The problem is that he always goes too far. The TH sees the world as if it were a box: We are all imprisoned by time (we have only so many years of life) and space (we have only so far we can move). He finds that reality too confining and tries to escape by banging his head against the wall. The result is a crushed skull.

• **Godlike act.** People who are successful often believe that they no longer have to play by the same rules as those who are less successful. They have proven their superiority to the common masses and may now make up their own rules. They may even justify this by rationalizing that whatever benefits them eventually benefits the rest of the community, since they employ many people or pay hefty taxes. The TH also believes this, and because of this false perception, eventually commits a godlike act that directly contradicts the rules that the SB has made known. This arrogant act means he's decided his judgment of what is good and evil behavior is superior to that of the SB.

• **The fall from grace.** The TH is punished for his lack of faith in the SB, the plan and the rules. The punishment is death, either real or symbolic. Real death is pretty straightforward: at the end of the story he's dead, as in all of Shakespeare's tragedies. Symbolic death means the TH is isolated from the community, which is what real death is anyway. Charles Foster Kane, in the film *Citizen Kane*, dies in the beginning, but death was not his punishment since it did not come immediately as a result of his actions. Rather, his punishment was self-imposed exile, to be cut off from the community and anyone who had ever loved him; to live in the mausoleum Xanadu, which he envisioned as his own heaven, but became his own hell (for what is hell but to be isolated from love?). In the film *Five Easy Pieces*, Jack Nicholson deliberately leaves behind his wallet (symbolizing his identity) and suitcase and hitches a ride on a truck going to Alaska, where the driver informs him it is "cold as hell." Alaska becomes a symbol of death. Nicholson is isolated from family and loved ones, which is as bad as death.

• **Inspiration.** As a result of the TH's inevitable death or isolation, the audience is supposed to experience a catharsis, a purging of our own desire to seek certain selfish goals. And we are meant to be inspired by the potential that the TH demonstrated. Imagine what he could have accomplished—the wrongs he could have righted for the community—if he'd only funneled his energies and talents for good.

**How it works:** Tragedy is a direct warning: Put yourself above the community and you will be banished from the community. The TH mistakenly believes his successes in life are solely because he's so talented and smart. He forgets that he owes everything to the SB and the plan. This arrogance leads him to commit an act that defies the SB's rules, which leads to his isolation from life or the things that make life worthwhile. The Biblical story of the Garden of Eden is a template for this vision. Adam and Eve have everything they could possibly want, including immortality. They just have to follow God's rule: Don't eat the fruit from the Tree of Knowledge of Good and Evil. God knows that, being humans and not gods, they can't handle this knowledge because they can't see the plan. However, they do eat, which is indicative of them trying to be godlike by having the knowledge that only God can use. They are banished from the Garden, losing their immortality, which is a sentence of death. This same story is echoed in the myth of Phaeton, son of Apollo, the Sun God. Apollo drives the chariot of the sun across the sky. Phaeton begs to drive the chariot but Apollo refuses, warning him that he's not yet ready. Phaeton steals the chariot, drives it across the sky, and is thrown to earth and dies. Icarus, who fashioned wings and flew too close to the sun, also falls to his death. The recurring language in these stories is of falling, as in "fall from grace."

**How it works in plotting:** The key conflict is between *what humans can know* and *what the SB knows*. For example, Morgan Freeman's detective character in the film *Seven* expresses this conflict when he tells a pregnant Gwyneth Paltrow about the one woman he truly loved and nearly married. She became pregnant, but he felt the world was too horrible a place to raise a child, so over a period of several weeks he "wore her down" until she got an abortion. He then tells Paltrow that he thinks—no, he *knows*—he made the right decision, but that not a day has gone by he hasn't regretted it. While that seems contradictory, it perfectly illustrates the issue: He's portrayed as a highly educated, brilliant man who regularly haunts the library (see Symbolism: Settings above). So, on a logical level, he knows he made the right decision; but his logic shows a lack of faith in the plan, a failure to acknowledge his own limitations as a human to see the SB's bigger vision. His regret is the part of him that recognizes his limitations and realizes that having children in a corrupt world such as this is, in itself, an act of faith and hope. But he is an admitted sinner (by strict Orthodox rules) in that he did not marry this woman, and that he promoted an abortion. His punishment is that he's alone—he lost his girlfriend, his possible child, and lives emotionally severed from the other cops.

In *Cool Hand Luke* and Ken Kesey's *One Flew Over the Cuckoo's Nest*, the protagonists struggle to expand their boundaries of selfdetermination against corrupt societies (prison and mental hospital, respectively). Each is killed. But they are Christ-like in that their deaths inspire others to gain freedom. For the prisoners of *Cool Hand Luke*, sitting around at the end talking about Luke as if they were his disciples is a form of freedom that makes them better able to endure their own imprisonment. *Cuckoo's Nest* creates a more tangible freedom when the Native American escapes the hospital.

Examples: The examples are vast because this is a favorite story: *King Lear, Othello, Hamlet, The Old Man and the Sea,* Budd

Schulberg's *What Makes Sammy Run*, F. Scott Fitzgerald's *The Great Gatsby* and the film *Champion*.

## Comedy: Happily Ever After

**The Template:** Don't confuse comedy with the Comic world vision. Slapstick physical humor and all the variations of making people laugh are indeed comic, but not necessarily a world vision. For this you need a specific formula, in this case one that fully embraces the Orthodox principles.

• **Boy meets girl** [or boy meets boy or girl meets girl]. Here our would-be lovers usually have to overcome an initial aversion to each other, but that's part of their charm and shows they are selective. Plotting here involves finding cute and amusing ways for the lovers to meet and minor obstacles for them to overcome before recognizing their mutual love.

• **Boy loses girl.** Inevitably, the boy and girl separate due to one or both of the following causes: (1) ego and (2) corrupt official or relative.

• **Ego.** People are reluctant to enter into romantic relationships (the familiar "fear of commitment") because they fear losing themselves, their individual identities. Couples fight passionately over minor infractions—a towel on the floor, a toothpaste cap left off—because these acts imply that their values, which make up who they are, are being deliberately ignored. This eventually results in being totally absorbed by the other person, a kind of death.

• **Corrupt official or relative.** This is usually embodied by a ruthless boss (Sigourney Weaver in *Working Girl*), a domineering girlfriend or boyfriend (Hugh Grant's fiancée in *Four Weddings and a Funeral*), Steve Martin's girlfriend in *All of Me*), an untrustworthy friend (Jason Alexander in *Pretty Woman*), or a wicked relative (stepmothers in many fairytales). These characters represent the person without faith in the SB or the rules; they only pretend to be virtuous (think Serpent in the Garden of Eden, trying to destroy Adam and Eve's faith). At the end, this corrupt character is either kicked out of the new "Garden of Eden," which has been formed by the couple, or he sees the error of his ways and is converted to a more loving, caring person with a Comic world vision.

• **Boy gets girl.** Boy and girl eventually get back together (or the audience would tear the pages from the book and the seats from the theater). But they only get back together because of divine intervention referred to as *deus ex machina* (Latin for "machinery of the gods"). Historically, this was literal in that ancient Greek and Roman plays would sometimes use a crane to introduce a god in the play. The god would miraculously unravel or resolve the plot, bringing order to the chaos the characters had created for themselves. For modern audiences, this device has been transformed into an obviously contrived coincidence. For example, there's no way Nicolas Cage in *Family Man*, or Bill Murray in *Groundhog Day* or Warren Beatty in *Heaven Can Wait*, could ever have come to find love without being thrown into a supernatural reality. But there are numerous more down-to-earth coincidences in such stories. Sometimes people criticize a romantic-comedy because of this device, "Oh, brother, that was such a *coincidence*." Well, stop it— because that *coincidence* is the whole point of the story. The reason lovers are brought back together is that they finally recognize that their love for each other is more important than the petty things that separated them (ego and/or corrupt official). Once they have that realization—on their own—they have demonstrated faith in the way the world works, which is faith in the SB and the plan. That's when the forces of the SB will bring them together through a coincidence.

• **Marriage.** At the end, the couple is together, and we are left with the impression that they will stay together. Traditionally, this is symbolized through marriage, though modern day has given us the option of living together to show that same bond. This final part of the formula is not just to make us sigh and smile, it has a specific thematic lesson. Marriage itself is symbolic of

**1. People overcoming their selfishness to love someone else more than they love themselves.** They recognize that the relationship is greater than the sum of its parts (the individuals). The ability to do this demonstrates that individuals are capable of doing this on a larger scale, eventually creating a world in which humans can be selfless. This would mirror the concept of heaven—where all people love each other—but it would exist on earth.

**2. People recognizing their responsibility to the community.** Marriage is more than a commitment to another person, it is a commitment to the community. By forming a family and having children, the characters demonstrate they are ready to take their place within the community, fulfilling the rules of the SB. In many of Shakespeare's comedies (*As You Like It, Twelfth Night, A Midsummer Night's Dream*), characters fall in love with characters in disguise. For example, Tom and Jane are in love. But Tom gets nervous about the relationship and runs off to live alone in the woods. Jane follows, but disguises herself as a man and calls herself "Jim." Tom and "Jim" become best of buddies. Lisa meets "Jim" and falls in love with "him." And so on. At the end of these stories, they are all revealed for who they are and have a mass wedding. Part of the message is that it matters less who you marry than the fact that you accept your social duty and marry. It also demonstrates that our concepts of romantic love can be narrow, but if we give people a chance we can love them beyond the "disguise" that we all present to the outside world. In the classic Billy Wilder film *Some Like It Hot*, Joe E. Brown falls in love with Jack Lemmon, who is disguised as a woman. At the end, when lovers Tony Curtis and Marilyn Monroe come together, a moony Brown cuddles beside Lemmon. Lemmon rips off his wig and announces, "I'm a man!" Without hesitation, Brown smiles and says, "Nobody's perfect." This, too, is an act of faith.

**How it works:** While Tragedy is a warning about what can happen to those who lack faith in the plan, Comedy is a celebration of those who maintain faith in the face of adversity. The TH complains about the limitations of the metaphoric room that is life and bashes his head into the wall trying to break out; the comic hero appreciates the room, is grateful to be allowed to live in the room, and sets about making it a happy place to live. The act of being able to love another more than oneself is proof of the divine within us. All that symbolism aside, the practical application is that those who are constantly upset about the way the world is are going to be unhappy; and if they arrogantly place their own values above those in their community, they will eventually be shunned by that community. Those who accept the limitations and imperfections of life and focus their attention on thinking about others rather than themselves, are happier.

**How it works in plotting:** Some may find the Comedy formula too rigid and therefore too predictable. That, folks, is the whole point of its popularity. No one goes to a romantic comedy hoping to be surprised at the ending by having the formula broken and the couple not get together. This recipe has worked for 2,500 years precisely because of its familiarity. People go to a romantic-comedy for the same reason they go to church—to have their faith renewed. In this case, it's faith in our ability to overcome our own selfishness in order to love another.

A typical plot would be something like this: Gypsy, 18, and Rob, 18, are in love. Gypsy has a little brother, Timmy, 12. Gypsy and Timmy's parents were recently killed in a car crash. Mean Uncle Steve, who was in business with the dead parents, comes to live in their home and take care of the business as well as the children. But he's stern: He demands that Gypsy stop seeing Rob and spend more time cleaning the house. And he's harsh with little Timmy. Frustrated, Rob tries to convince Gypsy to run away with him. "If you really love me," he pleads, "you'll come with me." But she's committed to taking care of Timmy. "If you really love me," she explains, "you'll stay." They argue and split up because of their egos (each wanting his or her own way) and because of the corrupt relative.

One day Gypsy is in her parents' study, cleaning. A bird flies into the room through the open window. She captures the bird and stands in front of the window, bird in hand, and sighs, "Go and be free, little bird, like I can never be." She opens her hands and the bird flies up, turns around, and pecks her on the forehead. Gypsy tumbles backward, falls onto her parents' desk, and a secret drawer pops open. Inside is a report from a private detective that the parents had hired. It shows gambling debts of Uncle

### Case Study: *Groundhog Day*

*Groundhog Day* (1993) is one of the funniest and most deliberately moral romantic comedies ever made. Even though its angst-in-cheek wit and black-comic tone make it appear up-to-the-minute contemporary, its traditional structure and moral lessons would make the ancient Greeks feel right at home, for it exemplifies the same type of comedies they watched in their drafty robes from the hard seats. At the same time, the Orthodox rabbis of Jerusalem, the Buddhist monks of Tibet, and Jesus' born-again disciples would all have endorsed this movie as teaching a fundamental lesson they all share, the most crucial lesson each person must learn. Bill Murray plays a character named Phil, a rumpled, cynical weatherman with a perpetual bad-hair day—the perfect romantic lead for a story in which love redeems. But the crucial lesson here is that it isn't romantic love that saves Murray from his deathlike existence, it is a greater more universal love of humanity. It is that broader focus that elevates *Groundhog Day* above morally superficial romantic comedies like *Sleepless in Seattle*.

When the film opens, the screen is filled with puffy white clouds rolling across a blue sky. The image, combined with the upbeat music, conjures a feeling that we are watching more than clouds, but glimpsing the billowing hemline of heaven. Cut to a pair of hands as Murray pantomimes against a blank blue screen: He is forecasting the weather for his TV audience. We see his hands against the blue backdrop, but the TV audience also sees the projection of the weather map. In a gesture of supreme arrogance, Murray blows hard, and the clouds that line the Midwest seem to blow away. This opening displays a man pretending to be a god; he foretells the weather as if he created it, or could make it go away

*continued*

197

with a mighty puff. But the movie audience is also shown the blue screen, which reminds us that it's an illusion, a trick of the eye. The problem is, Murray acts as if his power is true. A few scenes later, he even tells a cop, "I make the weather!"

He is ambitious, anxious to rise higher in his profession. He wants to be rich and famous, and he thinks he deserves it more than others. His attitude gives him license to treat others rudely, dismissing them as beneath him. The Groundhog Day assignment is also beneath him and he complains about it throughout the whole drive there. When MacDowell tells him it's cute and people like it, Murray replies, "People are morons." This attitude and behavior follows the traditional egomaniacal behavior of some romantic heroes. They're lovable jerks. They believe themselves to be so superior to others they have isolated themselves from the rest of the world (like the groundhog in its hole, who is also named Phil). This isolation—exemplified by greed, avarice, ambition and a parking space with your name on it—is symbolic of death. When a character places himself above others, he also cuts himself off from them, which is in essence what death is. It's not just symbolic: Researchers led by University of Michigan sociologist James House have concluded that social isolation is statistically as dangerous to one's life as smoking, high blood pressure, high cholesterol, obesity, or lack of exercise. Companionship, they discovered, whether human or animal, significantly reduces stress. (It is a further irony that Murray awakens each day to Sonny and Cher singing "I Got You, Babe." It is a like a cosmic clue: As long as you care more for yourself than anyone else, you are trapped in the swirling waters of a flushing toilet.)

Murray is attracted to MacDowell. We see this in the opening when she is playing on the weather set that he has just left. While he was pretending to be a god, she unconsciously parodies him by positioning herself so that when she is viewed on the monitor, her smiling face appears to be surrounded by clouds. She looks like an angel, and we can see Murray is affected by this image, though he quickly tries to hide it. For her part, MacDowell finds Murray amusing, but she cannot love him because he is incapable of receiving or giving love. As the film progresses, Murray pursues her, but his problem is that he mistakes *desire* for *love*. He wants to possess whatever he wants, because that will make him feel like he's got power. Because her ideal of love is so pure, MacDowell becomes a type of angel in this magical myth, though she doesn't know it.

So, we now have our two lovers, separated by ego—mostly his. What brings the lovers together? The *deus ex machina*, machinery of the gods. Well, you can't have much more of a supernatural intervention than to have Murray waking up everyday, still in the same day, reliving it over and over for months, perhaps years (an early draft of the script suggested thousands of years).

But the lovers are not yet ready to come together. Murray's first reaction—after the initial shock to his unusual situation, is to satisfy sensual desires (the infantile stage of all human beings). He seeks pleasure at 150 mph no matter what the cost, steals money, eats whatever he wants, drinks, smokes, drives fast, tricks women into sleeping with him; yet this begins to wear thin after a while, and pursuing these desires is no longer satisfying or fulfilling. At first he was like an infant, living only to satisfy hunger. Now he is a spoiled and bored adolescent who is angry and depressed when he realizes that fulfilling one's desires does not make one the master, but the slave to those desires. Instead of a god, he is merely a dependent. This is a teenage stage in which teens feel the expectations of everyone, but lack the maturity to gain control over their own lives. The dressing in black and heavy-metal music

*continued*

of groups that speak of death (Megadeath, Marilyn Manson, Cypress Hill), reflect the feeling of isolation from society, as well as the fear that they will soon be entering that society and the person they are now will be lost. This is the stage Murray now enters.

This is a crucial stage in comedy, for it is the key theme: Humans have very little control over the way the universe, or their own world, for that matter, works. We are born and we die; we cannot change that. We are prisoners of time and space, unable to escape either, like people locked in a room. Once we recognize that, we can rebel, as do THs, or we can accept the fact that we are not gods, we are not the center of the universe. If we are trapped in a room, let's decorate that room, throw a get-to-know-your-neighbor party, and make the best of these limitations. Accepting our own limitations is actually freeing. Instead of worrying about what we cannot change, we can concentrate on what we can do, which is to treat each other as nicely as possible, since we're all trapped in this same room. In other words, we can behave ethically.

Murray is not at that stage yet, though. His problem is that his dream has come true. He has gotten all that he has ever wanted—money, women, the ability to have anything he wants. When he tries to explain his situation to an unbelieving MacDowell, she asks him if he thinks he's God. He replies, "I'm *a* god—not *the* God." Yet, having achieved the ultimate power to have whatever he wants (the dream of many people), Murray is miserable. By reliving the same day over and over, he discovers what many people take a lifetime to learn; that their goals were selfish and ultimately unsatisfying, that they sacrifice everything they start out believing in to get more money or power, only to have lost what they'd hoped the money and power would bring them. (One irony of this plot device is that all the lessons of life can be found in one day, if we pay attention.)

Murray's discovery of his own (figurative) impotence is when he offers help to a homeless man who he's been ignoring during each daily incarnation. He feeds the man, tries to help him, but the man dies anyway. Nothing Murray can do will prevent this. This drives him to despair because it further emphasizes his lack of power. So, if fulfilling his desires bring him no satisfaction, and he cannot prevent the death of someone he's come to care for, what is the point of living? So he tries to kill himself.

This proves to be impossible. No matter what he does to himself, he reawakens to Sonny and Cher. Similar to Buddhist and Hindu concepts of reincarnation, Murray must return until he purifies himself of the bad *karma* in his soul. This karma is created by actions that show how one clings to the illusions of this world. On a basic level, this means that the more you care about buying that expensive watch because you think it will make you happy, the more vulnerable you are to disappointment and unhappiness; the less you care about those things, the less having or not having something affects you. Murray's means of salvation from this lonely death-like existence is to make MacDowell fall in love with him (a nifty variation of the Flying Dutchman story). Through cunning and deceit, he learns everything she likes and keeps changing himself to fit her ideal of the perfect mate. But no matter how much he fakes it, or how close he gets to having her care for him, she always stops short, because she can sense his insincerity. As an angel-like figure, MacDowell represents the purity of love. She could only love honestly, which is why he thinks if he can get her to love him, he will believe he has proven that he is worthy of love. But this is still illusion, like his weatherman persona in front of a blue screen pretending to control weather. He is a false god she will not love. He wanted her for selfish reasons and that is not what love is.

*continued*

Eventually, Murray even abandons pursuing her. Now that he is stripped of his own false illusions about what life is about, what is valuable and worthy in life and what is not, he slowly undergoes a change. He takes piano lessons. He learns to ice sculpt. He begins to help people. Nothing monumental, mostly the everyday slings and arrows of life: he changes a tire for an elderly woman; catches a boy who falls out of a tree, etc. Soon he is on a schedule, running around every day helping the same people over and over. What makes this so remarkable is that these people won't remember what he's done; they will continue to make these same mistakes over and over. There is no reward for him, not even the undying gratitude of those he's helped. But he does it anyway! He can't prevent the homeless man from dying because death is out of the human realm; he accepts that. We all will die. Still, if we can't prevent death, we can at least make life more pleasant. We can ease suffering, promote happiness—in other words, we can love. Romantic love is only one manifestation of this universal love, the larger concept is the love of humanity. Once the character stops thinking of himself as above others, he is no longer isolated, no longer "dead." He sees that humanity is the body and he is merely one small part of that greater body. (Christians would liken this to the body of Christ, of which we are all a part. Buddhists would think of it as the Great Universal Soul, of which we are all a part.)

On the last day, Murray is no longer trying to impress MacDowell. He is not faking sincerity or love; he exudes it, he lives it. MacDowell observes this and that is what makes her fall in love with him. (His ice sculpture of an angel is a nice symbolic touch, for that is what he has become; instead of seeking salvation in others, such as MacDowell, he has refashioned that part of existence he can control—himself.)

Finally, MacDowell sleeps with him, though they do not have sex. Ego has been overcome, and the lovers are now one. They wake up in a new day, ready to start a new life together. For Murray, he is truly alive for the first time, since he now has embraced his part within humanity rather than trying to escape it. Not only will they marry, but when they step outside into the town that has been his private hell, he declares, "Let's live here!" In romantic comedy, turning hell into heaven is merely a change of perspective.

Steve, proof that he embezzled money from the company, and photos of him chatting with a car mechanic (who may have caused the crash). Gypsy takes this information (achieved through *deus ex machina*) to the police and Uncle Steve is arrested, Timmy is safe, and the lovers are together.

Examples: Too numerous to list, but aside from those already mentioned, includes just about every romance novel, many glitz novels and popular "women's fiction." Also includes films such as *His Girl Friday*, *When Harry Met Sally*, *You've Got Mail*, *Pretty Woman*, *Runaway Bride* and *French Postcard*.

An interesting variation of the formula is the film, *My Best Friend's Wedding*. This follows all the same traditional conventions, but it's told from the POV of the corrupt "relative," the friend who is out to destroy the wedding.

Musicals often follow this same formula. In fact, they emphasize the pattern through five common songs that appear in most romantic comedy musicals: the hero's song, the heroine's song, the villain's song (think corrupt relative or official), the love song, and the setting song. The setting song is of particular interest here because it is the defining song of the theme. Notice how many musicals are named after a place: *West Side Story*, *Camelot*, *South Pacific* and *Oklahoma* to name a few. That's because setting—community—is even more important than the couple that falls in love. The reason they fall in love is to contribute to the community. Even the language of the setting song is similar: it's always described as a magical place where the usual rules of nature don't apply; you'll feel younger, happier, you might even be able to fly (as in Peter Pan's "Never-Never Land").

## Naturalism: It Ain't Necessarily So

**The Template:** Contrary to the Orthodox vision, Naturalism does not believe there is a planned reason for whatever happens. People are on their own to create the kind of moral order they want.

• **No Supreme Being.** There is no SB, no plan, no soul, no universal absolute moral values, no sacred scriptures.

• **Natural order.** Instead of a divine order, there is a natural order, indifferent to humans, based purely on the science of the material world interacting. Nature doesn't care what happens to people; if we become extinct, the natural order continues along, always adapting, always changing. Humans need to turn away from the heavens for answers and concentrate on helping and comforting each other. At the end of Thomas Harris's *Red Dragon*, the protagonist, after capturing the serial killer, ruminates of the green machine, a metaphor for an impersonal natural order that allows the horrible things he's seen.

• **Free will.** Each person has free will, but with that free will comes the awesome responsibility to choose one's actions carefully. It is one's actions, not intentions, that define a person. The problem is, without Orthodox rules, how can one be certain of choosing the right action? Well, it can't be done—and therein lies the conflict that drives the Naturalistic plot.

• **Courage.** The theme is about courage. When faced with making a moral choice in a world in which there are no absolutes, will the character have the courage to do the right thing? Knowing what the right thing is can't be determined by a law or community consensus—only by the person making the choice.

There are three levels of choice (borrowed from existentialist philosopher Soren Kierkegaard):

**1. Aesthetic.** Here the protagonist chooses his actions based on his passions and bodily desires. He takes many lovers, indulges himself, pursues whatever lusts he has, regardless of who gets hurt. He may feel bad about the consequences of his actions, may even question them, but in the end, he chooses to satisfy his own needs over those of others. This is the lowest level of choice because it involves the least amount of personal freedom. Although the person thinks he is free because he does what he wants, this is an illusion. He is in fact enslaved by his passions, a servant to his desires, always running around servicing them, even though the consequences often lead to alienation from others (Sammy Glick in Budd Schulberg's brilliant novel *What Makes Sammy Run*). This is the level of *instant gratification*. It is ruled not by pleasure, but fear—of death, of alienation, of missing something. This is the weak thinking of adolescents or immature adults. They are doomed to live life *reacting* to their emotions rather than controlling them and *acting* by free choice.

**2. Ethical.** On this level, the character makes choices that reflect his commitment to community values, not just his own pleasures. Rather than indulging in many lovers, he takes a wife and raises a family. He accepts his responsibility to the group over that to his own desire. This is the level of *delayed gratification*. The concept of delayed gratification is the cornerstone of civilization: We teach that rather than strike someone when you are angry, steal food when you are hungry, take advantage of someone for sex when you are horny—wait and the reward for waiting will be much greater. If I don't strike someone when I'm angry, I am creating a society that does not harm others on a whim, which means I can feel free to speak my mind without fear of harm, the reward being that my family will be safer. [For Orthodox believers, delayed gratification can also mean that doing good in this life will reap rewards in the next life.]

**Vampires vs. Saviors.** Vampires are symbolic of beings that seek instant gratification. They feed off others in the community because they want to live forever. They do whatever they want to whomever they want. This is the behavior of someone—vampire or not—who lives on the aesthetic level. His flaw is that he seeks to live forever in the material body that, like all things material, is inevitably temporary. And his lifestyle makes him hunted by the ethical community.

Saviors represent people who recognize that life is temporary and that it is more important to do what is right for the sake of what isn't temporary (*soul* if it's Orthodox or *humanity* if Naturalism). Where vampires feed off the blood of the community, saviors give their own blood in order to "feed" the community. Saviors sacrifice their lives to help others as an acknowledgment that this life is not what's most important. This is the behavior of someone who lives on the ethical level (delayed gratification).

**3. Religious.** The word is misleading because it has nothing to do with traditional religion. This level is rarely achieved because it requires that the character make a choice that might actually go against what society believes is right. To make this choice requires an enormous amount of courage, because one can't rely on reasoning alone.

The rational mind is a faulty machine, both in how it records information and in how it processes it. You make many choices based on your memories of experiences, yet you know that those memories are not always accurate. You have altered them through time. Perhaps you retold an event from your past, embellishing it so often with clever remarks you made that you no longer can remember whether you actually said those things. In courtroom cases, studies have concluded that eyewitness accounts are the least reliable sources of evidence. Add to that your ability to rationalize: to use false logic to convince yourself to make a choice you *want* to make rather than *should* make, such as, "Beating this child is for his own good," or, "Women are emotionally erratic and therefore should not hold public office." Even Orthodox believers reinterpret sacred texts in order to change rules they don't want to follow, which is why there are so many variations within the same basic religions, such as 28,000 sects of Christianity.

The only way for a character to make a religious choice is by balancing reason and intuition, an innate sense of what is right beyond the illusion of reason. This is difficult to do and requires making "a leap of faith." Just as the Orthodox vision asks adherents to make a leap of faith, to believe that there is a SB and a Plan; here too, a leap of faith is required. But the leap here is that you have made the best possible choice, regardless of what anyone else thinks or says.

The Religious Level confronts one of the conflicts of the Ethical Level. Sometimes the group morality is wrong, but people lack the courage to break from the crowd. They convince themselves that they are ethical people because they are doing what everyone else considers ethical, and therefore never have to confront the fact that they are living an illusion. This is called *"bad faith,"* and is explained on page 212 under Tragicomedy.

Example: In the classic Western film *The Man Who Shot Liberty Valance*, the three main characters represent the three levels of Naturalistic choice: Lee Marvin (aesthetic); Jimmy Stewart (ethical); John Wayne (religious). Marvin plays Liberty Valance, an evil man who does whatever he wants to whomever he wants. Stewart is an idealistic lawyer who comes West to bring law, but through books. Books prove to be impotent against Marvin's ruthlessness and fast gun. Wayne is something of a loner, a good man who lives by his own standards but is somewhat removed from the community. He's not afraid of Marvin, but he's not willing to take him on just because it would be best for the community that Marvin terrorizes. In the end, Stewart is goaded by Marvin into a gunfight that he can't possibly win. What do you think happens next? (Take a moment before reading on.)

If you answered, "Wayne comes in to save Stewart by facing Marvin," you're half right. Wayne saves Stewart, but by shooting Marvin from a distance with a rifle and making it look like Stewart won. Wayne's action isn't legal (it's murder), nor is back-shooting considered morally right by the community; but he makes a leap of faith and does what he thinks is best for the community, even if they wouldn't recognize it as such. Now the community will be more willing to accept the laws represented by Stewart, because they recognize his courage in risking his life to enforce them.

**Important plotting note:** These three levels sometimes represent the character arc in a Naturalistic story. The protagonist starts on the aesthetic level in Act 1; progresses to the ethical level in Act 2;

and in Act 3 is faced with a leap of faith to achieve the religious level—sometimes succeeding; sometimes failing.

**How it works:** Because there is no SB no plan and no rules, people are responsible for choosing their own set of moral rules, and then acting upon them. This requires courage, especially in facing the pressure of the community to adhere to its rules. Individuals should choose their moral rules so that they benefit all of society. However, they must accept the challenge that what's best for society may not be acknowledged by that society due to its own lack of vision or bad faith (see Tragicomedy).

**Why bad things happen to good people:** Because nature doesn't recognize human notions of good and bad. It's an indifferent tornado that crushes the trailer homes of good and bad people alike.

**How it works in plotting:** A common plot pattern involves a character who believes in the Orthodox vision suddenly confronting some catastrophic event—often life-threatening—that forces him to re-evaluate his former beliefs. He realizes that nature doesn't care about human notions of fairness. In Stephen Crane's much-anthologized story, "The Open Boat," four characters have survived the sinking of a ship and are floating on the ocean in a lifeboat. Their food and water has run out and they realize they must make for shore or die. The problem is that the surf is very rough and dangerous, and they could just as easily be drowned heading for shore. Nevertheless, they risk it. Survival would logically depend on two things: physical fitness and knowledge of the sea.

- Captain: not fit (wounded); knowledge of the sea
- Cook: not fit (overweight); knowledge of the sea
- Oiler (Billy): fit; knowledge of the sea
- Journalist (protagonist): fit; no knowledge of the sea

Of the four, only Billy has both requirements needed to survive. However, when they make their desperate run for the shore and are capsized, only Billy is killed. Why? Because human notions of logic don't apply to the natural order. All humans live in an "open boat," exposed to the indifferent forces of nature—weather, disease, accidents—and we need to make the best of it and be more compassionate toward each other, recognizing that we're all in the same "boat."

The story opens: "None of them knew the color of the sky. Their eyes glanced level, and were fastened upon the waves that swept toward them." These lines tell the reader that the characters are so focused on the waves (the immediate cause-and-effect events in their lives), they can't see the bigger picture of what those events mean. The last sentence of the story reveals a change has taken place as a result of their experience: "When it came night, the white waves paced to- and-fro in the moonlight, and the wind brought the sound of the great sea's voice to the men on shore, and they felt that they could then be interpreters." Now that they've experienced the might and indifference of the sea, they understand the bigger picture. [Note: Stephen Crane was on a ten-foot dinghy as a survivor of the sinking of the Commodore in 1897. His accounts of the sinking of the ship and his thirty hours in the dinghy became widely read. Yet, despite the popularity of his reporting of the "facts," he felt compelled to write a story that would reveal the truth behind the facts.]

The film *The Maltese Falcon* promotes an Orthodox view: Sam Spade is a good man who resists (or seems to resist) various temptations in order to bring the murderer of his partner to justice. The novel is more subversive. Spade's face is described on the first page as resembling a blond satan. He then proceeds to break, or is revealed to already have broken, every moral code of the (fictional) detective: He has slept with his partner's wife as well as his secretary, and he then sleeps with the client. His motive for solving the case isn't justice or enforcing the Orthodox rules, rather it's because it is bad for business if one's partner is murdered and the case goes unsolved (the same "it's just business" justification the mobsters in Mario Puzo's *Godfather* used to rationalize their crimes). The final chapter shows Spade reading about himself in the paper, gloating. His secretary walks in, and he puts a friendly arm around her. She backs away, not wanting to be touched by him—the kind of man who could sleep with his client and then turn her in to the police. And so it ends, with no clear sense of good winning or evil being punished.

## Case Study: What Makes "A&P" Naturalist

In John Updike's short story "A&P," the narrator is Sammy, a nineteen-year-old checkout clerk at a grocery store. He's portrayed as judging everyone and everything based on its appearance. He has a vague dissatisfaction with his job, but he's unable to articulate why. The story starts with the line, "In walks these three girls in nothing but bathing suits." Sammy is immediately attracted to the one girl whom he refers to as the "queen bee." She's innocent, sexy, but confident. Her presence helps him articulate his dissatisfaction with the A&P: It's a world of false order—shelves lined with crap, frequented by "houseslaves" in pincurlers. We can tell from Sammy's grammar that he's not very educated, and we soon realize that one of the things that bothers him, though he hasn't yet admitted it, is that he might end up working in the A&P for the rest of his life. When the manager, Lengel ("Lengel's pretty dreary, teaches Sunday School and the rest. . . ."), sees the girls in their bathing suits, he tells them that they must dress decently in the A&P. In an intuitive moment of outrage, Sammy quits his job. The girls don't wait to see what happens and leave. Now Lengel gives Sammy the chance to back down—but Sammy refuses. In a keen moment of insight, he tells us, "But it seems to me that once you begin a gesture it's fatal not to go through with it." What he means is, that given the opportunity to make a choice that defines who you are and what you stand for, you kill the person you want to be by not following through with it. It's important that Sammy not be very educated, because he makes his choice based on a balance of reason and intuition. Had the story ended here, it might have been Orthodox: Good triumphs over evil as he exits the A&P with a smile on his face and bounce in his step, looking forward to all the possibilities life has to offer.

Instead, Sammy looks back into the A&P and sees Lengel at Sammy's register, checking "the sheep" through: "His face was dark gray and his back stiff, as if he'd just had an injection of iron, and my stomach kind of fell as I felt how hard the world was going to be to me hereafter." Here's what he means: Sammy saw how easily he was replaced, that the world of the A&P doesn't care about his moral resolutions. A person shouldn't look for applause or reward from the world for doing what is right. The reward is that you are becoming the person you want to be. Sammy's not sorry for this choice (he tells us that a few paragraphs earlier), he's just aware of the consequences. Basically, this is a retelling of the Garden of Eden story. The "queen bee" is a variation of Eve, and Lengel (God) boots Sammy from the Garden of A&P, where he would have had job security and a set of shrink-wrapped moral values. Sammy eats from the Tree of the Knowledge of Good and Evil by choosing his own definition of good and evil, and is expelled. Orthodox finds this a cautionary tale; Naturalism presents it as a celebration of being courageous enough to question the status quo.

Examples: Naturalism is the dominant world vision of much of modern literary fiction, especially since World War II. Ambrose Bierce's short story "An Occurrence at Owl Creek Bridge;" Jack London's novels *The Call of the Wild* and *The Sea Wolf*; Theodore Dreiser's novels; Leonard Michaels's short stories; J.D. Salinger's *The Catcher in the Rye*; and Thomas Harris's *Red Dragon*, *Silence of the Lambs* and *Hannibal*.

### Tragicomedy: Having a Bad Faith Day

The Template: Tragicomedy combines some elements of both Tragedy and Comedy. Although it acts as almost a parody of Tragedy, it does end on a serious note. Like Tragedy, it is a warning against lack of faith—except instead of lack of faith in a SB, it punishes lack of faith in oneself. Generally, it follows this pattern:

• **Tragicomic Hero.** Unlike the TH, the Tragicomic Hero (TCH) is not admirable. He reflects not the accomplished, successful person, but rather the average person with all his neurotic insecurities. He will be likable, however, probably because of a strong sense of humor.

• **Conflict.** The TCH is faced with a major conflict that challenges him to choose between acting courageously or doing what others pressure him to do. He chooses to follow the latter. This conflict usually focuses on helping a friend in need. The TCH eventually refuses to help. In some literature, this is meant to parallel the denial of Christ by the apostles, not as a religious metaphor, but to show how we often refuse to see how our actions are harmful to ourselves.

• **Bad faith.** While the TH acts out of arrogance and confidence, the TCH acts out of lack of courage and bad faith. Bad faith is made up of two components:

1. **Denial of who he is.** He refuses to see that he is a coward, an alcoholic, a bad parent—that his view of his life is an illusion. He will think that he is a good person because his intentions are good, even though his actions are not. Illusion vs. reality is a major theme in fiction, often signaled by an unreliable narrator.

2. **Denial of ability to change.** Even if he acknowledges these flaws, he will deny his ability to change who he is. He will rationalize with statements such as, "That's how I was raised," "It's genetic," or "Everyone else is doing it."

The film *The Matrix* offers a nice metaphor for bad faith. In reality, people live in pods, attached to tubes, acting as batteries for a giant computer. To keep them content, the computer generates a mental life for them so that they all think they're living lives just as you and I are living ours (or think we are). The rebels are a group who have broken out and are living in fear and squalor, but at least seeing the truth. However, one of the rebels betrays the others because he prefers the illusionary world to the real one. That's bad faith.

• **Punishment.** The TH is punished with death or symbolic death. The TCH is punished with failure, which results in alienation from others, or just misery as he realizes the kind of cowardly person he is and probably always will be.

**How it works:** The average person faces the same great moral drama as the TH. The stakes are more realistic, though. Rather than the high drama of death, the TCH faces what we sometimes fear even more, failure and humiliation as we realize that we are moral cowards.

**How it works in plotting:** The pattern is simple: Show us a person we like because she's humorous, witty, intelligent. Then give her a moral dilemma that at first seems like a no-brainer—of course she will do the right thing. Then show all the influences on her life start to wear her down until she makes the immoral choice, which usually is not helping a friend in need. This act of betrayal results in her either being an outcast or embraced by the equally corrupt community, but with her aware that she has killed a part of herself by this betrayal. The TCH is often very educated and articulate (professors, lawyers, doctors). This is meant to show the impotence of our knowledge when it comes to doing the right thing.

Woody Allen's film *Manhattan* is a good example of how Tragicomedy works. Allen plays a middle-aged man who is dating seventeen-year-old Tracy (Mariel Hemingway). The film starts with Allen sitting in a bar with Hemingway and some friends. They are discussing some intellectual crap (remember, TCHs are often very educated and articulate) when Allen interrupts by proclaiming that courage is the most important character trait a person could have, thereby announcing the movie's theme. Allen continues to complain that he shouldn't be in this relationship, that she's way too young for him; he even encourages her to attend a semester in England where she can meet other guys her own age. She protests that she doesn't want any of that because she loves him. However, Allen is unable to live under the pressure of having a relationship that is not acceptable by community standards. He breaks it off and begins dating Diane Keaton, who's more his age. But he soon discovers that Keaton, who was previously having an adulterous affair with his best friend, is not a good person, she only thinks she is. She starts to cheat on Allen and the romance ends. Alone, lying on his couch, he begins to list the little things that make life worth living, when he suddenly says, "Tracy's face." He realizes that he loved her and she loved him, and that he only gave her up because he didn't have faith in himself to withstand social pressures. He tries to call her, but the phone is busy. He runs down to the street and tries to hail a cab, but can't. Finally, he runs full-speed down the streets to her home. When he arrives, she's loading her suitcase for her semester in England. He tries to talk her out of it. She has to go now, she explains, but she still loves him and they can pick up again when she gets back. "You have to have a little faith in people," she says with a smile. He forces a weak smile in return, and the film ends. He has no faith, which is why he ends up alone.

Examples: Novels include Muriel Spark's *The Prime of Miss Jean Brodie*, Philip Roth's *Portnoy's Complaint*. Short stories include Tobias Wolff's "In the Garden of North American Martyrs," Leonard Michaels's "City Boy," and Joyce Carol Oates's "Naked."

## Satire: Things Are Worse Than You Think

The Template: Satire is the most focused of the world visions in that it tries to elicit a direct change in the audience. There is a difference between satiric and Satire. Skits on *Saturday Night Live* and *Mad TV* are often satiric, but they aren't really a fully developed satire. Satire seems to gain popularity during times of social conflict; during the Vietnam War, satire appeared in abundance in theater, film, literature and on TV. Some conventions of satire follow:

• Comic seduction. The opening of the satire is often very funny; this is how the author seduces the audience into what will eventually become a much darker story. The humor will be broad, perhaps even bawdy, involving slapstick and fart jokes.

• Exaggeration and surrealism. Satire creates its world by exaggerating the characters and/or setting until it's not realistic anymore. Surrealism, in which the story takes on a dreamlike quality in which the rules of the physical world are bent, is also a common tool here. The reason for both of these techniques is the theory that the audience is so locked into its world of "reality" that it refuses or is unable to see the real truth. By stripping the audience of the familiar, the author makes them more open to looking in the mirror—and finally recognizing, to use *The Matrix* metaphor—the dismal pod they are really living in.

• **Bleak ending.** The comedy of the opening scenes soon starts to spiral into a darker and darker humor until the final scene is usually one of deep despair. The level of this despair must be intense enough to want the audience to respond by either changing something about themselves so they don't end up there, or more commonly, to change something about society so we don't all end up there. For example, the ending of Jonathan Swift's novel, *Gulliver's Travels*, leaves the reader with a protagonist who is so crushed by all that he's seen that he no longer wants to leave his home or interact with other people. Or the ending of Stanley Kubrick's *Dr. Strangelove*, in which the pilot, played by Slim Pickens, rides an atomic bomb as if it were a rodeo bull as he plummets toward Moscow—which is quickly followed by the mushroom cloud and the awareness that the world is again at war.

How it works. A very funny opening seduces the audience into a world that quickly turns dark and frightening. The story must provoke enough fear and outrage to inspire the audience to change. "Good satire is correctly identified dysfunction," says Rob Sitch, director and co-writer of the Australian satiric film *The Dish.* "By pointing out dysfunction, you hope somebody will fix it up." This reflects the general Naturalistic belief that we can't look to outside supernatural help in solving our problems. We have the free will to do what we wish, but we have to see what needs to be done. Satire tries to slash through the veils of illusion we've hung between ourselves and the awful truths about ourselves.

How it works in plotting: Typical targets of satire include government, big business, the military, religion, society—pretty much anything with a vast, faceless structure that dehumanizes people. Generally, Act 1 is filled with hilarity about the ineptness and hypocrisy of the target. During this time the hero, usually an innocent, good-hearted person, is buffed about by these forces. Act 2 has the target gaining the upper hand on the protagonist, but in a much more sinister way; the stakes are raised considerably. Act 3 has the target defeating the protagonist in a way that the audience finds emotionally devastating.

Satire can also be very personal, with the target being our own foibles. For example, Bruce Jay Friedman's play *Steambath* begins with a man named Tandy, who walks into a steambath wearing a towel but is confused as to how he got there. Surreal things happen: Two men start singing and dancing to a number from the musical *Gypsy*; a woman walks in, takes off her towel and, completely naked, showers in front of all the men. Tandy realizes he's dead and that this is some sort of afterlife. He's told that God is the Puerto Rican attendant who cleans up the place. After a long period of doubting God, he finally believes and goes about trying to convince God that He made a mistake by killing Tandy. God says it's possible and lets Tandy make his case. Meanwhile, there are two other main characters: an old man who always tells stories of his exotic past, and a nerdy man who prattles on about how the movies shaped his life (and caused his death). What the audience comes to realize, after all the comedy of the opening scenes (God trying to prove he's the Supreme Being by doing simple card tricks and drinking a tray full of martinis), the story gets darker. By the last act, Tandy tells God why he should go back to his old life, that everything is just starting to get good. But what the audience comes to realize is this: The old man wasted his life by living in the past; the nerd wasted his life by living in fantasy; and Tandy has wasted his life by living for the future. Tandy represents the average person: always chasing after a goal, convinced that achieving that goal will make him happy; yet once he achieves it, he immediately sets another goal. By the end of the play, without God saying one word, Tandy has talked himself out of going back to his old life because he realizes he wasn't happy at all. Tandy is a TCH in a satire formula. This shows you how world visions can sometimes overlap.

Examples: Science-fiction often uses satire as a way to caution us about the way the world is going: If we don't change our ways, we could end up like this. Black comedy also uses a lot of satire. Satire films include *A Clockwork Orange*, *MASH*, *American*

*Beauty, Brazil, The President's Analyst* and *Being John Malkovich*; fiction includes Jonathan Swift's *Gulliver's Travels*, George Orwell's *Animal Farm* and Joseph Heller's *Catch-22.*

## THE PSYCHOLOGICAL MODEL

Psychoanalyst Sigmund Freud spent a lot of time reading fiction. In fact, he credited his study of fiction with helping him formulate his theories about human behavior. He believed writers were the best students of human conflicts and motivation, so by studying literature throughout the ages, we could better understand the patterns that we seem to follow. The simplified version of Freud's model of the psyche, shows how writers have envisioned conflicts within characters that result in the plots of their stories. Warning: The following presentation is for the study of literature only. It's not endorsed as being scientifically proven. However, Freud's theories were very influential on many of the twentieth century's greatest writers: Thomas Mann, Hermann Hesse, Ernest Hemingway, Jack London and Philip Roth, to name a few. These writers influenced other writers, and so on.

**What Were You Thinking?: How a Character's Mind Works.**
There are three parts to the mind; the interaction of these three parts is responsible for generating the conflicts within stories.

• **Superego** (a.k.a. the conscience). Everything you've ever learned from any source is stored in the filing cabinet known as the superego. Whenever you face conflict about what choice to make, the file drawer pops open and your superego declares,

"This is what you should do!" The pronouncement may come from your religion, your parents, your education, your peers, etc. In cartoons and comedies, the superego is presented as an angel on your shoulder—for what is an angel but an archetype of someone who acts out of compassion, who sacrifices self for the sake of the community? We have access to it through our memory of what we've been taught.

• **Id.** You know that terrible thought you had, the one that popped into your mind at an inappropriate time and made you wonder about whether you're some kind of sicko pervert? That carnal thought came straight from the id. The id is pure desire. When you are forced to make a decision, the id doesn't hesitate to say, "This is what I want!" You're horny? Go ahead, tell that woman you love her if it gets you what you want. She should know better anyway. Somebody makes you mad? Go ahead and hit the bastard. This is the cartoon devil that sits on your shoulder—for what is the devil but an archetype of someone who chooses his personal desires over the good of the community? Because the id resides in the unconscious, there is no conscious way to access it in order to better understand it. The only way to get in there is through dreams.

• **Ego.** How you see yourself is your ego. That's why when someone acts cocky and confident, we call him egotistical. However, the ego has a difficult life. On one shoulder sits the superego pleading for it to do one thing; on the other sits the id demanding it do the opposite. That's serious conflict. Worse, no matter what choice the ego makes, part of it will feel the choice was wrong. For example, place an apple and a slice of cheesecake in front of the ego. Choose one. If it chooses the apple, the superego will be happy: "You chose wisely. A healthy snack, low in fat and good for the heart. Your weight will not increase." But the id is saying, "What's wrong with you, moron! You love cheesecake! Who knows when you'll get the chance to eat it again! You deserve it after working so hard all day! What a wimp!" But if you choose the cheesecake, you have the opposite battle.

The key to the ego's survival is rationalization. For example, the superego says lying is wrong; the id says lying is a perfect tool to get what you want. You lie to someone, but you rationalize that it was for her own good.

Situation: The ATM gave you too much money.
Superego: Stealing is wrong.
Id: Stealing gets you what you want.
Ego: Banks are huge corporations who are always stealing from people. They won't miss it. It's not really stealing since it's not from a person. I'm still a good person.

This rationalization gives rise to the unreliable narrator that writers so often use to show characters in conflict. The challenge for such characters—indeed, what the story is usually all about—is doing away with such rationalizations so the characters can become the people they would like to be.

**The ego conflict: superego vs. id.** The ego is like a mother who constantly has to step between her battling son and husband. She is torn between loving both people and understanding both sides, but forced to stay neutral to maintain an uneasy truce. Every time she has to take a side (choose between the superego and the id), she feels bad (see "Angst" below). So the ego feels inadequate, because no matter which side it chooses—id or superego—the other side will berate it. Each time, the ego takes this bad feeling and shoves it deep down inside, where it festers.

**Angst.** A character in a story, when faced with choosing between what she wants and what she should do (especially if what she should do goes against what others tell her she should do), faces a great internal conflict that creates angst (anxiety). In tragicomedy (see page 212), when the protagonist is faced with this conflict, she folds and does what others expect her to do, or what her id tells her to do. Because choosing often generates such angst in people, we tend to avoid the responsibility of choosing by just doing what everyone expects us to do. This is following the "herd instinct." Part of us recognizes that choosing according to the herd is fatal, it kills the person we wish to become, instead making us a "Stepford" person. These bad feelings must also be shoved deep down.

**Neurosis.** Eventually, all these bad feelings will bloom into a neurosis. Don't panic, everyone has some neurosis, which is an imbalance between illusion and reality; the character sees the world one way, though the reader realizes he is not recognizing the reality of the world. [On a more extreme level, when a character loses the ability to distinguish between reality and illusion altogether, he is psychotic (psycho), like the protagonist in Brett Easton Ellis's novel *American Psycho*.] A character is out of balance when he relies too heavily on either the superego or the id to make decisions.

• **Id character.** In stories, when we see a character who is compelled by id, he is usually portrayed as a selfish person who exploits others to get what he wants. This results in others shunning him until he is friendless and alone. Examples: Bobby Dupea in *Five Easy Pieces*, Fast Eddy Felson in *The Hustler*, Sammy Glick in *What Makes Sammy Run*.

• **Superego character.** The character who is dominated by superego is no better off than the id-dominated character. He is portrayed as excessively judgmental and critical (think Dana Carvey's Church Lady character from Saturday Night Live) of others until he too is shunned and ends up alienated from the community he thinks he is protecting. Such characters often do something self-destructive involving their id, as if all that repression finally burst. If the character is meant to be loathed by the audience, he will be found in a motel room with livestock (or something equally morally compromising); if the character is more sympathetic, he may die alone or just end up alone, or he may even see the error of his ways and change. Example: Aschenbach in *Death in Venice*.

**The cure.** Characters are often in conflict because of their neuroses. They can't see their circumstances for what they really are. The core of the neurosis is the suppressed angst, which resides in the unconscious. Part of the plot of the story is having the character finally acknowledge these suppressed feelings and confront them, thereby freeing himself. The problem is that, since they are in the unconscious, the only way to them is through dreams. However, *dreams* has many meanings here. One reason we can't confront them directly is that we are so comfortable with the illusions we've created about ourselves and our lives that we refuse to recognize the reality. So it takes an alternative reality, a dreamlike event, to shake up our perception. That alternate reality could be recurring dreams, with symbolism that leads us to discover the truth about ourselves. Or it could be that the character goes on an adventure that is completely different from his usual lifestyle, especially in a foreign country, and he is able to see himself more clearly. Another alternative reality is literature itself. A character is confronted with a moving story that parallels her own conflicts, and that story helps her to better confront her own problems. For example, the structure of the film *The English Patient* is the patient telling his story to the nurse, and his story acts as a catalyst for her to make the right decisions about her own life.

The cure is the character rebalancing her world between superego and id. She is supposed to recognize that we can't be too much of either, that both are part of who we are as human beings. Passions can be regulated by the superego, but they can't be suppressed. Morality can be tempered by the id, but it can't be ignored.

**Putting it all together.** Joseph Conrad's short story "A Secret Sharer" is a clear example of how this works. Plot: The protagonist is a new captain of a ship. He's inexperienced and fears that the crew won't respect him and follow his orders. The day before the ship is to leave, he paces the deck at night alone. He sees a naked man climbing up the side of the ship. The man is described as being very similar to the captain, though not looking like him. The man tells the story of how he was on a ship in the middle of a storm and was forced to kill a man who froze in his duty in order to save the ship from sinking. However, his captain had not seen it that way and had him locked up. He escaped and now wants the protagonist to hide him. The captain hides him in his bed. When the other ship captain comes looking for the prisoner, the protagonist denies seeing him. Later, the ship begins its voyage. The captain agrees to let the prisoner escape over the side of the ship, even giving him some of his own clothes. As they approach treacherous waters where there are many shallow rocks, the prisoner slips over the side. But before he swims away, he leaves his hat behind to mark the shallow rocks. The captain, understanding what the hat means, commands his crew with confidence. They respect him and the ship moves safely through the waters.

**What it means:** The captain is afraid because he's about to leave the Realm of Light to enter the Kingdom of the Dark. He knows the rules, but he doesn't know how to command respect. The prisoner represents the id (climbing aboard naked): he's a killer and a liar; he'll do whatever is necessary to save himself. Through contact with each other, both the captain and the prisoner come away with some characteristic of the other. The captain has adopted some of the ruthless strength of the prisoner, shown in lying to the other captain and in how he commands his own crew. The prisoner has gained some of the superego qualities of the captain, shown in the fact that he does something selfless, like marking the rocks. The original *Star Trek* TV series had an episode similar to this: Captain Kirk is divided into two beings. One is good, but meek and indecisive; the other is evil and aggressive in getting what he wants. There is a crisis that requires Kirk to make a crucial command decision. However, he is unable to choose. Only when the two halves (id and superego) are reunited is he able to command.

## JOSEPH CAMPBELL'S ARCHETYPAL MODEL

Legend has it that when George Lucas was first mapping out the *Star Wars* saga, he invited an obscure literature professor to his lavish ranch to help with the plotting. This professor was Joseph Campbell, known mostly in universities for his study of patterns in myths from around the world, *The Hero With a Thousand Faces*. The success of *Star Wars* catapulted Campbell to cult status, and many beginning writers rushed out to order *Hero*, some shocked to discover the book had first been published in 1949! Since then, not only have all of his books become best-sellers (he died in 1987), but books *about* his books have been used by writers to better employ Campbell's teachings in plotting their own stories. The good news is that this has resulted in more writers attempting to write stories with more thematic depth. The bad news is that this has resulted in many writers not bothering to understand the themes, but merely including plot points the way one paints by numbers. I've read many Campbell-influenced stories in which you can picture the "Quest of the Hero" chart taped to the writer's computer screen. A photocopy of a photocopy of a . . . (See also Overly Mechanical Plots [Joseph Campbell Syndrome] on page 28.)

Campbell once said, "The latest incarnation of Oedipus, the continued romance of *Beauty and the Beast*, stands this afternoon on the corner of Forty-Second Street and Fifth Avenue, waiting for the traffic light to change." His point, and the point of his book, is that there are a limited number of patterns in telling stories. For the writer, that means that understanding those patterns helps us control our plot choices for maximum effect on the reader.

Not only are the plots similar, but certain types of characters reappear in stories throughout history. These characters are called *archetypes*. Sometimes it's difficult to distinguish between an archetype and a *stereotype*, especially when bad writers who create stereotypes defend themselves by saying, "He's an archetype; he's supposed to be familiar." The difference is that an archetype, though she will have familiar characteristics and/or behavior, will still be a compelling, rich and surprising character. The stereotype, however, will just be flat and predictable. Also, the archetype serves both a practical purpose of furthering the plot and a thematic purpose of enforcing theme. Following is an example of one archetype and how it is used in fiction:

**Type:** Ferryman

**Origin:** In Greek mythology, Charon is an underworld deity who ferries the dead in his boat across the river Styx to the realm of Hades. Because he must be paid his fare, the Greeks buried their dead with a coin in the mouth.

**Practical purpose:** To transport a character from one place to another, usually from a world that the character is familiar with and comfortable into a world that is unfamiliar and chaotic. For example, the character may go from a quiet town to New York City (*Midnight Cowboy*); from the U.S. to a foreign country (*Midnight Express*; *Brokedown Palace*); from a safe mainstream life to involvement with dangerous and/or illegal professions (*Analyze This*; *Target*).

This character can also serve the very practical purpose of educating the protagonist—and the reader—about this unfamiliar world. For example, if the story is about someone who joins the military, he will usually run into a character who is his guide to the ways of military life. All the while he's informing the protagonist of the rules and buzz words of this new world, he's also informing the reader. Or a character goes to Jamaica to search for his missing brother. As soon as he steps out of the airport, he's greeted by a gaggle of local taxi drivers who want his business. One of them manages to outdo the others to gain the protagonist's attention and business. This taxi driver will continually feed information about the local culture, customs, history, and geography in order to educate us about this "dark world." It's possible that the guide may eventually betray the protagonist, for he may also be a guardian of this world. Or he himself may die protecting the protagonist (as in Rudyard Kipling's poem *Gunga Din* and story *The Man Who Would be King*, both of which are excellent movies).

**Thematic purpose:** The ferryman takes characters from their controlled lives to a place where the characters are unable to control their environment. The purpose for this is that while we are busy scrambling to maintain the numerous minutia that makes up our daily lives, we can't see the larger picture of what our lives add up to. We have to be shaken out of our rut— exploded out of it high into the air—and while we're falling back to earth, we can see our lives, and the actions that comprise our lives, for what they really are. This experience allows us to re-evaluate our priorities and values and get our lives back on track. Or, if the character denies what he sees; the readers see, through the character's failure, a need to re-examine their lives.

**Examples:** In Thomas Mann's novella, *Death in Venice*, the protagonist, Gustav von Aschenbach, is a disciplined German writer whose work is somewhat formal and passionless. He travels to Venice for a vacation. Venice, a decaying and sinking city, represents desire and passion. So the protagonist is traveling from his disciplined and passionless world to one of passion (from superego to id, which is explained above in the Psychological Model). A ferryman, in the guise of a gondolier, takes Aschenbach from his boat to the hotel. The trip is disorienting for Aschenbach, who accuses the gondolier of taking him on a long route in order to jack up the fare. When Aschenbach threatens not to pay him, the gondolier sinisterly replies, "The signoir will pay." The reader clearly knows that the gondolier/ferryman has taken Aschenbach to a world that he will not be able to control, one that will change him forever.

The same purpose is served in the Martin Scorsese film *After Hours*. The protagonist is taken by a cabdriver/ferryman from his well-lit offices and well-organized life in upscale Manhattan, to the dark, gritty streets where he continually runs into situations and characters that he can't control.

There are many other archetypes: virginal girlfriend, prostitute with a heart of gold, wise elderly person, generous thief, etc. Two of the most common are the *Snow Maiden* (virginal girlfriend) and the *Dark Lady* (prostitute with a heart of gold).

**Type:** Snow Maiden

**Origin:** She will possess some, if not all, of the following characteristics: She comes from a cool climate (or was sent there to be raised or educated); the daughter of a wealthy family; educated; blonde and fair-skinned; religious or demonstrates clear moral values (usually exemplified by her virginity or near-virginity). She embodies all the best characteristics of civilization. Her blonde hair and fair skin symbolize coolness, meaning rational thinking (what's good for community) over mere passion (what's good for self). Think Grace Kelly.

**Practical purpose:** The Snow Maiden is the girlfriend, the one the male protagonist is chasing after. Because she is so good, it's often more difficult for him to win her heart. This contrast provides more conflict and higher stakes.

**Thematic purpose:** The Snow Maiden symbolizes all the principles the protagonist wishes to embrace. He often starts out as either a bit of a rogue or someone with a dark past. Exposure to her demonstrates that he's willing to change from someone who exploits the community to someone who contributes to the community.

**Examples:** Many Westerns use this archetype. For example, the Snow Maiden will be the daughter of a wealthy rancher. She was sent back East to be educated, and now has come home to run the ranch, teach school, and/or build a church.

**Type:** Dark Lady

**Origin:** She will possess some, if not all, of the following characteristics: She comes from a poor family in a hot climate (Mexico, Greece, Italy—usually a foreign country that represents passion); is uneducated; works in a bar or in a profession that exploits the community by preying on its desires; sensuous, often with dark hair and dark skin; and has had many lovers, usually including the protagonist. She represents passion and desire (instant gratification) over rational thinking (delayed gratification). Think Angelina Jolie.

**Practical purpose:** The Dark Lady provides temptation for the protagonist, thereby creating a major conflict. Suspense is generated because we are now unsure whether the protagonist will choose the Snow Maiden that we want him to pick, or the Dark Lady.

**Thematic purpose:** The Dark Lady symbolizes the temptation to make instant-gratification choices that satisfy our passions and desires. When we make such choices, we are alienating ourselves from the values of the community, which results in long-term unhappiness. In some stories, particularly noir and Westerns, the Dark Lady will have once been the lover of both the hero and the villain, back when they were friends rather than antagonists. She now symbolizes the dark past that the hero is trying to leave behind as he moves more toward embracing the community he once exploited.

**Examples:** Marlene Dietrich in *Destry Rides Again* and Katy Jurado in *High Noon* exemplify the Dark Lady. They are foreign, sensuous, sexually experienced, run saloons, and want to see the heroes dead. Both are girlfriends of the villains, but eventually are won over to the side of goodness by the heroes.

**How archetypes work.** The reason writers use archetypes—most of which in Western literature are modeled after characters in Greek and Roman mythology—is to let the readers know that the story is not just about the plot conflicts—it's also about certain themes. The familiar characteristics of the Dark Lady and Snow Maiden signal the readers, in a shorthand way, that the turmoil the protagonist goes through isn't just a superficial decision about which woman he should choose; rather, it's about which values he should choose.

**Quest of the hero in a nutshell.** If you want to know all the details of Campbell's model, read *The Hero With a Thousand Faces*—it's only a couple hundred pages. Or you could read Chris Vogel's presentation of Campbell's principles in *A Writer's Journey*. In the meantime, I'm going to present a stripped-down version of Campbell's teachings that gives you the basic idea of what he's saying. Campbell aficionados beware: I have changed some of his terms and phrases to make it easier to follow.

**Writers like books with charts and writing recipes because they can then tack them to their bulletin boards and follow the structure provided. It feels like writing, but a lot less stressful because you don't have to make as many decisions.**

These models are meant to help you ask the right questions about your story and characters. They help you figure out what it is you want to say and give you some guidelines for how to say it. Blindly following any pattern without tailoring and enhancing it to suit the needs of your particular story produces bland, lifeless stories that may have great meaning but lack any energy and freshness that make us want to read them in the first place. The message is useless if we don't pay attention to the messenger.

**Two worlds.** Stories generally involve a protagonist who faces a conflict that takes her from the world she is familiar with to one she is not.

**1. Realm of Light.** This is where the story usually starts, in the world the protagonist is familiar with. It could be her home, her neighborhood, her job. It could also be more general, such as her country or even land vs water. **Symbolism:** This represents the superego, the world of rules and order. This is our perception of the world, of ourselves. **How it works:** The protagonist will be forced to go from the life she is familiar with—and over which she believes she has some control—to a world over which she seems to have no control.

**2. Kingdom of Dark.** This is where much of the story takes place. It could be a foreign country, a cruise, a different job, an unfamil-

Joseph Campbell's "Quest of the Hero"

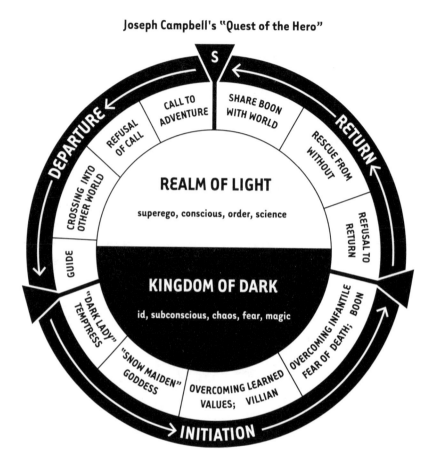

iar neighborhood. The point is to place the protagonist in a setting in which everything they know is useless, making them vulnerable. The fish-out-of-water story is a typical example. A hick in the big city (*Coogan's Bluff, The Beverly Hillbillies*), a city boy among hicks (*Deliverance, Doc Hollywood*). **Symbolism:** This is the id, the world of passion and chaos. Here characters are exposed to temptations they have avoided or suppressed, such as the protagonists in *Death in Venice* and *The Blue Angel*. **How it works:** Once exposed to the passions of the Id, the characters no longer act in the predictable way they did before; they now indulge in the temptation, thereby getting in touch with that sensual side they've repressed. Ironically, the character is exposed to this alternative reality of chaos and uncontrolled passions in order to better see his world so that he can restore order to it.

**Three-act plot structure.** The two worlds are incorporated into a traditional three-act plot structure: Act 1: Departure, Act 2: Initiation and Act 3: Return.

**1. Departure.** The protagonist receives a *Call to Adventure*. This can be very direct: "There are a bunch of terrorists holding schoolchildren hostage. You're the only guy who can handle the situation. You need to come out of retirement and take them on." Or it can be more subtle: a first date, a parent or child coming to visit, a job offer. Anything that will shake up or alter the world you live in. However, at first the protagonist usually *refuses the call.* He will say, "I'm too old for this shit," and slam the door. Or she'll refuse the job offer, turn down the date, etc. There are two reasons for this:

1. Increase suspense. The reader knows that the character will eventually accept, otherwise there's no story. The suspense is now focused on what will cause him to change his mind.
2. Establish personal conflict. Whatever the reason she refuses, it is related to her personal demons. This reveals more about the character and increases the stakes. Finally, the character accepts the call to adventure and heads straight for the Kingdom of Dark.

**2. Initiation.** Here is where the protagonist endures a *Road of Trials.* These trials are the plot conflicts and complications that occur in a story to keep the character from achieving whatever goal he has set out to accomplish. The character's goal is the *boon.* The boon is what he thinks he wants (the golden fleece, a cure for cancer, the Ark of the Covenant, etc.), but it's not necessarily what he eventually gets or what's best for him. Along the way, he has to confront a series of archetypes, including the supernatural guide (ferryman), snow maiden, dark lady, villain, etc. Remember that the purpose of the archetypes is to provide challenges for the protagonist to overcome. The ferryman may be a true friend and help the protagonist, or he may betray him. The snow maiden may be a true lover, but she's also a temptation to stay in this world and forget about the boon. So is the dark lady.

**About the villain.** The villain is out to destroy the protagonist. The psychological take on the villain is that he represents the father. Before you sigh and roll your eyes, take a closer look: The father is the figure that the son attempts to emulate. The father teaches the son what is right and wrong and how to behave. But at some point, if he is to become his own person, the son will have to choose for himself what is right and wrong. Otherwise, he will always be a clone of his father. So he must slay the father (symbolically), overcoming the villain who is trying to kill him (prevent him from being his own person). In some stories, the protagonist comes to understand that the villains in his life aren't villains at all, but are antagonists only because he's projected that onto them.

**About the boon.** Although the protagonist may very well find the original boon, the story is really concerned with the *Ultimate Boon*. The original boon is the misdirection; what the story hopes the protagonist discovers is a more mature vision of the cycle of life. The Road of Trials is an opportunity for the protagonist to demonstrate courage, because that is what is needed to face life and see each decision for what it is: another step in creating yourself, in becoming the person you want to be. Rationalization and justification are techniques we use to delude ourselves so that we can avoid choosing what we know is right in favor of what might benefit us materially (see bad faith in Tragicomedy on page 212). The ultimate boon is the ability to recognize the temporary world of things of the flesh so that we can embrace and live by things of the spirit. This would be true whether or not you believe in an afterlife. In fact, the ultimate boon is that the character overcomes his infantile fear of mortality. That means he loses his fear of death, which is an obsession with the material world, and accepts that death is part of the cycle. And because it is an inevitable part, we should emphasize more spiritual, and less temporary, aspects of our lives, such as moral choices that benefit community over selves.

**3. Return.** Once the protagonist achieves the boon, he now faces the return to the Realm of Light, his old familiar world. Sometimes he doesn't want to come back (*Refusal of the Return*). He comes to love the alternate reality because it is seductive. Someone might have to come from the outside (*Rescue From Without*) to rescue him (Marlow coming after Kurtz in Joseph Conrad's "Heart of Darkness"). The character might return home with the material boon only to tell everyone about the ultimate boon. Sometimes the people back home don't want their perceptions changed and they may kill the protagonist (savior stories such as that of Jesus Christ). Or they may hail him as a hero. However the return, whatever the reception, the protagonist is now *Master of Two Worlds* in that he accepts both the superego and id and lives a life balancing the two rather than suppressing one.

 **Physical Therapy**

Pick your three favorite stories. First, determine exactly where you think the departure, initiation, and return begin and end. Second, locate some of the characteristics of each (call to adventure, refusal of the call, etc.). Third, identify specific archetypes. Now, do the same with one of your stories. If you are able to do this, you should be able to answer the critical thematic questions:

- Why did the events in your story take place?
- How are the characters changed by what they went through?
- What insight into the situation does the reader gain as a result of experiencing your plot?

# CHAPTER SIX

# The Writer's Life

## FAQs Frequently Asked Questions

? How can I find more time to write? see below
? How can I tell if what I'm writing is good? page 238
? How much outlining do I have to do? page 241
? How can I get the most out of a writing workshop? page 246
? What is the best way to revise my manuscript? page 255
? How can I improve my own writing by reading fiction? page 278

### Q: HOW CAN I FIND MORE TIME TO WRITE?

Those of you brave and foolish enough to take up writing sometimes don't realize that you will also have to take up juggling: your job, family, friends, recreation—and writing. It's not easy. I've seen many exceptionally talented writers from my workshops grow weary of the balancing act and give up writing altogether. In fact, the question I hear most often at workshops and conferences is the desperate plea of "How do I find time to write?" Fortunately, there is a simple and painless solution.

### Why Writers Don't Write

Even professional writers sometimes use little tricks and rationalizations to delay their daily writing: cleaning the desk, organizing CDs, watching videos, teaching the parakeet to say "Call me Ishmael." But eventually they get down to the business of writing with fierce dedication and discipline.

But when delays turn from a few minutes into a few weeks, even months, then you've got a serious problem. The two most common reasons writers don't write are that they don't love writing and life demands interfere with their efforts.

1. They don't love writing. They like being thought of as a writer, but they don't want to be bothered with the perfection of their craft. Such a person will eventually fixate on something else that sounds romantic, say photography or smelt fishing. If you've read this far, you obviously are passionate about writing, so that doesn't pertain to you.

2. Life demands. People are always saying, "Get a life." Well, you've got one, baby, and it's riding you hard and putting you away wet. It seems like every Sunday night, just as you jot down the new week's to do list, you wonder, "Where did the week go? I had every intention of writing." Perhaps you even have one of those books, *Getting Organized for Idiotically Dumb Morons*— you know it's somewhere, you just can't remember where. And no doubt you're sick of hearing stories from other writers who claim to get up at 3 A.M. every day to work on their novels. You're the person this section can help.

## The Zen of Scheduling

Novelist Anne Tyler (quoting novelist Reynolds Price) once told an interviewer that she had these words of wisdom for aspiring novelists: "Creative inspiration is like a small child; it loves routine." Accept this fact: *There's no way to do this without some form of scheduling.* Yes, you've probably read about some successful first-time novelist who wrote only when the muse entered his body and he jumped down, spun around, typed a page of prose. That may be how he remembers it, but it's highly unlikely that's what really happened. More likely the writer would hit the typical roadblocks of writing, struggle daily with how to proceed, then have a breakthrough moment and leap back to work.

When I first started out as a writer, I too wrote only when I felt inspired. I thought that was how "real writers" wrote. Any kind of a schedule seemed artificial, as if I were tampering with the universal creative spirits. Plus I'm lazy. However, when I sold my first novel and was suddenly under contract for three more, I realized I didn't have the luxury of waiting for that poky muse to drop by. So I fashioned a daily schedule of writing in defiance of my artistic philosophy and toiled away at the same time every day. Here's what happened: I became a better writer. A much better writer. I quickly discovered that forcing myself to write every day meant that I had to actually *have something to write about.* Therefore, instead of thinking about my story and characters only when I sat down to write, I had to think about them when I wasn't writing. This resulted in more cohesive and clever plots, more richly developed characters and more polished prose style. I also discovered that I do my best work when I don't feel like writing because that's when I'm most critical.

Business gurus will tell you that the most important factor in achieving success is showing up for work. The writing guru's variation is put your butt in a chair. When novelist Jonathan Lethem (*Motherless Brooklyn*) was asked for the best advice he ever received, he answered, "Work every day." Colson Whitehead (*The Intuitionist*) responded to the same question, "My friend, the poet Kevin Young, always says, 'Get off your ass and do it.' By whatever means necessary, get to work." To become a good writer, it is more important how frequently you write than how many hours you put in. For example, it is better to write three times a week, two hours each day than it is to write four hours every Saturday and Sunday. Even though you're putting in two fewer hours, you'll probably produce more and better pages. The three benefits of this are planning, pressure and practice.

**1. Planning.** The most difficult part of writing is not the writing or polishing. It's the planning. What should happen next? Should I set this scene in a restaurant or in the kitchen? Why would she leave him? By having a consistent schedule of writing, you give yourself time between writing sessions to think about what you're going to write.

**2. Pressure.** Writing for long blocks once or twice a week creates too much pressure to produce. It's inevitable that sometimes you will get stuck and have to fidget and sweat your way through some writing sessions, perhaps walk away on occasion. If you write only once or twice a week, a mini-block can mean you don't write again for two weeks, thereby losing track of your story. But if you have a regular schedule, you know that no matter what happens today, whether you write three pages or one sentence, you'll be back tomorrow. Or the next day. That reduces a lot of pressure.

**3. Practice.** To become a better writer, you need to continually practice and hone your skills. Think of it as a sport: To improve your golf or tennis game, it's not enough to go out once a week. Repetition trains the muscle memory.

## Scheduling for the Scheduling Impaired

There are two basic methods of scheduling, each suited for different personality types. Both are equally effective, so choose the one that best suits you.

The *gridlock method* involves a rigid schedule of writing that you adhere to diligently. Follow these steps:

**1. Complete the scheduling grid.** Using the accompanying grid, fill in every hour that you have a commitment. Don't hold back. Include everything that you routinely must do and like to do, including job, family time, meals, favorite TV programs, sleep, sports, etc.

**2. Schedule writing.** Look at the empty blocks on the grid. Fill in the blocks where you are *positive* you can write. The best schedule will include at least two-hour blocks, at least three days a week. The reason for the two-hour blocks is that it can often take twenty minutes or more to get a writing rhythm going. You may have to reread some of your previous writing or endure a few false starts. With only an hour, you may just be into the swing of the story when you have to rush off. On the other hand, be realistic. Don't overbook your writing schedule to such a degree that you're bound to fail. Limit it to three to five days a week, two to three hours a session.

**3. Prioritize.** If you can't find a reasonable number of hours in your week, reexamine your priorities. Go back over your

schedule of obligation hours and assign each one a priority number of either
1. Must Do: job, family, sleep, exercise, etc. or
2. Like to Do: Monday Night Football, cooking class, mall shopping, etc. Are there any two's that might be drafted to your writing schedule? (If not, you should skip ahead to the next method of scheduling.)

**4. Engage.** Once you have a workable schedule, commit to sticking with it for a month. Announce to everyone that this is your writing time, and be sure they realize it's sacred. Many beginning writers feel so guilty about their writing time (after all, you're not making money; you're taking time away from the family, etc.) that they sabotage their own schedule. Don't do it. If you need to run errands or walk the dog, put that in your schedule, but *do not sacrifice your writing time.* You must show others that you take your writing time seriously so they too will take it seriously. Do not answer the phone unless it's an emergency. People will call up and ask, "What are you doing?" If you say "writing," they say, "Good, I'm not interrupting anything" and keep yammering.

Those who prefer a more flexible schedule should try the *spare-change method.* Rather than filling out a grid and adhering to a set writing schedule, this establishes goals for each day and week. It's still important that you write as many days of the week as possible for all the reasons outlined above, but here you are free to choose what times of day you will write. How will you find this time? The same way you find spare change when you need a few coins to do the laundry or tip the pizza delivery person: search the sofas, empty pockets, go through dirty laundry. You look for minutes to write, and it all adds up to hours.

With the spare-change method, your goal is not putting in a certain amount of time (as with the gridlock method); rather your goal is producing a specific number of pages each day you write. All that matters is that you complete that number of pages each day, no matter when, where or how you do it. This method works best with the kind of writer who doesn't require quiet and solitude or a lot of warming up. She is able to sit down and begin working as soon as the opportunity arises, accept interruptions without being affected and resume writing hours later as if nothing happened. (This is also best for those who don't require a lot of sleep.) Here's how to implement it:

**1. Goal.** Decide whether you are going to adhere to a daily or weekly goal. A daily goal means that every day you write, you expect to complete a specific amount—for example, two pages. A weekly goal doesn't rely on daily production, nor does it require that you write the same days each week. All it requires is that at the end of the week, you have achieved the number of pages you've promised yourself.

**2. Schedule.** Take a calendar and write the page number you expect to be on at the end of each week. For example, the Sunday after you start this regimen, write "page five" (or three, ten, twelve—whatever you decide). On the following Sunday, write "page ten." Keep marking the calendar until you've reached the number of pages you think this story will be. (Don't worry that you aren't certain or that the length may change as you write. The point is to establish a goal, a rough estimate, and work toward it.) You do not go to bed that Sunday night until those five pages are complete.

**3. Polished.** Polished prose means that by the end of the week, it's no longer a rough draft. It's very close to how you imagine the final version will read. To accomplish this, you should carry hard copies of the pages with you at all times. Whenever you have a few minutes, pull them out and start reading the pages—with pen in hand. Mark the pages, make notes in the margins, replace words. As soon as you can, type in the changes and start carrying the new pages with you. Rinse and repeat.

The most challenging obstacle to becoming a successful writer is not the competition from the hordes of laptopped workshop rats, the whimsy of erratic editors or the uncertainty of the marketplace. It's actually finishing your book, script or story. This should help you do just that.

## Q: HOW CAN I TELL IF WHAT I'M WRITING IS GOOD?

*"I am profoundly uncertain about how to write.
I know what I love or what I like, because it's
a direct, passionate response. But when I write,
I'm very uncertain whether it's good enough.
That is, of course, the writer's agony."*

SUSAN SONTAG

I've never known a writer who did not express grave doubts about his or her ability. Even successful and acclaimed writers wonder: Am I any good? Most of them secretly harbor a wish for some sort of supernatural machine, the repository for the world's greatest writing, an arbiter of its highest level of literary taste, in which you could deposit your manuscript and five minutes later it would spit the pages back out with "genius!" or "stinks!" stamped across it.

The difference between the novice and the professional writer is that the pro knows these doubts are merely an occupational hazard, like stage fright for an actor. Do not see it as a hazard to be overcome but rather a companion that constantly challenges you to become better. Without that anxiety, we might settle for less than our best. Here are four tips to help you determine if what you're writing is any good.

### Tip #1: Set the Standard

Before you can decide whether your writing is any good, you need to establish your standard. If you're wondering if you're as good as Shakespeare or Melville, the answer is, "Probably not." But neither are some of our greatest writers. One of my favorite novels is Budd Schulberg's *What Makes Sammy Run?* Is it as good as *King Lear*? No. But it is a brilliant, compelling work with memorable characters and thematic depth. I doubt Schulberg said, "Either I write as well as Faulkner, or I don't write at all." More likely, he might have said, "Either I write to the best of my ability, or I don't write at all."

First, make a list of your favorite authors, the ones whose writing you most would like to emulate. If Tolstoy is one of them, then go for it; you might very well be the next Tolstoy. But if you're writing genre fiction—mysteries, science fiction, romances—then include at least three authors on that list who write within your genre. Keep stacks of works by these authors on your writing desk (you'll see why in tip #2).

Second, be honest with yourself. This needs to be filled with people you are currently reading. If you love Danielle Steel, then put her on the list. Putting Charles Dickens on the list won't help you if the last time you read his work was in high school. Who would you rush home to read?

Third, make an informal list of what exactly you like about these writers. If it's plot, then write out a brief synopsis of several of your favorite plots. If it's style, mark passages in the books that exemplify that style. And so forth. This will become your writer's bible, to which you can add new authors and works any time. Keeping this list in mind as you read your own work will help to make sure your own work exhibits the characteristics that draw you to your favorite authors.

## Tip #2: Read for Comparison

First, place your own manuscript, partial or completed, on your desk. Next, begin reading one of the authors on your list. As soon as you come across something you like in her story, *stop reading*. Now begin to read your own manuscript. Do you see any differences? If so, specify them in writing. For example, your favorite author uses more poetic descriptive language. Or her dialogue is shorter and punchier.

Go back and forth between your favorite authors and your own writing. It's important that you don't keep reading the books on your list until you've finished them. This is not for your reading enjoyment; it's for your writing improvement. Read those authors only in small sections as a means of comparison with your own work.

Don't take the list of differences as gospel. Perhaps you are developing a style that is different from those of your favorite writers. You may admire another writer's descriptive language, but you have no desire to write like that. This, too, is valuable information that will help you gain confidence in your own unique writing skills. Decide which items on this list are ones you'd like to change and which are merely examples of your own budding style.

239

### Tip #3: Mining for Gold

There's a rule of thumb in sitcom writing that you must have three laughs per page. Some TV critics might say that rule is ignored more than it's practiced, but it's still a good idea to have such rules of thumb. Decide what your goal is, then read through your manuscript to see if you've lived up to it. My goal is to find one "good moment" per page. That moment might be a metaphor, a descriptive phrase, a dialogue exchange. But if I can find one shining moment per page, I am pleased. If I find more, I'm delighted— and usually surprised.

The more you reread your work, the less enamored you are over each word. I often carry pages of my manuscript with me all day so that any time I get a few minutes, I can reread them and continually polish. After a while, I'm a much more objective critic and can more easily separate the wheat from the chaff.

### Tip #4: The Outside World

Nobel Laureate Jean-Paul Sartre once said, "Hell is other people." While this may be true in one's daily life, for writers, especially beginners, "*Help* is other people." The good writer needs good critics. Most professional writers have other professional writers they give their work to for criticism. To do so is not just an acknowledgment of doubt in one's ability, it is an announcement of desire to be a better writer.

First, you need to choose who this select group of critics will be. (It's better to have more than one for comparison's sake.) The best critics will be those who are also writers, usually in a class or in a private workshop. It's fine to give your manuscript to nonwriter loved ones, but there's a downside. Because they aren't also writers, you tend to respect their opinions less. If they love it, you still have doubts. If they hate it (and are courageous enough to admit it), you resent the input. You smile, but you're thinking, "What do they know about writing?" Either way, you're putting a strain on your relationships. Give it to them only if you have other, more skilled critics to share with. That way you can appreciate your loved ones' opinions for what they are: sincere efforts to help.

Local community colleges usually offer a variety of creative writing courses. If possible, contact the professor to ask if her particular class includes the critiquing of student manuscripts in a workshop atmosphere. If not, seek out a writer's group that you might join. Don't be afraid to sit in for a couple sessions and then move on if you don't like it. It's crucial that you respect the people in the workshop.

Second, be realistic about criticism. Even professionals disagree about the quality of manuscripts. I've had conflicting editorial advice about the same work from major publishing houses. I even had a novel rejected by one house, only to have the same house accept the same manuscript six months later when it was submitted to a different editor. Only you know what you intend to accomplish; the critic judges what he perceives. Sometimes even the best critics are wrong. However, if you start to get a lot of similar comments ("I don't like the protagonist"), then you should start taking them seriously.

### As Good as It Gets

No one said writing was going to be easy. In fact, most experienced writers warn you how difficult it is. Novelist Henry James joined that chorus of warnings when he remarked, "We work in the dark—we do what we can do—we give what we have. Our doubt is our passion and our passion is our task. The rest is the madness of art." That just means that, despite all our doubts, we'd do it anyway because we love it. So if you're going to do it anyway, why not get better at it—and maybe even get paid for it?

## Q: HOW MUCH OUTLINING DO I HAVE TO DO?

Some writers prepare detailed outlines of their novels before they start. They know everything that will happen from the moment the hero pulls out his gun on the first page until he kisses the love interest 358 pages later. For example, when Edgar nominee Robert Irvine once spoke to my writing class about outlining, he brought with him a typical outline that he uses when writing a novel. It was seventy pages long! It included dialogue, character sketches, chapter-by-chapter breakdowns—just about everything but what to eat while writing the book. On the other hand, when novelist Ross Thomas spoke to my class, he claimed that he never started with an outline, that it took away the thrill of discovery. When his protagonist walked into a room, Ross told us, he wanted to be looking over his shoulder, just as surprised as his character.

### The Slap-Dash Outline

I fall somewhere between. I use what I call a slap-dash outline, one that describes only the chapters immediately ahead of me. This allows me to maintain the spontaneity of discovery, yet provides a compass that points me in the general direction I need to go.

**How it works:** When I write my first chapter, I often have no idea what the novel is about. And for the next chapters, I avoid thinking too much about what will happen down the road in the novel. Technically, the beginning of a novel should establish tone, character and plot. But let's face reality: The *true* purpose of the novel's opening is to grab the readers by the throat and not let go until they are compelled to find out what happens next. So when I start a novel, I'm thinking only about writing a novel that does that—to me. It must interest me so intensely that I'll want to write the rest of the novel just to discover what happens next. If it works on me, then I know the rest of the readers will also be satisfied.

However, if I plan it out too specifically at the beginning, if I know too much about where the novel is going, I might try to get fancy with the opening, do things that are stylistically satisfying but not grabbing. You must keep alive the sense of adventure a reader feels when opening a novel. Remember, if the readers aren't compelled by the first chapter, they will never reach those other gems you're waiting to spring on them.

Once you've written that riveting opening chapter or two, you will need to create some kind of outline. Many writers already know the ending of their books before they start writing the first word. They may not exactly know how they're going to get there, but they know the general destination. Will the protagonist survive? Will the couple get together? Will the ending be happy or sad? Outlines are just road maps to these destinations. For me, the slap-dash outline is road map enough because it encourages my curiosity, which helps me intensify the suspense, yet still lets me know enough about where I'm going not to panic.

## Scribbling Toward Bethlehem: What and When to Outline

First, neatness doesn't count. The slap-dash is so named because you're not looking for a formal outline with a lot of letters and numbers and subheadings. That's daunting and either discourages you from outlining or encourages you to over-outline. Second, for the first third to half of a novel, you can *limit your outlining to three or four chapters* ahead of where you are. This is enough to keep you from getting stuck, but not enough to kill the momentum or the freshness of your writing.

Here's an example of the slap-dash outline I used while writing my suspense novel *Masked Dog*.

Chap. 8

[ Lisa R ]
- talks w/ Alexei
- her background
- wants to see Price

Chap. 9

[ Dees ]
- talks w/ Hesse

[ Devane ]
- going after Hesse
>> Hesse killed (?) <<

Chap. 10

[ Price ]
- w/ Trinidad & Rebecca
- "sees" Lisa R
- cigarette scene

Chap 11

[ Rawlings / Dees ]
- R. chews out D.
(maybe R knew about
D secretly withdrawing
so; put somebody on
Price; Price spots Lisa R)

Chap 12

[ Devane ]
- waits for Price / Reb. /
Trin. to leave apartment
- remembers Price's
smoking habits
- poison planted

Chap. 13

[ Jo / Price ]
- she's back ((crush is
out w/ agents)
- tells of murder
- sex scene

At first glance these notes look like the drug-induced scribblings of someone who claims frequent sightings of UFOs, but they make sense to me. Here's what it means:

- **Bracketed names.** The names of the characters in brackets (Lisa R, Dees, Price, etc.) under each chapter are the POV characters.
- **Action.** Identifying which scenes will have action helps me gauge the pacing. If I know where a major action scene is, I know where I need to place chapters that might create more suspense before the action scene or where to place a nonaction emotional scene.
- **Dashes with ingredients.** The dashes followed by an activity ("—talks w/ Alexei") or a direction ("—her background") indicate the key ingredients of the chapter. These things must happen here. However, you'll notice under chapter nine I have double arrows and a question mark (>>Hesse killed(?)<<). I wasn't sure if he would be killed. I just wanted it there as a possibility; the arrows indicate that this was important and required some hard thinking.
- **Rearranging chapters.** Notice the arrow indicating that I should move chapter ten to before chapter nine. Once I'd jotted this outline down, I could see that it had been too long since we'd been in the protagonist's POV.

Although this is the outline I used, some of the final chapters are quite different from what the outline reveals. As I was writing them, I could see I needed to add a chapter or move a chapter or even combine chapters. But the outline served its purpose in forcing me to see the larger picture. I was able to see the shape of the book's next few chapters as I wrote, building and adding texture because I knew what was coming up.

The further along you get in your novel, the more detailed your slap-dash outline will become. For the first half of a book, you might only need a few lines under each chapter heading, such as the example above. However, as the novel becomes more complex, with all the subplots coming together, you may need to write much more under each heading. Also, you may need to outline more than a few chapters in advance. In fact, there will be a definite point, usually around two-thirds of the way through, where you'll have to outline the rest of the novel. Again, you may not stick to the order or even the events you outline, but you'll at least know the basic elements that need to be in the novel.

## The After-the-Fact Outline

Even with the slap-dash outline, once chapters or scenes are written, a more formal outlining procedure will help you keep an overview of where you've been so you better know where you're going. For this outline I use notecards, with each notecard representing a chapter. It looks like this:

```
chapter:      10
pov:          Nick
major action: • Nick follows Tina.
              • Tina goes to tattoo parlor.
              • Nick phones Buzz.
key info:     Tina has birthmark on rt. shoulder, looks like profile
              of Hitchcock.
pages:        122-130
no. of pages: 9
```

The first three entries are self-explanatory. The "key info" entry tells me if there's anything revealed that I'll need to bring up later. The last two entries help me with the structure and rhythm of the novel. "Pages" tells me where in the novel the chapter takes place so I can see if certain events come too soon or too late. The "no. of pages" informs me of how long the chapter is, which lets me know if there's room to expand if I'm looking to place an additional scene somewhere. Once you place these notecards on the bulletin board, you may see that chapters can be moved. For example, you might have three twenty-five-page chapters in a row, all intense emotional scenes. You might decide to move a short, comic scene between two of them to heighten the emotional impact rather than have all three chapters overwhelm the reader.

## Q: HOW CAN I GET THE MOST OUT OF A WRITING WORKSHOP?

What do frozen giblets, worker bees and writing workshops have in common? They each have a life span of about three to six months. There's not much we can do about the giblets (those who eat gizzards pretty much get what they deserve) or worker bees (who at least outlive the male drones by a few months). But there's no reason why a group of amateur writers gathering to help each other become better writers cannot continue to thrive and offer crucial support for many years. They just need to follow a few simple guidelines.

### Are Workshops Necessary?

"Hey, if you're a writer, you just *write*," some hopeful best-selling author might argue. "Who needs a workshop? Just a bunch of wannabes sitting around yammering."

I've been teaching writing workshops at a community college for twenty years. I teach novel workshops, poetry workshops, short story workshops and scriptwriting workshops. I also run an annual writing retreat in Palm Springs, California, that involves a solid week of writing with nightly workshops. As a graduate student in creative writing, I also attended my share of workshops. So I've seen it from both sides: as the omnipotent leader who critiques manuscripts from behind a burning bush and as the quivering writer behind a too-tight desk in a too-hot room with the nearest bathroom too far away. And I'm here to tell you that the writing workshop is one of the most valuable tools a writer has. I can't tell you how many workshop students have come up to me and said, "If only I'd taken this workshop earlier I would have saved myself a couple years of writing around in circles."

I don't flatter myself that they mean my workshop specifically. Any good workshop would do, whether through a community college or even a private workshop organized by like-minded writers seeking honest feedback about their work.

Many of my students repeat my workshops many times. Sometimes for years. They may finish one novel and come back to work on another. Currently in my novel workshop I have a man who in the last year has published a novel and five short stories.

In my script workshop I have a writer/director whose first movie (written in my workshop a few years ago) has been picked up for distribution after he won the best director award at the Los Angles International Film Festival. They return because they find working with an audience of readers helps them hone their craft better. It makes them aware that at some point, someone will be sitting all alone in a room reading their work.

Here's a little secret of my own: Although I never submit my own work to class, the workshop continuously helps me become a better writer. I have published over thirty-five books, fiction and nonfiction, but I come away from every workshop inspired about my own work. Sometimes a student's manuscript will contain a phrase, a description or an exchange of dialogue so good that I can't wait to go back over my own manuscript to make it better. Or I will read a passage that contains flat characterization, clichés or a predictable plot and I will hurry home to rewrite my own to make sure it doesn't have those same flaws.

### What Do You Get from a Writers Workshop?

A good writers group will provide three crucial benefits:

• **Feedback.** You learn how to read your own work and discover not only what needs to be changed, but how to change it. It's no easier judging your own work ("Is this character sympathetic enough?") than it is judging your own looks ("Do I look fat in these pants?"). We all need someone outside the world we've created to look at it and make sure others will see on the page what we're seeing in our heads. Many professional best-selling writers still use workshops, though their workshops usually consist of three or four close friends and fellow writers.

• **Discipline.** Most writers are prolific in their minds, creating many masterpieces. But when it comes to the actual writing, we are one lazy bunch. A writing group is like a literary chain gang, forcing each member to stay on a schedule of writing so he has something to submit when it's his turn to be critiqued.

• **Competition.** The competitive atmosphere in a writing group is helpful, the same as on a sports team. Seeing the person next to you turning in ten great pages makes you want to do the same. Reading a powerful passage by another writer in the group is different than reading a powerful passage in a published book. You feel that if the person sitting next to you can write that well, so can you. With a little work.

### Starting Your Own Writers Workshop

Writing workshops are fairly easy to start. Because my classes often contain thirty or more students, I encourage the better, more disciplined writers to start their own groups of five or six students. This allows each of their manuscripts to receive more personal attention much more often than they would get in my larger workshop. So, if you want to start your own, attend a writing class, meet students whose work you respect and whose personalities complement yours and invite them over to form a group. It's often that simple.

There are other ways as well: Post a notice asking for interested writers to show up at a coffeehouse or restaurant to discuss forming a group (it's better not to have any meetings with strangers in your home). Such notices can be posted in your apartment building, housing complex, school, coffee house, athletic club or church. You'd be surprised at how many secret writers there are out there eager for an excuse to show their work to others.

Starting a group is the easy part. Maintaining it is the hard part. Just like any relationship.

### What Goes Wrong: The Symptoms

Writing workshops often have a short life span, despite the best intentions and oaths of loyalty sworn by the participants at the group's inception. I have been called in as a consultant to many such groups that were once healthy, vibrant gatherings, but are now gasping on their deathbeds. They want me to heal them. Fortunately, there is a cure, but first you have to diagnose what is wrong with your particular group. Let's look at the two major symptoms.

**1. Hostility.** (Usually manifested by clenched teeth and deep sighs during meetings and muttering to oneself on the drive home after each meeting.) The participants start fighting amongst themselves, either outright or in their heads. They don't respect the comments of some of the group members who may seem too harsh or completely off base. For example, if you write science-fiction and no one in the group reads science-fiction, their comments will ultimately seem useless. Sure, they could comment on general things such as characterization or style, but other comments may seem damaging to your work because of their ignorance of the genre.

**2. Lack of focus.** (Usually manifested by a few people talking all the time, often using the manuscripts as an excuse to discuss their opinions about the world and their own lives.) This occurs when there are significantly different levels of writing ability in the group and/or different levels of commitment to writing. If most of the people are serious about their work and are striving to improve toward some ultimate goal of publishing, then having two or three members who consider writing a hobby or an excuse to meet other people (on a par with golf or quilting), can really demoralize everyone. This has nothing to do with how nice a person is: A very sweet and kind person can unknowingly kill off a promising writing group.

The result of these two symptoms is that the writers soon write less and don't show up at the meetings as often. Other things start to take priority, and pretty soon they've stopped writing altogether.

**The Cure**
The more organized a group is, the better its chances of survival. The following is a good place to start:

• **Scheduled meetings.** Regularly scheduled meetings are crucial. Avoid the free-floating "Let's call each other later in the month and set up the meeting" syndrome. This wastes time and makes the group seem too casual. Meetings can be used as goals ("I will have twenty pages to turn in by the next meeting.") But irregular meetings are like an irregular diet or exercise plan— self-defeating.

• **Regular attendance.** Participants need to commit to the group. Those who continually miss meetings need to be replaced. Such a cavalier attitude can become contagious, and soon everyone is skipping meetings until they have to be cancelled altogether. It may be difficult, but pull the offenders aside as soon as they start missing and say, "I realize you have a busy schedule, as we all do, so maybe you should rejoin us when things slow down for you."

• **Writing level of members.** Some groups have prospective members submit a writing sample before accepting them into the group. Some also have prospective members sit in on a critiquing session first, to hear what kind of insights and comments they might offer. This does help to eliminate the person who simply likes everything or loathes everything but can't articulate why.

• **Leader.** Select a leader who is responsible for running the meetings. This leadership can change at each meeting or it can be one person each time. But meetings go much more smoothly and efficiently when one person is able to keep the discussions focused and cut off digressions. For example, in my workshops when someone starts going off about "That plane couldn't have landed there because that model wasn't built until 1914 and . . ." I give the T sign with my hands meaning "technical info." It's great to have expert help from the group, but such technical information can be jotted down on the manuscript for the author to research or chat with the expert after our meeting. Entire meetings can be swallowed whole by digressions like this.

• **Read manuscripts before arriving.** Some groups have their members read their manuscripts aloud to the group after which the group critiques what they've just heard. This is a bad idea. True, you do get the rhythm of the words, which is especially helpful with poetry. But your target audience will be *reading* your work, starting with agents and editors. Seeing the words on the page is much more helpful to your group than hearing them. Manuscripts that are going to be critiqued should be handed out at the previous meeting, giving the members plenty of time to read the words. They should then write directly on their copies any praise or suggestions for improvement. A cover sheet should be attached to the front of the manuscript. Each member should summarize her reactions on this sheet. When the group begins to discuss a particular manuscript, the leader should ask only for general comments as summarized on the cover sheet. After everyone has given their reactions, begin a page-by-page analysis.

Leader: "Anyone wish to comment on page one?"
Bill: "I liked the opening paragraph. It hooked me immediately and made me care about what was happening to the narrator."
Susan: "I agree. But this metaphor in the third paragraph needs to be polished. It's a bit confusing."
Leader: "Anyone agree or disagree?"
Jim: "Yeah, I didn't get the metaphor either."
Leader: "Anyone else? OK, what about page two?"

This systematic approach actually moves much more quickly than the free-wheeling approach. And, because it's specific, the writer will better remember the comments. When the session is over, each member should hand his copy of the manuscript back to the author, who can then take the stack home and decide which comments to follow and which to discard.

Some authors are nervous about this method because they're worried about copies of their work floating around for someone to steal. Relax. Your ideas are pretty safe. Your chances are much better of dating George Clooney or Nicole Kidman. (For more on protecting your work, see "Stop Thief!: Protecting Your Words and Ideas," on page 252.)

• **Cover sheet.** It helps to have a cover sheet attached to each manuscript. The cover sheet may vary according to the level of the group, but such a sheet will force the members to more clearly identify and articulate strengths and weaknesses before the discussion begins. This will reduce pointless digressions as participants struggle to say what they mean. Also, it allows the author to take these cover sheets home and compare people's reactions.

### Workshops Aren't All Work

When a writing group is working well, the members can't wait to show up. They look forward to seeing each other and they respect each other's opinions about the manuscripts. This doesn't mean they always agree, it just means that they believe their fellow writers gave thoughtful and sincere analyses.

When a workshop really works, the writers go home inspired to write more and better. That is the main purpose of the workshop, to keep us writing. There's only so much technique I can teach a student, and they can probably learn those techniques from just about any competent writing teacher. But I try to also maintain an atmosphere of support and inspiration that combats all the self-doubts that writers have thrown in their paths. The result has been that the writers in my workshops have produced hundreds of published poems, stories and articles as well as over two dozen published novels, half a dozen produced movies and a long-running TV series.

These authors would have produced this work without me. I had nothing to do with their successes. All I provided was an atmosphere where they could take themselves seriously as writers. More than anything else, that's what a writers' workshop must do.

### Stop Thief!: Protecting Your Words and Ideas

Inevitably in a writing group, someone will ask, "How can I protect my writing from being stolen?" While it's an understandable concern, it's a little like a cab driver asking, "How can I ensure that I'll never be in a car accident?"

Practically speaking, you can't. But the odds are extremely slim that anyone will steal your material. I've been conducting workshops for twenty years and have never once had anyone complain of it actually happening. However, just as you can increase your odds of protection when driving by using a seat belt, having an air bag and driving safely, you can also take a couple precautions with writing.

There are two things that can be stolen: your words and your ideas. Words are easy enough to protect because it's so obvious when someone steals them. It's like getting caught shoplifting with the stolen goods shoved down your pants. Hard to claim you don't know how they got there. That's why it rarely happens.

Ideas and concepts are harder to protect because it's harder to prove that they've been stolen. I can't tell you how many times I've been working on a novel or a script, only to read that someone had recently written a similar story. It's annoying, but most of the time it's really just coincidence. I'm not so arrogant as to think I'm the only writer who ever had this particular idea. Besides, it's not so much the idea as it is the execution and presentation. However, if it's someone I know—who's read my work and then comes out with a startlingly similar idea—then I'd be suspicious.

There are three things you can do:

1. Copyright your material. You can register with the Copyright Office by calling (202) 707-9100 and requesting Form TX for novels or manuscripts of nondramatic literary work; or Form PA for scripts. The cost is $30.

2. Be cautious about who's in your group. If theft is a genuine concern of yours, then join only a group that consists of people you know well enough to trust. Or, if you've just joined a group of strangers, hold off submitting your work until you've gotten to know them better.

3. As an added precaution, your group might all agree to sign a nondisclosure agreement that states: "We, the undersigned, promise not to discuss the details of each other's manuscripts outside the group." Of course, this won't stop someone from chatting about your manuscript with his or her spouse or friend, but it might act as a reminder to be cautious.

A final word of advice: You're more likely to be struck by lightning than have someone rip off your work. It's true that someone might steal your car while you're at the movies, but does that mean you won't go to the movies or that you'll always be thinking of your car while you're watching? Relax and enjoy your writing group. The benefits far outweigh this miniscule risk.

## Online Workshop Etiquette: You Talkin' to Me?

Although you may be participating in an online workshop from the comfort of your home, it's important to remember the words you send aren't confined to your home. You don't know these people except as disembodied words; in many cases you don't even know their real names. So, just as if you were walking alone in a strange neighborhood, it's best to be cautious and polite.

The general rules for critiquing a manuscript should apply: (1) Always start with the strengths of the work. Praise the things you like or that the writer does well. It would be an extremely rare manuscript that doesn't have some kind of promise. (2) When offering a criticism, phrase your words as a positive suggestion rather than a negative complaint. For example, rather than say, "Your prose style is filled with clichés," say instead, "You could look for fresher, more original descriptions and similes." Avoid saying "don't," as in "Don't rush the scene." Instead, "The scene may move too quickly; take a little more time with the characters so we're more involved." Of course, this takes more thought and care on your part, but if you want people to be thoughtful and caring about your work, you must do it with theirs. Also, by approaching critiquing this way, you are actually developing better skills with which to critique your own manuscript.

If you are on the receiving end of criticism, keep a couple things in mind. First, people who offer rude, crude or nasty criticism are to be ignored completely. It doesn't matter who they are (or say they are), or how many times they claim to have been published—they clearly are not interested in improving your work. Their goal is to promote themselves, which makes their analyses suspect. It is important not to respond to this type of person with anything more than "Thank you for your help." Sure, you may be trembling with anger when you type those words, but you have nothing to gain from attacking him or her. You don't want to spark a cyber version of road rage, with someone hunting you down or sending you hostile e-mails.

Second, remember that inexperienced critics, despite the best of intentions, don't always know how to articulate precisely what they mean. They may complain that your story is too slow when they really mean the dialogue is choppy (which causes the story to slow down). Don't explain or make excuses for what you were trying to do. Just ask the critic questions to try to get a clearer sense of what she means. For example, you might ask, "Can you name specific passages that seemed to be slow?" Or, "Did you care enough about the character in this scene?" (If the character isn't developed enough, we may not care what happens to her, which makes a scene seem slow.)

Finally, the nice thing about cyberspace is its vastness. If you don't feel comfortable with a particular group, you can join another with just a few keystrokes. You should always come away from your group feeling inspired to write. If you don't, start surfing.

## Q: WHAT IS THE BEST WAY TO REVISE MY MANUSCRIPT?

> *"I think to understand an idea you have to wade in, write your way through it, and throw away big hunks until you get it right. . . . I think of a story not as a part of myself on a page, but as a thing that can be better or worse depending on what I do to it. I really do think of it as a thing to be shaped, made, and perfected."*
>
> LEE SMITH

Remember this golden rule of writing: No one gets it right the first time. I have a little writing secret that has seen me through the completion of over thirty-five books, ten screenplays and dozens of stories and poems. Just when I'm most frustrated with my daily writing and the demons of common sense are whispering, "Find another profession, you no-talented hack," I summon up this little secret and the demons vanish like relatives after you announce you need to borrow money.

My secret is this: My first few drafts are always crap. Guaranteed.

This is not self-deprecation or false modesty. I know when I sit down to write the first few versions of a chapter, story or article, that whatever appears on the screen is a far cry from what I'm imagining in my mind. But that doesn't bother me anymore because I know that I can fix it. I have come to learn that good writing has nothing to do with the first, third or fiftieth draft. In fact, good writing has to do with *not* counting drafts, *not* keeping track of how many times you've revised something. The only draft that counts is the final draft.

This is the last chapter of the book because it is the most important. The other chapters teach you how to write various specific scenes, but this chapter is about the whole work, how to put all those separate scenes together to form the whole work—which is the point of it all.

**Getting to "The End"**

Revising can be daunting. There's so much to look for—pacing, characterization, plot, theme, style, etc.—that a writer can get lost in the labyrinthine process. When I sit down to write the first few versions of a chapter, the jumble of clumsy words appearing on the screen is a far cry from the perfect passages I'm imagining in my mind. But that distance doesn't bother me anymore. Because during the course of writing and revising all of my novels, I have learned that the more I keep revising that jumble, the closer I can bring it to my imagined perfection.

The difference between the early and final drafts of writing is that early drafts lay down the basic story and characters while the final drafts fine-tune what is already there. The early stages of writing and revising resemble first aid on a battlefield: You see a gaping wound (such as a clichéd description) and you slap a Band-Aid on it (change a few words). This is because early drafts are part of the discovery process. This is when the writing is most liquid, meaning that you feel free to add or delete passages, go in a different direction than you had first intended, suddenly expand minor characters into major ones. You are more daring because the area is still uncharted. But once you have charted it—that is, once you have the characters you want, doing and saying the things you want, in the order you want—now you're ready for the final drafts. Early drafts are like selecting the members of a sports team; final drafts are teaching them to play together as one cooperative unit.

Although the phrase "final draft" suggests the last time you'll revise, that really isn't the case. "Final drafts" really refers to the final *process* of revising. It's when you are satisfied with the basics, but now want to erase any persistent flaws. Sometimes the process is minor—just touch-up painting here and there. Sometimes it's more major—knocking out walls and adding windows.

## Ground Rules

The key to successful final revisions is to *compartmentalize your approach*. Instead of trying to revise all the aspects of the text at once, concentrate only on one element at a time. The following four-step method of revision is a simple way to examine each of the most crucial elements. The strength of this method is that by doing only one step at a time, you are fully focused on that one area and not distracted by other problems. Don't give in to the temptation to fix something that is not part of the step you are pursuing. If you're revising for dialogue and come across a choppy narrative passage, just mark the narrative passage and return to it later when you are concentrating on that particular step. Keep in mind that each step has an ultimate goal, and achieving that goal is the whole point of a particular revision.

The other important element to remember is *to apply this process only in short, self-contained sections*: If you're revising a long story or a novel, use this method on scenes or chapters. My students always ask if they can't just keep writing ahead rather than revise scenes or chapters as they go along, then fix everything once they've completed the entire first draft. Although I am usually very much against any "rules of writing"—because each writer must find the method that works best for her—in this one area I strongly discourage the method of writing the full draft and then going back to revise. The reason is that the act of revising is not just applying makeup and accessories; sometimes it involves rethinking what you're writing about, what you want to say, who these characters are, where you're going with the story. Sometimes you only discover the answers to these questions during a rewrite. There's usually a reason you get stuck in a particular place: You realize something is wrong with what you've written or intend to write.

You just don't know yet what that something is. You need to take the time to figure out what the exact element is that is bothering you to know what comes next. Pay attention to this crucial instinct because it's the writer's gag reflex: It keeps you from swallowing bad writing.

Also, by not writing ahead, you'll feel more free to follow any of the many options you have, whether eliminating major characters, changing settings or drastically altering plot. Sometimes you may even end up changing protagonists. (After writing ninety pages of *The Thin Man*, Dashiell Hammett dumped his popular *Continental Op* protagonist and replaced him with Nick and Nora Charles). But once you've written ahead and have already structured the whole story, you have a greater commitment to what you've already written. Now, instead of experimenting with all the options of improving your story, you're more likely to try to build bridges to force scenes to meet.

Revising calls for a certain degree of ruthlessness. You must question the worthiness of every aspect of what's in your story, and if anything is found wanting, you must jettison it. The following steps will help you find those weak spots—and offer some suggestions for how to fix or cut them.

### Step #1: Structure

**Goal:** Develop a clear and compelling plot.

**Problems to look for:** (1) Too passive/talking heads, (2) no buildup/anti-climactic.

**How to fix:** We start here because structure is the skeleton of the scene. Once these bones are all correctly aligned, stuffing the internal organs in the right place and stretching the skin over it is a lot easier. Basically, you're looking to see that the plot events are in the right order and that, if they are, the scene builds toward a satisfying climactic payoff.

The passive/talking heads scene occurs when characters are sitting around yammering back and forth without any tension to the scene. They are called talking heads, not because they are speaking a lot, but because what they are saying seems removed from any sense of characterization. It's as if they are puppets speaking the words of the author rather than real people speaking their own minds.

One simple way to fix this is to change the setting so that the scene is more active. Instead of the husband and wife sitting in the airport waiting for his mother to arrive while discussing how horrible she is, put them in a car stuck in horrendous airport traffic that may make them late. This additional element is a misdirection device, shifting the readers' focus to the urgency of the couple being late, which makes the readers anxious and therefore more apt to pay attention to the dialogue. Also, it gives the couple more to talk about (the awful traffic, her awful driving) so the conversation seems less contrived and more natural. And it gives a concrete focus to the mother's character by introducing the fact that she hates it when people are late; this fact *shows* us who she is and takes the place of long descriptions of how controlling she is. The son can even throw in an anecdote about something outrageous the mother did when someone was late (e.g., stood up and left the hospital because the surgeon was late; or left her daughter's wedding because the groom was late).

Each scene is like a mini-story: It has a beginning, middle and ending. The beginning introduces the conflict of the scene, the middle complicates it, and the ending resolves it. That means every scene has to have a "hot spot," a point in which the action and/or emotions reach an apex. Usually the scene builds toward this. When revising for structure, make sure you locate the hot spot—and make sure it generates enough heat to justify the scene even existing. You'll know if it has enough heat if the readers' anticipation is satisfied during this moment. One of the main reasons scenes weaken here is that writers end the scene too early—as if it were a TV series and they were breaking for commercial. An argument doesn't end when someone makes a witty or stinging comment—it keeps on going to the point where people are uncomfortable, frustrated, at a loss for words. So must the scene.

So far, I've discussed revising structure within a scene or chapter. However, once the whole story is completed, you must also revise the structure of the larger work. This means making sure all the scenes are in the best order. It can also mean eliminating some scenes. This is a time when you have to do what's best for the whole work, even if it means cutting a wonderful scene that no longer fits. John Steinbeck once warned writers to "beware of a scene that becomes too dear to you, dearer than the rest."

Before moving scenes around, I suggest you create notecards for each scene or chapter. Tack them up to your bulletin board in order. Now you have a clearer visual sense of the rhythm of the story. Do you have too many passive scenes together, thereby dampening the momentum? Are the settings too similar? Just by studying the cards, you can sometimes discover structure problems. Move the cards around, and see if changing the order of the scene helps. Or perhaps you'll notice that you need an additional scene between a couple characters; if so, the notecards will show you where.

### Step #2: Texture

**Goal:** Sharpen descriptive passages to make characters, setting and action more vivid.

**What to look for:** (1) Too much or too little description, (2) clichéd word choices, (3) too many adjectives, (4) research info dump, (5) info in wrong place.

**How to fix:** This step has a lot to do with you defining your unique style. Some writers use a lot of description, others use very little. There's no right way. But when there's so much description that the story's momentum bogs down, that's too much. Or if there's so little that the characters or settings are bland and non-memorable, that's too little. Most writers, myself included, have many descriptive passages that they love, but that they wisely cut from a story because they call too much attention to themselves and detract from the story. Any time you see a passage of description that is so poetic and involving that the reader stops to admire the author—cut it. You've just intruded into the story to take a bow, thereby smothering your own creation. Save all those wonderful passages you cut in a folder; you may be able to use them in another story.

On the other hand, telling the reader too little can be equally annoying. While some writers insist on telling us every detail of a character's description and background, right down to the number of freckles on her ear and where she bought her blouse (Bloomingdale's during a Memorial Day sale, reduced from $98 to $38 because of a slight stain on the sleeve), others are stingy with any details. The reader emerges from a scene not having any idea of the characters' ages or physical descriptions or a feel for the settings. Even though the writer may tell us the scene takes place in an alley, the reader never experiences the alley and therefore is never fully involved in the scene. The danger in fixing this problem is to overdescribe—as discussed above—by assaulting the reader's senses with every sight, smell, sound, taste and feel of the alley. Instead, concentrate on one aspect of the alley: "The alley bordered several low-cost restaurants competing for the lunch money of the secretaries on a budget in nearby office buildings. The cloying smell of things being fried—french fries, tempura, extra-crispy chicken—lay trapped between the buildings like a heavy fog. Randy was grateful for that aggressive odor, otherwise he'd have to deal with whatever was spilling out of all those Dumpsters, especially the one with the chicken feet sticking out like branches from under the lid." In this case, focusing on the smell provides enough texture, while also implying visuals: the types of food being fried tell us what kind of restaurants they are. Ending with a visual snapshot of the chicken legs provides the emotional reaction that the writer wants, something that couldn't be achieved if the reader were flooded with too many visual details.

Directly related to this is the dreaded "info dump" (see Clumping ailment on page 129). This is where the writer decides to stop the story cold to give a lot of details about the history of the house the characters live in or how to pilot a plane. Yes, sometimes those details are not only important to your story, but they add a level of credibility. But novice writers either include too much info or they include too many such passages. Scenes that involve technical information should remain short. For example, one of my students is writing a novel that involves sailing a yacht. This author has great expertise about sailing, so he includes page after page of description about the technical aspects of sailing. Workshop reaction to these scenes is always the same: There's so much technical information that the readers get lost and no longer care about what's happening to the characters. However, there's another student in the same class who is also an expert sailor and also writing a novel involving a lot of sailing. Reaction to his sailing scenes are always very enthusiastic because we get just enough info to accept the realism of the scene, but not so much as to numb us. The purpose of the scene is to make the sailing realistic, which only requires a few lines here and there to make the reader a believer. Remember, these novels aren't about sailing, they're about the *people* involved in sailing.

Aside from adjusting length, writers can vastly improve the impact of the texture by concentrating on word choices. Read through the manuscript one time with the sole purpose of circling words that could be stronger. Then go back and take your time replacing them. Do not rely on a thesaurus; many times you'll just be replacing one dull word for a more complex and even duller word. The word you're looking for often isn't a synonym, it's just something richer, more evocative.

A common reason that passages can bog down or lose their snap is that the writer has burdened it with too many adjectives. The beginner's logic is that if one adjective is good, three is great. Not so. Clustering adjectives together actually causes them to do battle with each other, one devouring the other until none has any impact. Most of the time when there are several adjectives together, at least two of them have the same meaning anyway. For example: "She was a quiet, introspective, shy girl." Do we need all those adjectives, especially since they are all quite similar in meaning? Think of every adjective as a hundred-dollar bill and spend wisely. Read through the manuscript one time doing nothing but cutting unnecessary adjectives. Add nothing or replace nothing this time through, only cut.

### Step #3: Dialogue

Goal: Elicit character personality through conversation.

What to look for: (1) Too many tag lines, (2) too few tag lines, (3) tag lines in the wrong place, (4) tag lines that contain too much info, (5) yet another info dump, (6) bland or melodramatic lines.

**How to fix:** The first four areas to examine involve the use of tag lines, which are the "he said" and "she said" parts of dialogue. Basically, the tag line identifies the speaker—such a simple task that you wouldn't think it could be such a big deal. Yet, the misuse of tag lines is one of the most destructive forces in dialogue. Some beginning writers feel that every line of dialogue requires a tag line. It doesn't. If there are only two speakers, several lines of pure dialogue can go on without ever telling us who the speaker is; the reader already knows. The proliferation of tag lines is really nothing more than lazy writing, used as a crutch to avoid making the characters' voices so individual that the reader can recognize their cadence and tone without being told. This is because beginning writers focus too much on *what* the characters say and not enough on *how* they say it.

Yet, there are times when the reader does have to be told who is speaking. This can be because there are several speakers, or the dialogue is interspersed with action or interior monologues, or just for the sake of the rhythm. Following are several examples of the same line of dialogue, each presented with a variation on the same tag line. Notice the subtle differences in the effect achieved by each.

> "Hi," she said, moving toward me.
> "Hi," she said. She moved toward me.
> She moved toward me. "Hi."
> "Hi." She moved toward me.

The first two examples are friendlier because the "she said" slows the pace, taking away some of the energy from her act of moving. The second two examples are more dramatic because they present just the dialogue and the action—which now seems more deliberate and aggressive. (Note about word choice: What does the word "move" imply here that "walk" doesn't? "Move" is less visual than "walk," but more sensual, implying that she is more of a force than just an average person, someone who the narrator has some nervousness about as she approaches.)

Where the tag line goes affects the emphasis on the dialogue. Look at the following variations. Which has more impact?

"This is yours. That is not," he said.
"This is yours," he said. "That is not."

The second version is stronger because the emphasis is now on "That is not." Placing the emphasis there adds an ominous tone. The first version has the lines together, which doesn't emphasize either and makes the dialogue seem breezier.

Another common error is placing the tag line at the end of a long speech. For example:

> "I just don't know what to do about James. He's always running around with delinquent types, like those nasty boys from over in Springfield, the ones with gun racks in their trucks and beer cans under their car seats," Tina said.

There are two problems with this: (1) If we don't know who the speaker is until we get to the end of the speech, then we're going to be confused while reading it; if we do know, then no tag line is necessary. (2) Even while reading the speech, we can see there's a tag line, so we don't fully commit to the dialogue until we see how the tag line will affect how we should view the speech. This problem can easily be solved by relocating the tag line:

> "I just don't know what to do about James," Tina said. "He's always running around with delinquent types, like those nasty boys from over in Springfield, the ones with gun racks in their trucks and beer cans under their car seats."

Now we know who the speaker is up front—and when we finish the speech, we are left with a vivid image of the nasty boys with gun racks and beer cans, not Tina speaking. If you are going to use a tag line in a long speech, do so as soon as stylistically possible. If you wait too long, the reader won't know who the speaker is until the end and you will have broken the rhythm.

Sometimes you need to identify the speaker, but you don't want to use the word "said"—for the millionth time. You can substitute an action instead. This still identifies the speaker but adds a visual image. The first two following examples are the usual "said" variations; the third demonstrates substituting an action.

"You always do this to me," I said.
I said, "You always do this to me."
I shook my head. "You always do this to me."

Don't overdo this technique, otherwise every line of dialogue will have a gesture attached and the characters will all seem like they're on a caffeine buzz.

Finally, keep your tags simple. The more complex the tag line, the more it detracts from the actual dialogue. Avoid adverbs (e.g., she said angrily). Every time you see a word with an "ly" at the end, scrutinize it to make sure it's necessary. In general, adverbs are often repetitious; the dialogue tells us she's angry; no need to repeat it.

Info dumps appear with alarming frequency in the dialogue of weak writers. It's pretty much the same problem as described under "Texture" on page 260. Here characters ramble on about the history of their family or how to make cheese. Now, this same information can be compelling—as long as it doesn't seem as if the author intruded just to unload all his research. Instead of having a lengthy monologue with one character spewing forth, let the information come out as part of conversation. Perhaps the speaker is reluctant to tell but the listener wheedles it out; or the speaker is blabby but the listener keeps trying to shut him up. Or the conversation takes place while the characters are doing something else that allows for interruptions: They may be at a garage sale looking for vintage bowling shirts; they may be on a ski lift preparing to ski down the steepest mountain they've ever been on. Now you have parallel topics, with one being the misdirection, the other being the real information you want to get across.

Punching up bland or melodramatic dialogue is trickier because first you have to be able to recognize it. You may think that if someone knew what bad dialogue was, they wouldn't write it in the first place. It's not that simple. A line of dialogue doesn't exist in a vacuum. Its power comes from the context—that is, the lines around it, the situation that prompts it, the character who says it. A line in one context may seem bland, but in another context it may be brilliant. Or some minor tinkering can sharpen a line. Here's an example from a student manuscript:

> "I'll see if I can do a trade so we can sit together."
> "I'd like that," Susan said, "but I'd be rotten company."
> "We can be rotten together," he said.

Not a bad line. It's meant to endear him to her. But a better line would be: "We can rot together." It's less expected and therefore a bit funnier, edgier, suggesting a character who isn't as predictable.

One of the things I do before editing my own dialogue is to read a passage by someone whose dialogue I admire (e.g., Elmore Leonard, Ross Thomas, Lorrie Moore, Jane Smiley, Peter De Vries, etc.). Don't limit yourself to just fiction writers; reading playwrights (like Beth Henley and David Mamet) is also extremely helpful. Which writer I choose to read depends on the tone that I want to achieve. If the scene calls for fast-paced edgy dialogue, I may read Leonard. If I want playful and desperate, I may read Mamet. Whomever you choose, don't read an entire story or play, just read the dialogue passages until you have a feel for the language, then immediately go to your work and start editing. In addition, John Steinbeck advised writers to say the dialogue aloud as they write it: "Only then will it have the sound of speech."

## Step #4: Editing

**Goal:** Tighten pace and continuity.

**What to look for:** (1) repetition through implication, (2) slow passages.

**How to fix:** Cut, cut, cut. This is often the hardest part for writers because they've worked so hard on every word. But this final step is the one that gives the work its final shape. Much of what you will cut is repetition, words that repeat what the reader already knows because it's been directly said or implied elsewhere. Nobel-Prize-winning writer I.B. Singer once said, "The writer's best friend is the wastepaper can." Apply this maxim to individual words and lines and you have the essence of editing. Following is a passage of an early draft from a student novel—literary mainstream. Susan and Bill are coincidentally on the same flight back to their hometown. They have feelings for each other, though not yet spoken. Draw a line through all the words you'd cut.

"Uncle Jake's had a heart attack."

"No!" Shock and regret clouded his face.

"Harry Tobin called me." The muffled drone of airplane engines, the smell of jet fuel and the odors of fast food and lavatory deodorizers were a sudden assault on her senses. She felt queasy. "I've been shuttling all over the eastern half of this country since 10 o'clock last night, trying to get the quickest connection home."

"I'm so sorry about Jake," Bill said. "How serious is it?"

They fell into stride, hurrying toward the gate.

"I'm not really sure," she said. "Harry said it was bad. When I called the hospital from Memphis, I couldn't get any information except 'guarded.' " She looked over at him, a wan smile barely turning up the corners of her mouth. Then it was her turn to look more closely. "You look grim. I take it things didn't go well?"

"Worse than not well." He kept his face forward. "But no comparison with your news."

"What happened?" Immediately she apologized. "Sorry. I think this is where you tell me MYOB."

Let's look at the same passage—edited. The words with strikethroughs have been cut; the underlined words have been added.

"Uncle Jake's had a heart attack."

"No!" ~~Shock and regret clouded his face.~~

"Harry Tobin called me." The muffled drone of airplane engines, the smell of jet fuel and the odors of fast food and lavatory deodorizers ~~were a sudden assault on her senses. She felt~~ <u>made her</u> queasy. "I've been shuttling all over the eastern half of this country since 10 o'clock last night, trying to get the quickest connection home."

"I'm so sorry about Jake," Bill said. "How serious is it?" They fell into stride, hurrying toward the gate.

"~~I'm not really sure," she said.~~ "Harry said it was bad. When I called the hospital from Memphis, I couldn't get any information except 'guarded.' " She looked over at him, ~~a wan smile barely turning up the corners of her mouth. Then it was her turn to look more closely.~~ "You look grim. I take it things didn't go well?"

"Worse than not well." He kept his face forward. "But no comparison with your news."

"What happened?" ~~Immediately she apologized.~~ <u>She shook her head at her nosiness.</u> "Sorry. I think this is where you tell me MYOB."

Here's why these cuts were made: (1) His exclamation of "No!" tells us he's shocked, regret is implied because we know from previous scenes that he likes Jake. (2) The fact that she gets queasy implies the assault on her senses. (3) "Harry said it was bad" is a strong line; the cut line weakens the speech. (4) The "wan smile" description is distracting because it focuses our attention on her face rather than the emotions of the moment. (5) We know she apologizes because we see the word "sorry." No need to tell us; however, the writer's instincts are correct in that there needs to be a rhythmic break there. Instead, she could insert an action that is related to her feeling. This makes it more vivid.

Once you have finished editing your manuscript, go through again to make sure there are clear transitions bridging where you have cut. Think you've cut enough? Kaye Gibbons (*Ellen Foster*), after working on her new novel for eighteen months, deliberately deleted all nine hundred pages. She said, "It was so bad, and it kept being bad."

### Step #5: Blending

Goal: Search and destroy any weaknesses.

**Problems to look for:** Soft spots: unclear character motivations, actions that seem contrived, etc.

**How to fix:** A month ago, a student of mine came to the house with her novel manuscript in hand, desperate because she seemed unable to fix some of the problems that were bothering her. I'd read the novel before, so I was familiar with the story. As she poured out all the problems in a rush of frustration and anxiety, I stopped her after the first problem and told her how to fix it: Add a scene early in the novel that showed a certain characteristic of the character. She wanted a stronger motivation for why the boy keeps a secret. All she had to do was make the secret bigger than the one she'd created. When she went to the next problem, the solution was the same: Either add a new scene or expand an old one that made the reader believe the thing that happened later. Then I told her to make a list of what she thought all the problems were—in writing—and see how many could be addressed merely by changing.

Yesterday, I read a former student's screenplay. He was concerned about whether or not there was enough suspense regarding the main character's quest. I suggested adding a scene in which he tries to use his new abilities, but fails. This heightens the suspense about the next time he tries.

I recently faced the same situation. An editor said he liked my novel but didn't believe the character was capable of the violence he eventually commits. I suggested adding an early scene that is either a flashback or a memory of a youthful indiscretion in which he was violent and how he overcame those tendencies. Fortunately, that added scene would work to our advantage in a couple additional ways.

This blending process is a sort of spot-welding. You find the troubled areas and add new scenes or expand old ones to fix anything you missed. Don't be embarrassed that you missed these things. All writers have to go back and do this same kind of repair work for the final product to blend together seamlessly.

## A Little Editing Help from Your Friends

During the course of completing a story, you should show it to as many *qualified* people as possible. Qualified means (1) people who read a lot, especially within the genre you're writing in, (2) workshop leaders, (3) teachers, (4) agents, (5) editors. Agents and editors should see it last, after you've shown it around, received feedback and made any changes you think are appropriate. Showing it to other people means they will give you opinions—that's the point. Yet many writers go ballistic when they get their story back and the person offers suggestions. What they really wanted was someone to say, "It's perfect. The most moving, funny, life-changing work I've ever read." I can tell you right now, unless it's your immediate family commenting, that won't happen. Instead of resisting editing advice, examine it as objectively as possible. If it makes sense, use it. If it doesn't, ignore it. But be open to it. I show all my work to my wife, who is one of the best writers and editors I've ever known. Still, when she is finished reading it and is reciting her list of suggested changes, I'm nodding on the outside while inside my mind is shouting, "What's wrong with you! Can't you recognize my genius? What kind of idiotic suggestions are these? Let's see you write the damn book!" And so on. However, I then take the list, read it over, think about it and change whatever I agree with, which is usually somewhere between 50 and 80 percent of what she said. Every book I've written that she's critiqued has been significantly improved because of her suggestions.

**Talent Is Fueled by Discipline**
There is no such creature as the final draft. It is as mythological as the unicorn. Just when you think you're done with a manuscript, you take another look at it and suddenly you're scribbling notes on every page. However, there is a point at which every manuscript must be abandoned, sent out to publishers and the next work begun. This five-step revision method will allow you to reach that "final" draft more comfortably because you know you will have examined every possible aspect of the work. But if you've completed these five steps and you still feel the work needs something, begin again with step one. You can apply these five steps more than once to the same manuscript. I do.

Eventually, you must kick it out of the nest to see if it will fly. This is the final—and most difficult—step a writer takes. But it must be taken. Once you've sent the manuscript out to the agent, magazine or book publisher of your choice, don't sit around waiting to see what will happen. Begin your next work as soon as possible. Not only will it distract you from the waiting, but all the techniques you've just learned and practiced in the completed manuscript are fresh in your mind and will make your next work even better.

It is the lot of writers to constantly question whether or not they have any talent. A book like this, with so much advice, may seem overwhelming: "So much to learn, can I ever take it all in? Maybe I'm just not talented." Don't let yourself off the hook that easily. I often tell my students that talent is a resource of limited value. Through the years I have seen many richly talented writers give up because they lacked the will to finish what was only promising. At the same time, I have seen many moderately talented writers complete novels and screenplays and sell them, and then go on to write others, all the time becoming better and better writers. James Baldwin thought will was the crucial element to a writer: "Do this book, or die. You have to go through that. Talent is insignificant. I know a lot of talented ruins. Beyond talent lie all the usual words: discipline, love, luck, but, most of all, endurance." American Book Award winner Chitra Banerjee Divakaruni (*Arranged Marriage*) also extols the virtues of disciplined revision: "I'll write a story over a period of a month, and then put it aside for eight or nine months." After that, she does a "prerevision" in which she identifies trouble spots and jots down suggestions in the margins ("This scene needs to be changed!" or "This sentence isn't right."). After an interval of time, she returns to the story with a "how-to-fix-it" revision. Here she writes suggestions, in a different color, to each of her original comments. Finally, she'll actually implement her suggestions. "You can't hurry writing if you're going to do it well," she says. "Otherwise, what is the point of being a writer? If you're going to create art, the least you can do is give it your best attention and as much time as it takes."

## Final Note: Get a Grammar Book!
After all the revising is complete and you have the best manuscript you're capable of writing, you need to take a serious look at the mechanics of your manuscript: grammar and punctuation. For the past twenty-five years I've been editing writers' manuscripts and

it's amazing to me that the same basic mistakes are alive and kicking the crap out of these otherwise well-written works.

☠ **A lot of writers are under the impression that editors will find all these little spelling, grammar and punctuation errors charming signs of an unjaded talent.**

Editors with stacks and stacks of manuscripts arriving every day don't have the time or the inclination to deal with writers who don't take their work seriously enough to fix the most rudimentary errors. There are two things you can do: (1) Get a grammar book and read it. Reading it first means you'll at least be aware of the types of problems that can occur. But don't worry that you can't memorize everything in the book; very few people can. I have several grammar books on my desk at all times because I know that I will have to look things up that I can no longer remember. Warning: Do not rely on grammar-checking software. They are incorrect at least 50 percent of the time. Instead, tattoo the following list of common errors to your arm (or pin it to your bulletin board), and check your manuscript against it before sending it out to an unsuspecting editor:

• **Hyphens in compound adjective.** This is the most common gaff. I would bet hard cash that if I looked at your manuscript right now, I'd find a whole gaggle of absent hyphens. A compound adjective is two or more adjectives working in conjunction to describe a single noun. She's a good-looking woman. He's a fly-by-the-seat-of-his-pants guy. **Tip #1:** The easiest way to decide if you need a hyphen is to apply each word separately to the noun. Look at the examples. Is she a "good" woman? Is she a "looking" woman? No, both words are required together to describe the woman. **Tip #2:** Don't hyphenate adverbs (the ones that end with "ly"), such as "Jim is an emotionally starved man." **Hint:** Phrases that begin with "self" are usually hyphenated (self-absorbed, self-starter, self-made).

• **Quotation marks.** In England and Canada, quotation marks come before a comma and period (or end-of-sentence punctuation). But here in the United States, we do the opposite. "Hi, Mom," she said. Jerry called me a "tramp." (Note how, even though "tramp" is the only quoted word at the end of the sentence, the quotation mark still goes *after* the period. The most notable exception to this rule rarely comes up, but here it is anyway: When using a semicolon or colon, the quotation mark is placed before semicolon or colon. (We are not, as the newspaper said, "New-Age hippies"; we are Newly Aware environmentalists.)

• **Comma before names.** Always place a comma before the name of a person being addressed. This will most often occur in dialogue: "Are you eating, Jim?" Without the comma, the sentence is much more gruesome. **Tip:** Words that are used instead of names are treated the same as names: "I'll be home late, Mom."

• **Mom vs. mom.** You capitalize Mom, Mother, Dad and Father whenever they are used instead of a character's actual name. You don't capitalize when the word is possessive, meaning you're treating the character as an object you own: "My father will pick us up after the movie," but "Could you come here, Dad?" **Tip:** If it has "my" before it, use the lowercase letter.

• **Dangling modifiers.** This is grammar's "silent killer" and is easy to miss. I usually find several in my own manuscripts when I proofread. When you start a sentence with a phrase that's supposed to describe something or someone, the first noun after the comma has to be the thing or person being described. Wrong: While driving home last night, the traffic lights kept turning red just as I approached. What's wrong: The first noun after that comma should be whoever is driving. Right: While driving home last night, I got red lights at every traffic signal. Wrong: Having completed extensive research on the death penalty, my paper should get a high grade. What's wrong: According to this version, the paper did the research, not the author. Right: Having completed extensive research on the death penalty, I should get a high grade on my paper.

• **Semicolons and comma splices.** A semicolon (;) is used to separate two independent sentences. You might wonder, "If they're independent sentences, why not just use periods?" You could. The only reason not to is because there's a certain connection between the two halves that gives them more impact when joined together. **Tip:** This is especially true if the two "sentences" are short. To make them separate sentences might create a choppy style; to join them together with a semicolon would give them better rhythm. This is particularly true when writing dialogue: "I am not a child; I am *your* child." **Note:** This is a tricky one because there are times when you may want to deliberately have a comma splice for stylistic reasons. Larry McMurtry (*Lonesome Dove*) does it extensively in some novels. Even though a semicolon would be correct, he uses a comma because it is less of a pause and the flow may be smoother.

• **Its vs. it's.** Whenever you use a contraction (won't, aren't, shouldn't), the apostrophe represents a missing letter. So, "it's" means there's a missing letter (for "it is" or "it has"). However, "its" without an apostrophe is possessive, meaning the word owns something. **Examples:** It's a heck of a world when a car can change its own oil. Paris has its share of faults, but it's still an exciting city to visit. **Bonus Tip #1:** decade apostrophes. Remember, the apostrophe represents a missing letter (or number). So, when writing about decades, the apostrophe goes *in front*: The '60s were a time of sexual awakening. **Bonus Tip #2:** The word "cannot" is *one* word.

• **Awhile vs. a while.** This is confusing because sometimes "a while" is correct and sometimes "awhile" is correct. Whenever the word follows a preposition (in, after, for, etc.), it should be two words (a while). **Examples:** After a while, we went home. Awhile ago, I saw a shocking sight. I've been here for a while. The hamburger will take awhile to cook.

• **Justifying margins.** There's a button on most word-processing programs that allows you to justify the right margin of your manuscript. When you click on that button, the right margin lines up perfectly like Prussian soldiers or a column in a newspaper— or even a published book. *Don't use this button!* To achieve this published look, the program adds extra spaces here and there. The result is that these extra spaces slow the reader down and make your story seem to drag a little.

• **Subject-pronoun agreement.** When a sentence starts with a singular subject, it must be consistent and not suddenly switch to a plural pronoun. Wrong: A person can't just decide that they don't like chocolate. Right: A person can't just decide that he doesn't like chocolate. **Tip #1:** Although we don't know the gender of the "person" in the previous sentence, we used a male pronoun (he). Due to tradition, this is technically grammatically correct. However, it can also be considered sexist to default to the male pronoun. One way around this is to use "he or she": A person can't just decide that he or she doesn't like chocolate. But this method can become clumsy and slow the pace. Another solution is to make both the subject and pronoun plural: People can't just decide that they don't like chocolate. But sometimes it's difficult or impossible to do this. In such cases, writers often alternate using male and female pronouns: A writer can be very temperamental when his writing is going bad. If a writer can't take the pressure, she should consider another profession. **Tip #2:** In fiction, if a character consistently defaults to either male or female pronouns in his dialogue or narrative monologue, this can be used to reveal a bias he may have.

• **Fewer vs. less.** Use fewer when referring to things that can be counted; use less when referring to general amounts. **Examples:** I have a few critical comments about your behavior. (The comments can be counted.) He's a lot less egotistical than I'd heard. (The size of his ego can't be counted.) **Tip:** In general, most people use "less" when they should use "fewer." Wrong: A lot less teenagers went to see that movie than the producers had hoped would go. If we had less people on this trip, there'd be more room to stretch out.

• **Whose vs. who's.** Writers confuse these two words because they mistakenly think the apostrophe in "who's" makes it possessive. "Who's" is a contraction of "who is" or "who has"; the apostrophe marks the missing letter. Once devious little grammarians did that, they were left without a possessive "who" and so created "whose." **Example:** Who's the idiot whose fancy Mercedes is blocking my Pinto? He's the guy who's going to be driving home without any tires.

• **Hopefully.** Don't start a sentence with "hopefully" because it will probably be wrong. Most people incorrectly use "hopefully" to refer to a person's hope that something will occur. Wrong: Hopefully, I'll sell my novel for a million dollars. Right: I hope I'll sell my novel for a million dollars. Technojargon: Hopefully is an adverb (notice the telltale "ly" at the end) meaning "in a hopeful manner." That means it's usually going to be located right next to a verb (which it's supposed to be modifying): I gazed hopefully at the editor as she pulled my novel out of her briefcase.

• **Farther vs. further.** Farther refers to *actual* distance. The gas station is farther down the road than I thought it was. Further refers to *unreal* distance. By training for the marathon, I've pushed myself further than I thought was possible.

• **Principle vs. principal.** Most people are OK writing about the principal of a school because we know that the princi*pal* is our "pal." The rest of the time we're confused. Principal is an adjective meaning "first" or "most important." Principal can also be a noun meaning "a sum of money" or "the head of a school or organization": The principal of our school told us that the principal rule for staying out of trouble was to obey his every command. (The second "principal" in this sentence means "the most important.") I can live comfortably off the interest of my investment without ever touching the principal. Principle is a noun meaning "a basic truth or law or rule of action": Gandhi was a man of unwavering principles. My principles forbid me to lie.

• **Ellipses.** Type three periods *with a space before and after each period* ( . . . ). In nonfiction, the ellipses is used to indicate words left out of a quotation. In fiction, it is used mostly in dialogue to indicate a pause or trailing off: (1) "Jimmy, there's something about you that's so . . . frustrating." Here the ellipses shows that the speaker was so exasperated that she needed to pause to find just the right word. (2) "I was wondering if maybe, you know, we could, you know . . ." **Tip:** Although four periods are used at the end of a sentence in nonfiction, in fiction, when indicating a trailing off, use only three periods. Common misuse: Beginning writers commonly use the ellipses to show an interruption during dialogue. (Some textbooks even suggest this.) Don't do it. Using the same punctuation to indicate trailing off and interruption is confusing to the reader and breaks the rhythm of the dialogue. Instead, use a dash. A dash is created by typing two hyphens in a row with no spaces between. Begin the dash immediately after the last word in the dialogue. (Note: Most word-processing programs automatically transform two consecutive hyphens into a dash):

"I won't give you the—"

"You don't have a choice, Chip."

• **Numbers.** Using numbers in scientific writing and creative writing is different, so don't follow what you see in magazines. The general rule of thumb is that numbers from one to one hundred, including all fractions, are written in words. For numbers over one hundred, if they are round numbers that can be shown in two words, write them out: six hundred apples, twenty thousand football fans. Otherwise, use figures: 621 apples, 20,245 football fans. Also, when beginning a sentence with a number, always use words. I have three sons at home with twenty-five pounds of laundry per son. Over three-fourths of the population loves chocolate. Five hundred angry protestors gathered outside the school.

Rather than use a lot of words for a big number, rearrange the sentence so that the number doesn't begin the sentence. Bad: Five thousand sixty-eight people gave blood yesterday. Better: Yesterday, 5,068 people gave blood. Exceptions: (1) For the sake of clarity and consistency, numbers can be used instead of words. If one part of the sentence uses a number larger than one hundred, you can use numbers instead of words for the other numbers in the sentence that are less than one hundred: When the police showed up at the protest, they arrested 25 boys and 112 girls. (2) With very large round numbers, it's sometimes better to use a combination of words and numbers: The population of the U.S. has surpassed 250 million.

• **Should of.** This phrase came about because when people speak they say "should've" as a contraction of "should have": He should've listened to me. Some writers merely transcribe what they heard, forgetting what the words mean. **Hint:** In general, you would only use the contraction "should've" in very informal writing or in dialogue to show informal speech.

These are by no means all the possible errors that writers can make, but they are the most common, and therefore the ones editors have come to most loathe. Don't give an editor an excuse to reject your manuscript without giving her the opportunity to know your writing. Think of it as a job interview with the appearance of your manuscript representing how you would dress. Slobs rarely get hired.

## Q: HOW CAN I IMPROVE MY OWN WRITING BY READING FICTION?

During the twenty-five years I've been teaching creative writing, I've tried to inspire my students by inviting a variety of editors, agents and writers as guest lecturers. One bit of advice was not only common among these professionals, but was always delivered with the greatest passion, the speaker leaning forward, eyebrows knit in concentration, voice raised as he sternly delivered his advice to the aspiring writer: *A writer must read.*

Often and a lot.

According to these successful writers, editors and agents, the depth with which a writer reads will be reflected in the depth of his own work. The first thing you have to do is learn how to read like a writer, not like a reader. The more you get out of reading, the more you can put into your writing. Although there's much to learn from instructional books like this, the heart of what you need to learn lies in effectively reading the fiction of the writers you most admire.

Like my students, you're saying, "Oh, I read all the time. The newspaper with breakfast, magazines while in the john, novels at night, short stories and poems when I'm in a literary mood." Quantity is certainly a part of reading. The more different styles and visions the aspiring writer is exposed to, the more models he has when approaching his own work. It gives him options. But it's not just the number of works you read, it's getting the most out of each work. Once you decide you are a writer, you no longer have the luxury of just flipping casually through novels dismissing them with a simple "This was good, that was bad." Now you must read them as if each were a pirate's map. Uncovering the subtleties within that map will help you discover the treasure within your own writing.

## Fascinatin' Rhythm

During my interview with Elmore Leonard, I asked him what authors he was currently reading. He told me Raymond Carver and Bobbie Ann Mason. I asked him why, since neither is a suspense writer, which is Leonard's claim to fame, and since Carver and Mason are quite different in style and content. "I'm not interested in content," he replied. "I'm interested in rhythm."

To the novice writer, rhythm seems like a poetic or musical term, yet a writer's rhythm is as individual as his fingerprints. How are the words arranged in the sentence, the sentences in the paragraph, the paragraphs in the chapter? Each writer's approach is different.

John Updike's short story "A&P" begins with a rush:

> In walks these three girls in nothing but bathing suits.
> I'm in the third checkout slot, with my back to the
> door, so I don't see them until they're over by the bread.

The rhythm is brisk, but smooth. He starts with a prepositional phrase, an old poetry trick, to give the sensation of interrupting some action already in progress. He hooks us with the pace and the image of three girls in bathing suits, obviously somewhere where their dress is inappropriate. Another thing we learn: The narrator's grammar is weak (it gets much worse), indicating he's just an average guy, not the kind of ironic wit that Phillip Marlowe is. He observes, he doesn't judge, which makes what he is about to tell us more objective.

Compare the above with the opening of Leonard Michaels's short story "City Boy":

> "Philip," she said, "this is crazy."
>     I didn't agree or disagree. She wanted some answer. I
> bit her neck. She kissed my ear. It was nearly three in
> the morning. We had just returned . . .

Michaels's rhythm is much more staccato. He uses the short, punchy sentences to build an abrupt rhythm that matches the narrator's mental state. Though he is the same age as the narrator in "A&P," we can already tell from the rhythm that they are very different characters, and these are very different stories. This almost surreal choppiness implies that, despite the romantic nature of what the narrator is doing, he is somewhat removed from his actions, emotionless. This effect is achieved by contrasting passion and description: "She kissed my ear. It was nearly three in the morning." Neither sentence has more significance to the narrator than the other.

In "A Poetic for Bullies," Stanley Elkin uses the same first-person point of view with a narrator almost the same age as the ones in "A&P" and "City Boy":

> I'm Push, the bully, and what I hate are new kids and sissies, dumb kids and smart, rich kids, poor kids, kids who wear glasses, talk funny, show off, patrol boys and wise guys and kids who pass pencils and water the plants—and cripples, *especially* cripples. Nobody loved I love.

The contrast here is even more obvious. Elkin's rhythm is more sophisticated, not as realistic as Updike's, yet not as surrealistic as Michaels's. He achieves this impassioned effect by shocking the reader with this strange list of things hated (things that the average reader would not hate). But then he follows the long chanting sentence with the short sentence that seems to contradict what has just been said. The first sentence is like someone yelling in our faces; the second is like a sharp slap to the cheek.

A novel's rhythm can sometimes better be discovered simply by reading parts of it aloud, as one would do with a poem. That allows you to hear how sentence structures can be counterpointed to create an internal tension in the prose. When you start to recognize these rhythms in other works, you will see how to energize your own style, sometimes merely by changing the lengths of sentences. One common mistake by beginning writers is to repeat the same sentence structure over and over (e.g., Thinking she was gone, he let himself in. Finding the refrigerator full, he helped himself to some beer.). By reading your works aloud, you can avoid this problem.

## Tables of Content

The following two steps will help you examine the content of a story.

**Step one: ask the right questions:** When you finish a novel or short story you should ask yourself one question first: *How did the main character change?* That is the key to understanding what a story is about. How is Holden Caulfield different at the end of *Catcher in the Rye?* Superficially, he's had a mental breakdown. But has he learned anything from his harrowing experiences? Has he grown?

A good story does not just give you a series of events, no matter how exciting these events are or how likable the characters are. In a good story, these events are related to the foundation of the characters. Either way they are changed by these events or they are not. If they are changed, what changed them, what realizations did they come to and at what costs? And if they are not changed, why not?

When you can answer those questions, you are on the way to asking the right questions about your own characters and how the events in your story relate to them. Many times my students come to me complaining that they're stuck in their books (they love to throw the old boogey man "writer's block" in my face); often the reason they can't go on is because they don't know how the plot relates to the characters. They know what they want to happen next, but not why. When they want to happen next, but not why. When they can use this process on someone else's story, it makes it easier to approach their own the same way.

**Step two: putting cause in your effect:** This is basically a refinement of one aspect of step one. Ever read a book where the characters seem to do things for no particular reason, just to spice up the story? Ever read a book where events beyond anyone's control keep occurring over and over? This kind of contrived story is melodrama, as opposed to the more believable dramatic story. The difference? Cause and effect.

If Johnny decides to leave his wife and family after ten years, the cause of this effect must be *significant* and *believable*. The cause must meet the effect in intensity. If he leaves simply because he's bored, the cause of the effect, it seems contrived. It's mathematical.

Much of cause and effect has to do with characters' motives. Why do they do whatever they do in a story? By understanding these motives, one can better understand the story.

Here's an example that may surprise you. As I mentioned in the style chapter, most people tend to clump Raymond Chandler's Philip Marlowe together with Dashiell Hammett's Sam Spade. Part of this error is due to the movies, since both characters were played by Humphrey Bogart. But when examining the motives of each character in the novels, we discover two very different characters.

Chandler's Marlowe follows the character pattern the author discusses in his essay "The Simple Art of Murder": "But down these mean streets a man must go who is himself not mean, who is neither tarnished nor afraid . . . He must be . . . a man of honor, by instinct, by inevitability, without thought of it, and certainly without saying it. He must be the best man in his world and a girl enough man for any world." Marlowe is indeed such a man, though cynical, his honor remains gleaming, a shield behind which a client can take comfort. Marlowe cannot be bought or frightened off a case. His one motive is Truth.

Hammett's Sam Spade in *The Maltese Falcon* is quite another man. He breaks all the unofficial moral rules of the honorable PI: He sleeps with his partner's wife, he sleeps with his client, and he turns his client in to the police, partially to protect himself. ("I won't take the fall for you.") Why does he pursue this case after his partner is murdered? For noble reasons? No, rather because "When a man's partner is killed he's supposed to do something about it . . . it's bad for business to let the killer get away with it." He isn't seeking Truth or Justice. His motive is business. While explaining this to the woman he supposedly loves and is about to send to the gallows, he lists the reasons for turning her in like a bookkeeper showing his ledger. He numbers them—seven in all—and says, "Now on the other side we've got what? All we've got is the fact that maybe you love me and maybe I love you." This unemotional balancing of accounts could never come from Philip Marlowe.

Has Sam Spade been changed by these events? The scary answer is no. At the end, he is sitting in his office, happy as ever. His incredulous secretary asks him if he really turned his own girlfriend over to the cops. He slips his arm around her waist and replies, "Your Sam's a detective." She pulls away from him, horrified and says, "Don't, please, don't touch me . . . I know—I know you're right. You're right. But don't touch me now—not now."

When the motives are examined, Marlowe is clearly the moral knight for right; Spade is the amoral businessman. By examining this kind of cause and effect in stories, the reader/writer will soon be able to develop the same thing in his own work.

### Better Well Read Than Dead

Many writers take writing classes or form writers groups in which they critique each other's manuscripts or listen to someone lecture on some of the things I just mentioned. But it's also important that you learn to apply these methods by yourself. This may be the single most important method of improving your own writing.

It helps to read with a pen in your hand, marking favorite passages or even weak passages. This will slow you down enough that you can get the full benefit of reading like a writer. It's akin to the tennis student watching a training film in slow motion.

Also, rather than just taking those writing workshops every semester, attend an occasional literature class. This will offer you some practice in analyzing stories, practice that will pay off when you analyze your own.

The benefits of changing your reading habits will become evident almost immediately. You will start to look at your own writing with a fresh, more informed eye, pinpointing trouble spots and polishing style according to the teachings you've learned from studying professional writers.

Eventually, some aspiring novelist will be hunched over her laptop retyping the first chapter of your novel so they understand how you make it all work so damn well.

# Index

# Index